# GOWNS BY
# ADRIAN

# GOWNS BY

# ADRIAN

## *The MGM Years 1928–1941*

Howard Gutner

Harry N. Abrams, Inc., Publishers

*Editor:* Ruth A. Peltason
*Designer:* Ana Rogers

PAGE 1: *Adrian in his studio with a selection of costume sketches from* Romeo and Juliet *(1936).*

PAGE 2: *Adrian on the set of* Our Blushing Brides *(1930) with Joan Crawford, making a last-minute inspection of her evening gown.*

Library of Congress Control Number: 2001091913
ISBN 0–8109–0898–0

Printed and bound in Japan
10 9 8 7 6 5 4 3 2 1

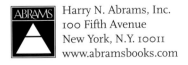 Harry N. Abrams, Inc.
100 Fifth Avenue
New York, N.Y. 10011
www.abramsbooks.com

# Contents

*Gilbert Adrian. Photograph, Clarence Sinclair Bull*

# Preface

In December 1932, *Fortune* magazine, one of America's preeminent business journals, ran an in-depth article on Metro-Goldwyn-Mayer in which they surveyed the studio's assets, production operations, and top personnel. "For the past five years," *Fortune* asserted, "all through the worst years of the Depression, MGM has made the best and most successful motion pictures in the United States." Furthermore, "everyone in Hollywood" thought that Irving Thalberg, executive vice-president in charge of production, was responsible.

Thalberg, however, knew better. When pressed by *Fortune* to elaborate on the reasons for MGM's success, he gave much of the credit to two people: art director Cedric Gibbons and costume designer Gilbert Adrian. Thalberg, the magazine asserted, subscribed to what the cosmetic business might call the law of packaging—that a mediocre scent in a sleek flacon is a better commodity than the best perfume in Paris poured into a gunnysack. *Fortune* concurred: "MGM pictures are always superlatively well-packaged—both the scenes and the personalities which enclose the drama have a high sheen. So high a sheen that it sometimes constitutes their major box-office appeal."

Gilbert Adrian began working at Metro-Goldwyn-Mayer in 1928, and by 1932 he had succeeded in transforming the studio's wardrobe department into a virtual one-man operation, becoming one of the first, and certainly one of the most highly publicized, of a Hollywood hybrid known as the costume designer/couturier. At the height of Adrian's MGM career in the mid-1930s, millions of women filled the cavernous baroque movie palaces that dotted the country to see his newest designs. At New York's Capitol Theater it was not uncommon for a patron to find herself seated next to an artist in the balcony with an electrically lighted pencil, hurriedly sketching in the darkness of the auditorium something he had seen on the screen. Weeks later, the sketch would appear in a modiste shop, adapted as a low-priced dress or coat.

Thirty and even sixty years later, the fashion world has continued to draw inspiration from Adrian's designs. In 1961 Halston took the pillbox hat that Adrian designed for Greta Garbo in 1932 and reinvented it for Jackie Kennedy. It became her signature hat for official engagements, a sort of crown substitute. In 1996, when Saks Fifth Avenue displayed Giorgio Armani's fall line in its New York windows, each female mannequin in its sleek suit was featured alongside photographs of Joan Crawford taken in the 1930s, her self-admiring stare resembling radiant pools of light, and her leonine form graced in suits and gowns by Adrian.

Throughout the thirties, Adrian was continually refining and experimenting with the design that would ultimately become his signature and give American fashion its own silhouette: the streamlined broad shoulder and tapered waistline that ultimately challenged Christian Dior's round-shouldered New Look in the late 1940s. The message in the Saks display window was clear: the sleek, flattering silhouette that Adrian pioneered in America has endured. It enabled women returning to the workforce in the 1980s and 1990s to compete confidently in the boardroom with men, and its resurrection can be seen not only in Armani's creations, but also in the tailored suits of Calvin Klein and Donna Karan. The recipient of a Coty Award in 1944 for his inventive ready-to-wear designs, Adrian would later be cited by many American designers, including Donald Brooks and Geoffrey Beene, as a mentor and major influence on their work. In 1978 Adrian was the first American designer honored with a retrospective by the costume division of the Smithsonian Institution.

Like so many of the young designers who gravitated to Hollywood in the silent era—Travis Banton, Orry-Kelly, Mitchell Leisen, Charles LeMaire—Adrian came to the West Coast after spending his formative years designing for the lavish Broadway revues that characterized the 1920s, and his clothes, like theirs, often possessed an innate theatricality. What initially set Adrian apart from his peers was prescience; his cognizance that the arrival of talking pictures in 1929 signaled a changing epoch for costume design as well as for acting and directing. For better or for worse, with the addition of dialogue movies gradually became more realistic, and less atmospheric.

"All the studio dress designers have been thinking in

terms of dramatic moments instead of the genuine, real moments that occur in life," Adrian said in 1930. "When sound came in, a great change came over movie fashions. With the entrance of the human voice actresses suddenly became human beings. A quality of mind came with the characterization and the story. Everything had to be more real. Roses became real roses, Chippendale chairs became real Chippendale. The clothes took on a genuine character. Now we're in a realm of reality where we can be more useful to women than ever before. She is as interesting in a smartly cut sport coat as she ever was in the eighteen-yard negligee covered with ermine tails. What I'm attempting to create for the screen are ultramodern clothes which will be adaptable for the street."

His instincts led him to seek out certain elements of fashionable dress from Parisian couture—details of cut and line—and translate them into the larger-than-life images seen on the screen. Frilly sleeves and padded shoulders had made fleeting appearances sauntering down the runways of Paris in 1930 and 1931. It was Adrian who selected these features, popularized them through the narrative drive of film, and made them standards of fashionable dress, ultimately turning them into American icons: Jean Harlow's bias-cut white satin evening gowns and Joan Crawford's puffed sleeves and broad-shouldered power suits can summon up an era in a few yards of cloth. "For years motion picture clothes were conceived in order to startle and amuse," Adrian said as early as 1929. "That the wife of a millionaire wore a gown whose train could only be looked at through a telescope seemed to delight so many ladies. We realize today that women of wealth do sparkle but not in quite such an obvious fashion."

Although Adrian became one of the most influential trendsetters of his time during the 1930s, many of the methods employed to bring his designs to the attention of the public had been established years earlier by the great Parisian couture houses. At the turn of the century, designers such as Worth, Paquin, and Doucet publicized their creations in women's fashion magazines such as *Les Modes,* which featured photographs of celebrity models, actresses, and singers wearing the latest styles. Popular performers such as Rejane, who was dressed exclusively by Doucet, were used as models by couturiers and regularly appeared in the pages and on the covers of French fashion magazines.

In the 1920s and 1930s, however, American publications such as *Vogue* and *Harper's Bazaar* chose to herald the latest designs from Paris on the rigid backs of East Coast socialites,

and in detailed sketches by such artists as Carl Erickson, Cecil Beaton, and Georges LePape. In 1933, for example, the readers of *Vogue* were invited to gaze upon Mrs. Rockhill Brevoort Potts in Chanel, and Mrs. Thomas Markoe Robertson in Molyneux (Mrs. Robertson "is particularly chic," said *Vogue,* "because [the suit] is of wool, because the hat matches, and because Mrs. Robertson has been individual enough to put her own stamp on the idea by wearing her skirts just a little bit shorter than all the others about town.")

By the mid-1930s these formal poses, which often featured the cream of New York society seated in stiff-backed chairs, could no longer compete with the whirling images of the motion picture. The die was cast in May 1938, when screen stars Dolores Del Rio and Joan Crawford made their debuts as fashion models in *Vogue,* with Crawford modeling a dress of white taffeta by Vionnet. The change had been building for years. "Screen presentation is vital and living," Adrian wrote in 1936. "It is dramatic yet natural. It is not a fashion magazine, nor a smart shop window. It lives and breathes."

More than a half-century later, American designers such as Ralph Lauren, Donna Karan, and Calvin Klein would rediscover the power of the kinetic visual image in television commercials and department-store video promotions with advertising campaigns that advocated a specific lifestyle. And the models these designers used were not socialites; they were chosen for many of the same reasons talent scouts once signed young women to movie contracts.

Adrian's association with Metro-Goldwyn-Mayer was the longest and most productive of his life, and during his tenure at the studio he worked with many of Hollywood's most notable directors: George Cukor, Ernst Lubitsch, Rouben Mamoulian, George Stevens, Frank Borzage, Howard Hawks, King Vidor, Clarence Brown, Dorothy Arzner, Jacques Feyder, Edmund Goulding, Victor Fleming, Tod Browning, Cecil B. DeMille, Mervyn LeRoy, Gregory La Cava, Victor Sjöström. While his high fashion designs for such stars as Norma Shearer, Joan Crawford, and Greta Garbo influenced American ready-to-wear throughout the 1930s, his sketches and architecturally-rendered costumes brought entire worlds to life on the soundstages of MGM.

Adrian designed costumes for the courts of Louis XVI, Nicholas and Alexandra, and Christina of Sweden, and his assignments ran the gamut from Eugene O'Neill's waterfront barflies in *Anna Christie* to the fantasy occupants of Oz. On mammoth productions such as *Marie Antoinette,* Adrian

*Adrian in his studio in MGM's wardrobe building. Photograph, Clarence Sinclair Bull*

designed thousands of costumes, including clothes for the lowliest extra. In sumptuous theatrical extravaganzas such as *Madam Satan, The Great Ziegfeld,* and *Ziegfeld Girl,* his unfettered imagination adorned the girls of the chorus in towering headdresses and elaborate capes woven of mirrored glass, sequins, marabou and ostrich plumes, transforming them into nymphs and sprites and snow queens. These elaborate confections would later influence a whole new generation of theatrical talent, among them Charles Busch, Bob Mackie, Ray Aghayan, and Howard Crabtree. A perfectionist and a tireless worker, Adrian never used a sketch artist, and sometimes produced in excess of 75 drawings in a single workday—a fact that elicited gasps from students at the Fashion Institute of Technology during a lecture in 1988 on Adrian's work at the school. Yet he treated the costumes of a chorus girl or extra with the same care, taste, and wit that he lavished on Garbo's crinolines in *Camille.*

The range of stars who have appeared on screen in his gowns, hats, and coats is worth listing: Katharine Hepburn, Rosalind Russell, Greer Garson, Jean Harlow, Marion Davies, Loretta Young, Ethel Barrymore, Mary Pickford, Irene Dunne, Lynn Fontanne, Marie Dressler, Janet Gaynor, Fanny Brice, Sophie Tucker, Vivien Leigh, Myrna Loy, Jeanette MacDonald, Judy Garland, Kay Francis, Hedy Lamarr, Ann Harding, Lana Turner, Helen Hayes, Paulette Goddard, Eleanor Powell, Claudette Colbert, Joan Fontaine, Maureen O'Sullivan, Tallulah Bankhead, Nazimova, Mrs. Patrick Campbell, Ina Claire, Marjorie Main, Luise Rainer, Constance Bennett, Carole Lombard, Billie Burke, Margaret Sullavan, Miriam Hopkins, Ingrid Bergman, and of course the three women whose images he helped to create for over twelve years, and who made his reputation—Greta Garbo, Norma Shearer, and Joan Crawford.

These actresses, shimmering against the sublime backdrops of Cedric Gibbons, each created an identity on screen that seduced the American public and sent them flocking to "cinema shops" in department stores across the country. In 1934 Adrian's costumes inspired a young girl in Los Toldos, Argentina, to go quite a bit farther than her local dress shop. Fifteen-year-old Eva Duarte saw Norma Shearer in *Riptide* at a local theater and found in the beautifully gowned star her ideal of elegance. She packed up her belongings and went to try her luck in Buenos Aires, and by the time she met General Juan Perón she had seen Norma Shearer in *Marie Antoinette* six times.

Adrian took his work, and his contribution to every film he worked on, very seriously. "Few people in an audience watching a great screen production realize the importance of any gown worn by the feminine star," he said in 1937. "They may notice that it is attractive, that they would like to have it copied, that it is becoming, but the fact that it was definitely planned to mirror some definite mood, to be as much a part of the play as the lines or the scenery, seldom occurs to them. But that most assuredly is true."

# A Predilection For Design

**G**ilbert Adrian's first public triumph as an artist and designer came at the age of five, soon after he started kindergarten. Alone in the empty classroom one afternoon, he picked up some colored chalk and began drawing. An ornate calliope was the first object to appear, surrounded by colored notes in a mist of steam. Behind it, a parade of circus performers, led by plumed horses. There followed a succession of prancing beasts: lions, tigers, zebras, and elephants, which Adrian outfitted in tassels and multi-colored draperies. When his teacher discovered the elaborate tapestry the following morning, she was unable to bring herself to erase it. For four days the results of Adrian's keen imagination decorated the classroom. Through word of mouth, his drawings soon became the wonder of his elementary school.

From the time he was old enough to hold a pencil, Adrian had always exhibited a compulsion to draw. On paper bags, the fly leaves of books, even on the wallpaper in his room, Adrian covered every available surface with pictures of people and animals. Both of his parents exhibited an aesthetic bent, and they encouraged their son's creative efforts.

Adrian Adolph Greenburg was born in Naugatuck, Connecticut, on September 3, 1903. His mother, Helena, had worked as a graphic designer in New York, and was the daughter of a milliner. When she married Gilbert Greenburg, a furrier, in the summer of 1895, her parents convinced the young couple to take over the family millinery business in Naugatuck.

*Billie Blythe towers over Patty Parish, left, and Lehman Byck in Adrian's designs for the* Music Box Revue *of 1924.*

The advent of the automobile at the beginning of the twentieth century made this a propitious business decision for the young couple. The U.S. Rubber Company was the chief industry in Naugatuck, and the small town was on the verge of becoming a booming industrial center. Its economic ascendancy was reflected in the increasing number of wealthy women who visited the Greenburgs' shop each month, placing their orders for huge motoring hats laced with feathers and elaborate veils. At least once a month, Helena or Gilbert would board the train to New York and return with boxes of material and trim. Their delighted young son would paste together scraps he found in the shop, creating tiny hats for imaginary, miniaturized ladies of fashion.

Adrian's mother had been an expert painter before entering the millinery business, and his father, on occasion, still produced lively caricatures for leaflets distributed by local organizations such as the Elks and Masons. A year before he entered kindergarten, Helena Greenburg offered her son a lesson on how to mix colors. Aside from this brief demonstration, however, Adrian resisted any individual artistic instruction his parents attempted to offer him.

It was a pattern he followed for the rest of his life. Enrolled at the Parsons School of Fine and Applied Arts in New York in the fall of 1921, Adrian found the freshman curriculum—slide lectures on the history of art; drawings made from plaster casts—to be stultifying. When his grades reflected the boredom he felt, school officials decided he might be more challenged if he were transferred to the Paris branch of Parsons.

This gave Adrian an entire summer to fill before the fall semester began in France. His parents wanted him to return to Naugatuck, but Robert Kallock, a lecturer at Parsons, came to Adrian's rescue. Kallock was a designer for the house of Lucile, and also a friend of Florence Cunningham, who ran the Gloucester Playhouse in Massachusetts, known for its ambitious sets and costumes. Through Kallock's connection, Adrian spent three months at the summer theater, surrounded by paint, sewing machines, dye pots, and fabric. Cunningham's contribution to the Adrian legacy, however, came in the form of a suggestion rather than any solid experience her theater could offer. Cunningham suggested to him that the name of Greenburg would not take him very far in the world of theater and fashion. Pointing out that Leon Rosenberg had taken the name Bakst, and that Romain de Tirtoff was now recognized on both sides of the Atlantic as Erté, she suggested that Adrian be known simply by his first name.

Adrian's father was outraged by the suggestion. He felt his son was simply trying to avoid using a Jewish name, until his wife pointed out that he had changed his own name from Greenburgh to Greenburg when he arrived in America. To ameliorate the situation, Adrian took his father's first name as his own, and it was Gilbert Adrian who set sail for Paris in the fall of 1922.

Florence Cunningham's interest in his work had changed Adrian. While his grades at the Parsons school in the Place des Vosges did not improve, he was nevertheless possessed by a new self-assurance. The Bal du Grand Prix, which was held each year at the Opera House, was an outlandish, popular event at which the artists and designers of Paris tried to outdo one another in a fantasia of exotic floats and costumes. Fabled couturiers such as Charles Worth and Paul Poiret were not above designing for this annual artists' ball; the year Adrian attended, actress Pearl White made her entrance down the marble staircase of the Opera House dressed by Worth to resemble an electric light bulb.

Adrian, like most of his peers at Parsons, considered the Bal du Grand Prix to be a sacred rite of initiation into the Parisian world of art and design. Whatever time he could spare from his studies he spent sewing, cutting, and stitching a costume for his friend Honor, a fellow student. "Neither of us had any money," Honor remembered almost sixty years later. "We both scoured the workrooms at

*A Chinese screen provides the backdrop for three chorus girls dressed in Adrian's Oriental-inspired costumes for the* Music Box Revue *of 1924.*

BELOW: *One of the Orientalist sets by Hassard Short from the* Music Box Revue *of 1924. The costumes are by Adrian.*

Parsons looking for whatever we might take that wouldn't be missed. I remember the costume Adrian created for me had a design of palm fronds, which he stitched in bright green thread. It shimmered under the lights like sequins."

Fortuitously, the bright color captured the eye of Irving Berlin. The composer was in Paris with his director, Hassard Short, in search of a costume designer for a Broadway revue they were planning, a sequel to their highly successful *Music Box Revue* of the year before. After reviewing Adrian's sketches the following morning, Short and Berlin signed him to a contract. Adrian made plans to sail back to New York after a scant four months in Paris.

The *Music Box Revue of 1921* opened on 23 September of that year and was an enormous critical and popular success. Adrian did some special artwork for the show, but he was not responsible for the costumes themselves, which were executed by Ralph Mulligan under the personal direction of Hassard Short. Aside from Berlin's music, the new *Music Box Revue* was, in almost every sense of the word, Short's show: "The new revue is ablaze with color," wrote Alexander Wollcott in his review, "wrought by Hassard Short

with a kaleidoscope of chic and fantastic and bizarre designs, with lovely curtains of black lace, with costumes of radiant pearls picked out against velvet blackness, with a hundred and one odd and conceitful costumes worked into gay designs."

If Hassard Short was not a mentor to Adrian in the fullest sense of that term, he nevertheless created a learning environment for the young designer that outdid anything he might have learned in a classroom. Short was responsible for many innovations onstage, both in costume design and especially in lighting techniques. While witnessing an error in the use of gelatin screens during a performance in Europe one night, he conceived the idea of using combinations of colored lights to make colored costumes appear black-and-white. As a result, he was able to achieve startling color transformations in the *Music Box Revue of 1921*. Short was also the first producer in the United States to use a light bridge and to eliminate footlights in favor of balcony spotlights.

The final cost of the 1921 revue was $187,613, of which more than a third went for costumes. Short insisted on using the very finest materials, a practice that Adrian would later follow. And while Adrian's contributions to this edition of the review were decidedly minor, Irving Berlin had not forgotten

his young designer. The following year, Adrian was given responsibility for three numbers, and in the 1923 edition he designed the bulk of the show, including the costumes for the opening number and the finale. The opening night audience included S. L. Rothafel, Samuel Goldwyn, Lee and J. J. Shubert, John Barrymore, Mary Pickford and Douglas Fairbanks, Martin Beck, Jascha Heifetz, Bernard Baruch, and, as luck would have it, Natacha Rambova.

Rambova was the wife of Rudolph Valentino, who was making the film *A Sainted Devil* across the river from Manhattan at the Famous Players-Lasky, Paramount Studios in Astoria, Queens. After production wrapped, Valentino and Rambova would begin discussions with a new company, Ritz-Carlton Productions, which promised the Valentinos a say in story selection, as well as a share of the profits from Valentino's films. Rambova was even able to win production head J. D. Williams's consent to go ahead with a story she was planning entitled *The Scarlet Power*.

Norman Norell had designed the costumes for *A Sainted Devil*, but Rambova "hated the designer's crabbed little sketches," and she found in Adrian's work a sympathetic attitude. Adrian's first film costume was a Spanish toreador outfit

*Highly stylized watercolor drawings of costumes by Adrian for the* Music Box Revue *of 1924.*

OPPOSITE: *A parade of chorus girls with huge feather fans. This kind of outsize accessory was a trademark of Hassard Short's revues, which Adrian would later adapt in his work for the screen.*

for Valentino in *Sainted Devil*. In the fall of 1924, Rambova
made Adrian an offer to design the costumes for Valentino's
first film under the Ritz-Carlton banner, which would be made
in Hollywood. Adrian had already made a commitment to
design costumes for Hassard Short, who was now working
on the yearly edition of the *Greenwich Village Follies*. In a
last-minute flurry of arrangements and good-byes, Adrian
hurriedly finished up his sketches for Short. When he met the
Valentinos at Grand Central Station for the trip west, he found
a retinue that included several maids and valets, a cook, a
business manager, a publicity agent, and Rambova's pet
monkey, who took an immediate shine to Adrian. Rambova's
love of animals matched her new designer's, and when the
monkey refused to be ousted from Adrian's compartment on
the train, Rambova felt she had made the right decision in
hiring Adrian.

*Swags of flowers frame the company and the stage for the finale of the*
*Music Box Revue of 1924.*

# Going Hollywood

A drian was euphoric in Hollywood. For the first time he had a steady job and income, as well as his own office and workroom at Paramount Studios. As they traveled west by train the Valentinos carefully read the script for a new film, tentatively retitled *The Hooded Falcon*. Set in medieval Spain, the story recounted the legend of El Cid, and the struggle between Moorish and Spanish forces for control of the country. As in his enormous hit *The Shiek* (1921), Valentino would once again find himself in Arab costume as a leader of the Moorish troops.

By the time the Valentinos arrived in California, both of them had decided that the script by June Mathis would have to be reworked. When Mathis was approached, however, she was too busy to do any further work on the scenario.

Natacha then busied herself with rewriting the script, while she set Adrian to work designing and overseeing the construction of the costumes for *The Hooded Falcon*. When J. D. Williams at Ritz-Carlton realized that the new film had been delayed for rewrites, he pressed Valentino to begin work in the interim on *Cobra,* a small modern-dress film based on a successful Broadway play that would feature the star as a young, debt-ridden Italian count, Rodrigo Torriani. When the count accepts a job offer in New York, he is pursued by an avaricious woman (Nita Naldi) who mistakenly assumes he is wealthy.

*Valentino with Nita Naldi in* Cobra *(1925).*

810-2598

Rambova called upon Adrian to interrupt his work on *The Hooded Falcon* and design the costumes for *Cobra*, which became his first completely realized work on-screen. Seen today, Adrian's work is not only notable for what it does, but for what it *doesn't* do. When Count Torriani arrives in New York to begin working at Dorning and Son, an exclusive antiques dealership, he makes the acquaintance of the firm's secretary, Mary Drake (Gertrude Olmstead). Not only does Adrian exercise restraint in his designs for Olmstead, but he repeats several of them over the course of the film. In an age of conspicuous consumption—the height of the Roaring Twenties—costumes in motion pictures were starting to be criticized for the money lavished on embroidery and other decorative frills without serious regard for narrative concerns. In *Cobra* Adrian created a wardrobe for a working girl that was startlingly realistic not only in its lack of ostentatious details and materials, but in the very real fact that this secretary, like most working girls on a budget, must wear the same three or four outfits day after day.

Lavish furs and rich materials such as velvet and silk, however, were used in Adrian's costumes for Nita Naldi's character. When she finally succeeds in seducing Torriani, she slowly removes her fur, revealing a stark black evening gown, its only embellishment a lightning bolt of silver sequins cascading from the right hip to the hem like a shock of sudden desire.

Rambova took very little interest in *Cobra*, and when the film was finished, she and Valentino took a vacation in Palm Springs, where they continued to plan *The Hooded Falcon*. (Valentino was so pleased with one of the designs Adrian had created for the film that he commissioned the Spanish painter Federico Beltran-Masses to paint his portrait wearing the costume.)

Rudy and Natacha's sojourn was interrupted, however, when J. D. Williams decided to terminate all plans for the production, citing budget overruns. Valentino's agent, George Ullman, then informed Rambova that he had an even more tantalizing prospect at hand: Joseph Schenck, the president of United Artists, was interested in signing Valentino. United Artists had been formed in 1919 to represent Hollywood's most popular and bankable stars: Mary Pickford, Charlie Chaplin, and Douglas Fairbanks, along with the director D. W. Griffith. In the early 1920s Norma Talmadge joined the corporation. Rambova was thrilled at the prospect of Rudy joining such exalted company.

What Rambova didn't know was that Ullman was attempting to discredit her in order to gain full control over Valentino's career. The new contract with UA called for Valentino to be paid $10,000 a week, in addition to receiving 42 percent of the profits from his pictures. But these lucrative terms were predicated upon one stipulation: Natacha Rambova would not be allowed to participate in the making of her husband's films. She would not even be allowed to visit the set.

Initially Valentino hesitated to sign the contract, but his lavish spending over the past three years—the purchase and renovation of two homes in California—had left him short of cash. After some deliberation, Valentino agreed to UA's terms.

Rambova was devastated. In an effort to salvage her wounded pride, she took an idea for a film to Ullman, whose duplicity in the contract negotiations with United Artists she had not yet realized. The script was a comic satire Rambova had written about the ridiculous lengths some women go to in order to make themselves beautiful. Ullman, observing the strain in the Valentino marriage wrought by the UA contract, and realizing that keeping Natacha busy would help facilitate the production of Valentino's first film under his new agreement, agreed to a $30,000 budget for the Rambova film, now entitled *What Price Beauty?*

Once again, Rambova engaged Adrian to design the costumes for the film, which would feature, in a small role, a young unknown dancer named Myrna Loy. They had met the previous year when Loy auditioned for a role in *Cobra.* In her memoirs, Loy later recalled the costume Adrian designed for her:

My only scene was a futuristic dream sequence depicting various types of womankind. Natacha dubbed me "the intellectual type of vampire without race or creed or country." Adrian designed an extraordinary red velvet pajama outfit for me, with a short blond wig that came to little points on my forehead, very very snaky. This bizarre film wasn't released for three years, but Henry Waxman took pictures of me in that outfit. They appeared in a fan magazine captioned "Who is she?" and eventually led to my first contract.

*What Price Beauty?* went $60,000 over budget, and despite a successful preview in Pasadena, no one at United Artists was interested in releasing the film. Lou Mahoney, who worked for the Valentinos as a handyman, and who became

their confidant, knew why: "No help came from anyone, no thoughts of trying to get this picture properly released. No help came from Ullman, Schenck, or anybody else. Their whole thought was that if the picture were a success, Mrs. Valentino would be a success. She would then start producing under the Rudolph Valentino Production Company. But nobody wanted this—except herself, and Mr. Valentino."

*What Price Beauty?* would not be released until two years after Rudolph Valentino's death in 1926. In 1925, however, Rambova left Hollywood, citing the need for time alone to sort things out. By then Adrian had received an offer from showman Sid Grauman to design a prologue for the world premiere of Charlie Chaplin's *The Gold Rush,* at his Egyptian Theater on Hollywood Boulevard. Adrian was right in guessing it would be an auspicious premiere. The opening of Chaplin's first film in two years would bring out virtually every star, producer, and studio executive in the film industry, from Gloria Swanson, Lillian Gish, and John Barrymore to Cecil B. DeMille, Samuel Goldwyn, Louis B. Mayer, and Irving Thalberg, on a first date with his future wife, Norma Shearer.

Weeks before the premiere, the newspapers speculated

about the prologue. Seven days before the opening, the *Los Angeles Times* reported that "no hint of the nature of the spectacular prologue offering that has been the subject of Grauman's plans for weeks has been disclosed by the exhibitor. He answers queries by smilingly stating it will be totally different from anything staged here before and that its features will be reserved for those who attend the premiere."

On opening night the curtain rose on a panorama of the frozen north, revealing a school of seals mounting a jagged crag of ice. The seals were quickly joined by a group of Eskimo dancing girls, who were followed, in the words of the critic for the *Los Angeles Herald-Examiner,* by a series of "impressively artistic dances by fascinatingly pretty young women wearing astoundingly rich and beautiful gowns all blending with the Arctic atmosphere and bespeaking the moods of the barren white country."

On the Monday morning following the Friday premiere, Adrian had five job offers waiting for him on Sid Grauman's desk. One of them was from Louis B. Mayer and Irving Thalberg at Metro-Goldwyn-Mayer, where the designer Erté had been working since March. Adrian weighed his decision carefully. MGM was a new studio with many possibilities, but he knew that with a renowned couturier such as Erté in residence, he would be just another designer under contract. He decided to accept an offer from Cecil B. DeMille, reasoning that the legendary producer-director would grant him the most latitude.

It proved to be a wise decision. Cecil B. DeMille's early Jazz Age films were largely responsible for significant changes in the demographics of film attendance that had taken place in the early 1920s. Although exhibitors still made distinctions between the middle-class patrons of the huge downtown movie palaces and the working-class audiences that tended to frequent smaller neighborhood theaters, DeMille's emphasis on sets and costumes appealed overwhelmingly to women across all social classes and ethnicities. In films such as *Don't Change Your Husband* (1918), *Why Change Your Wife?* (1920), and *The Affairs of Anatol* (1921), problems such as sexual frigidity or incompatibility are solved by a trip to the boutique for a new wardrobe. "Paris fashion shows had been accessible only to the chosen few," Cecil's brother William once remarked. "C. B. revealed them to the whole country, the costumes his heroines wore being copied by hordes of women and girls throughout the land, especially by those whose contacts with centers of fashion were limited or nonexistent."

Adrian designed the costumes for twenty-six films during his tenure at the DeMille Studios, although he worked with Cecil B. DeMille himself only twice, on *The Volga Boatman* (1926) and *The King of Kings* (1927). Still, his work on bread-and-butter studio fare such as *For Alimony Only* (1926), *The Country Doctor* (1927), *His Dog* (1927), *The Forbidden Woman* (1927), and *The Angel of Broadway* (1927) gave Adrian experience designing clothes for a broad spectrum of characters— social outcasts, female spies, and cabaret dancers, among them.

DeMille supervised each of the directors under contract at his studio closely, and a great deal of attention was given to the wardrobe on each picture. Money was no object at the fledgling studio, and when the subject matter was appropriate, Adrian was encouraged to purchase rare furs and costly fabrics such as silk and velvet. Before production began on each film, DeMille staged a fashion show with the costumes, complete with special lighting and individual staging. He watched the actresses closely, ever alert to an unflattering seam or cut. These lessons were not lost on Adrian, and as early as 1926 he was already articulating his own thoughts on successful ideas for costume design in the movies:

> The dramatic situations in a picture must be costumed according to the feeling of a scene—therefore there are some clothes that are not in good taste if worn off the set. They are put into the picture like futuristic scenery in some plays to help the drama and are out of place anywhere else.
>
> A picture may be exotic in theme, in plot or in characters. Never attempt to copy a gown worn in an exotic story on the screen, for it is certain to be exaggerated for the effect of the whole picture.
>
> I think I may say that women in moderate circumstances who cannot afford many changes of costume should avoid wearing the exotic type of gown. It is usually so extreme that one becomes tired of it presently; it is out of place at informal affairs and is perhaps too conspicuous for the average woman. . . . A jeweler, you know, shows his finest diamonds on a plain bit of black velvet, not on a gorgeous piece of metallic embroidery.

DeMille's famous dictum to his designers—take the current mode and exaggerate it beyond all measure—may seem at odds with Adrian's ideas. Yet Adrian's arguments won

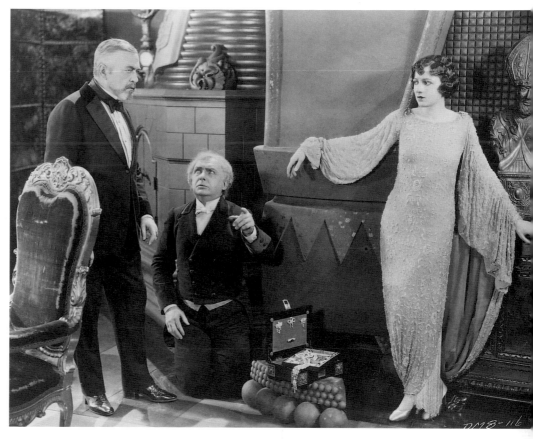

*Elinor Fair as Princess Vera in* The Volga Boatman, *wearing Adrian's evening gown. Note that the train of the gown is swept up to form the sleeves, which punctuate each movement of Fair's arms, allowing her to dominate the scene.*

out when he worked with the director on *The Volga Boatman,* an epic set during the Russian Revolution, which in essence was a romantic melodrama. The film starred William Boyd as Feodor, a Russian laborer forced to pull barges up and down the Volga River. Singing loudly with his companions as they tote their payloads, Boyd is overheard by Vera, a Russian princess (Elinor Fair). Attracted by his rich, strong voice, she begins to secretly yearn for him.

Meanwhile Vera has been seeing Prince Dimitri, but before she can seriously consider the idea of marrying him, the Russian Revolution erupts. Feodor leads the assault on Vera's castle, and when a member of his battalion is killed, the Red Army calls for Vera's death. Locked in a room with her, Feodor is impressed by her bravery. Instead of carrying out the death sentence, Feodor runs away with Vera.

Thankfully the absurd premise of the scenario would not be further intensified by the costumes. Adrian, who had researched court dress in the last days of the Romanovs (which had ended only ten years before), had been instructed by DeMille that Fair be dressed in the formal, elegant gowns that were the height of 1927 fashion. Adrian compromised, and when Feodor and his compatriots gain entrance to the castle, Princess Vera is dressed in an evening gown of nude chiffon embroidered in crystals and pearls. It might not be a gown that would have been worn by a member of the Russian imperial court, but neither was it as fantastic as some of the costumes worn by royalty in DeMille's other productions.

Before any artistic differences between Adrian and DeMille could come to a head, however, the DeMille Company was dissolved by its founder. In his autobiography, DeMille explained the position he found himself in less than three years after his company had been formed:

Less than a year after my break-up with Famous Players-Lasky, I offered Jesse Lasky the presidency of Cecil B.

DeMille Productions. He preferred staying where he was, and I had to retain the executive position I had assumed in the hope of building the DeMille Company to a point where it could independently finance and produce its own pictures. This was not happening under the tie-up with New York financiers; and my chosen work, directing, was suffering both from restrictive outside control and from the mass of administrative detail involved in my being head of a studio. When Joseph P. Kennedy brought his strength to the Pathé organization, I decided ultimately that it would be better for DeMille Productions to sell its Pathé stock, at a very handsome profit, and for me to form another connection free at least from the uncongenial burden of studio administration.

The "other connection" turned out to be Metro-Goldwyn-Mayer, where on August 2, 1928, DeMille signed a contract, which included a commitment of three pictures in two years. Talent was Metro-Goldwyn-Mayer's major asset, and Louis B. Mayer had good reason to celebrate Cecil B. DeMille's arrival at the studio in August. The director agreed to bring with him a number of key personnel from the DeMille Studios, including screenwriter Jeanie Macpherson and Adrian. They would all eventually be signed to studio contracts.

# A Studio Takes Shape

*Metro-Goldwyn-Mayer 1924–1928*

The merger of the Metro and Goldwyn film studios with Louis B. Mayer Productions in the spring of 1924 had created, almost overnight, a huge new production and film distribution center, organized expressly to supply feature films for its parent company, the Loew's theater chain. The new studio, Metro-Goldwyn-Mayer, took over the old Goldwyn plant in Culver City, a 43-acre property that featured 6 glass-enclosed soundstages, 8 additional stages, and 45 buildings that included labs, dressing rooms, storage facilities, and offices, all of them connected by three miles of paved road. The lot had actually been built by the movie pioneers D.W. Griffith, Mack Sennett, and Thomas H. Ince when they formed the Triangle Film Corporation in 1915. It was sold to Goldwyn three years later.

Although Samuel Goldwyn did not play a part in the newly formed company—Loew's Incorporated bought Goldwyn's remaining stock for $5 million—his trademark, a roaring lion encircled by a banner carrying the inscription *Ars Gratia Artis* ("Art for Art's Sake"), was taken over by MGM. More important, his insistence on highly crafted production values and his belief in the star system found a ready reception in the new company. From its inception in 1916, the features produced by Goldwyn Pictures were promoted in national magazine ads that trumpeted the "Goldwyn Quality." In 1918 Goldwyn had hired a number of well-known artists and theatrical designers such as Hugo Ballin and Robert Edmund-Jones, and then launched a publicity campaign focusing on the improvement of the set designs in Goldwyn films.

*Claire Windsor in her boudoir in MGM's* Dance Madness *(1925) wearing a costume designed by Erté. Technical and artistic skills notwithstanding, Erté failed to make the leap from decorative sketch to full character dress when designing costumes for film.*

The following year, Goldwyn began to focus attention on the costumes worn by his stars. *Moving Picture World* reported in 1919 that Goldwyn refused to let one of his stars, Geraldine Farrar, appear in public wearing the same gown twice; instead the dresses were donated to the Stage Women's War Relief. The wardrobe department on the Goldwyn lot had been under the general supervision of Sophie Wachner, who owned and ran a couturiere shop on Hollywood Boulevard at the same time.

Stars—and, to a lesser extent, directors, technicians, and craftspeople—were the chief asset of the new studio. The combined talent of the merger made it the most envied studio in Hollywood. The Mayer Company had brought in actors such as Norma Shearer, Lon Chaney, and Renee Adoree. From Metro came Ramon Novarro, Buster Keaton, Alice Terry, Mae Busch, and Monte Blue, while Goldwyn's contributions to the talent roster included Mae Murray, John Gilbert, Conrad Nagel, Blanche Sweet, Aileen Pringle, William Haines, and Eleanor Boardman.

The studio management team was equally impressive. Louis B. Mayer got his start in the movie business managing nickelodeons, and during his first five years in Hollywood had built up a profitable production company, releasing his pictures through First National and Metro. With the formation of MGM, Mayer became first vice-president and general manager of Loew's West Coast operations at a salary of $1,500 a week.

Mayer's hard-headed business sense was complemented by the abilities of his principal aide, production supervisor Irving Thalberg, who had worked for five years at Universal before joining Mayer in 1923. Thalberg was already famous for his ability to take a motion picture that had failed in previews, recut, reshoot it, and turn it into a hit. Although his reasons for reshaping a film usually involved a plot problem, Thalberg was also known to rework a completed film when production values did not meet his standards. From its inception, Metro-Goldwyn-Mayer was a studio where a director's conflict with a producer's authority usually ended in an ultimatum—from the producer.

Irving Thalberg believed that the film industry, like other modern industries that relied on mass production and mass merchandising, needed to develop its own version of the assembly-line system, with an appropriate division and subdivision of labor. He had put together the beginnings of such a system before he left Universal, and now, at MGM, Thalberg cultivated a coterie of close associates to facilitate actual production. By 1927 five of them were in place: Harry Rapf, Bernard H. Hyman, Hunt Stromberg, Al Lewin, and Paul Bern. Generally referred to as supervisors, these five men were forerunners of the present-day Hollywood producer. They worked closely with Thalberg to prepare projects for production, and then they monitored shooting, keeping an eye on budgets and schedules as well as the day-to-day activities on the set.

Once this system was stabilized and proven cost-efficient—by the end of its second year of operation, MGM had delivered close to 100 feature films to Loew's Incorporated, which prospered as never before—it was mimicked by other departments within the studio, beginning with the art department under the direction of Cedric Gibbons. Gibbons became one of the most autonomous of department heads, personally assigning each film to an art director, approving all budgets and sketches, and representing his staff in meetings with studio executives. In addition, his likes and dislikes—he hated wallpaper, for example, but loved decorative plaster—were helping to create a rich, glossy MGM look.

Other departments, however—notably the wardrobe department—were still experiencing growing pains. In 1925 there were three costume annexes, or storerooms, that dotted the MGM lot, some distance from the main wardrobe building. Shades of a golden past still hovered about these annexes from the Goldwyn studio; wardrobe left there by the Triangle Film Corporation included many original costumes that had been created for the films of D. W. Griffith and Thomas Ince, as well as gowns that had been designed for Gloria Swanson and Pauline Starke by Triangle designer Peggy Hamilton, who had since become a fashion columnist for the *Los Angeles Times*.

The main wardrobe building, a massive three-story concrete structure located next door to the executive offices, was a virtual honeycomb of workrooms and storage space. MGM had inherited over 100 employees from Metro and Goldwyn who worked in this building alone. The Modern Men's Wardrobe occupied the third floor. Fitters, cutters, drapers, figure makers, beaders, dyers, and milliners for the female stars and featured players were located on the second floor. The wardrobe department was managed by Ethel Chaffin, a genial middle-aged woman and former Goldwyn employee who supervised the sewing and tried to keep everyone on schedule, although no one was officially in charge. Designers came and went on a freelance basis. By the winter of 1924, when the studio was barely eight months old, Louis B. Mayer began negotiations with the designer Romain de Tirtoff (Erté) in an attempt to rectify this problem.

Romain de Tirtoff—he adopted the pseudonym Erté

*Erté in his sumptuous MGM office. Louis B. Mayer went out of his way to make the designer feel at home in his new California surroundings. As described in a number of Hearst newspapers, Erté's new office was nothing if not extravagant: "Ivory walls and an ivory barrel ceiling are set off by long black narrow beams running along the ceiling two feet parallel. Long black tassels hang along each end of the ceiling, with small cubical black lamps at the end of each beam. Narrow black wall seats surround the entire room, piled with black and ivory cushions of satin and velvet. Vases of flame gladioli and blue delphinium in dull green vases add a color note."*

BELOW: *The firepower attending a special tea and fashion show for the official opening of Erté's studio on May 27th included 20 members of the press and assorted welcoming hostesses. Among those present, and shown here with the designer outside his office are, left to right, Irene Mayer, Edith Mayer, Sylvia Thalberg, Helen Carlysle, Mrs. Harry Rapf, Mrs. William Thalberg, Don Acosta, Dorothy Donnell, Nola Luxford, Frank Nugent, Erté, Claire Swanner, LuRee Wiese, John Calhoun, Mona Gardner, Rose Plante, Barbara Miller, Mr. Alexander, Jean Loughbrough, Mrs. Carr. Notably, Nola Luxford, Claire Swanner, and LuRee Wiese are wearing Erté fashions.*

from his initials, R. T., when he began to work as a fashion designer—had worked as a sketch artist for Parisian couturier Paul Poiret, and through Poiret had the opportunity to design costumes for several theatrical productions in Paris in 1914 and 1915. By the early 1920s, Erté was on Broadway designing for Florenz Ziegfeld and George White. Influenced by the lavish, Oriental-inspired costumes of the Ballets Russes and the designers Leon Bakst and Ernst Stern, Erté soon developed his own technique: he united stylized designs and a minute attention to detail with the bold outlines and geometrical forms of the Art Deco style. The result was essentially modern, with a dash of romantic escapism.

The negotiations that resulted in Erté's contract with MGM were most likely brokered by William Randolph Hearst, the newspaper tycoon whose magazine *Harper's Bazaar* had

employed Erté to design covers beginning in 1915. Hearst had organized a production company in 1919 to promote actress Marion Davies, whom he had discovered working in the Ziegfeld Follies the previous year. Cosmopolitan Pictures had released the Davies features through Goldwyn, but after the merger Mayer offered Hearst a berth at MGM, no doubt with an eye to the publicity potential of the vast Hearst press.

Mayer's expectations were borne out when Erté arrived in New York in February 1925 aboard the steamship *SS France*. Accompanying the designer was his companion, Prince Nicholas Ouroussoff, two assistants, and fifteen trunks filled with fabrics and other material. "Erté's advent into motion pictures," wrote a columnist covering the designer's arrival for Hearst's *New York Morning Telegraph*, "is considered of special significance to the film industry as it is the first notable recognition paid to the importance of the costuming phase in motion picture production." Indeed, on June 20, Erté's designs decorated the MGM float in the first Motion Picture Electrical Parade and Pageant at the Los Angeles Coliseum.

Some months prior to Erté's arrival, Mayer had ordered

*An Erté design for Aileen Pringle in* The Mystic.

OPPOSITE: *Aileen Pringle wearing the finished costume in the film.*

but on black-and-white film, his designs proved too intricate. Worse, he often treated the actress as an ornament, or decorative object, rather than as a character in a narrative. "Somehow," fashion historian David Chierichetti has written, "the final garments were never as impressive as Erté's bizarre sketches."

And then there was Erté's temperament. In October he was assigned to create costumes for Renée Adorée and Lillian Gish in King Vidor's production of *La Bohème.* Adorée refused to wear the corset Erté had designed for her costume. Gish, however, was at first delighted when she heard that Erté had been assigned to create costumes for the film: "I thought he would know just how Mimi should look," she wrote in her memoirs. But when she met with Erté, she found that all the costumes he had designed looked like brand new dresses. Actress and designer soon came to blows. Gish suggested that on camera old silk would look more like the poor rags that her character would wear rather than the new calico Erté had chosen. As she said, calico "just won't act." Erté's final declaration: Miss Gish could take his

construction to begin on a lavishly decorated suite in the wardrobe building for the designer, modeled after Erté's own studio in Sèvres, France. Erté would work out of this studio for a scant six months, designing costumes for Aileen Pringle in Tod Browning's production of *The Mystic,* and for Carmel Myers in the role of Iras in *Ben-Hur,* as well as costumes and sets for *Dance Madness, Time, The Comedian,* and *Pretty Ladies* (Joan Crawford's first film). In a public relations short, *Inside the MGM Studios,* released in 1925, Erté is glimpsed at a fitting with the young Crawford, still known by her real name, Lucille LeSueur.

In truth, Erté's career at MGM may have been doomed before it really began. Through his *Harper's Bazaar* covers, Erté had succeeded in defining the reigning style of the flapper,

sketches and do what she wanted with them, but she was never to enter his studio office again.

From a public relations standpoint, this was not a smart move. Gish had signed an exclusive contract with MGM the previous spring, giving her costume approval as well as the right to select her own directors and scripts. Mayer had arranged for Gish to be greeted with flags and multicolored bunting when she arrived at the studio on April 14, and though her fortunes at MGM would fall in a few short years, for the moment she was the studio's biggest, and most prestigious, star.

Lillian Gish took her problems with Erté to Lucia Coulter, a genial seventy-year-old woman who worked as a wardrobe supervisor under Ethel Chaffin, and who went by the affectionate nickname "Mother Coulter." Before she began working at

For the character of Mimi, a destitute French peasant, Coulter and Gish collaborated on achieving a credible, more realistic look. Furthermore, as Erté had barred Gish from his studio, MGM turned to freelance designer Max Rée to design the rest of Gish's wardrobe for the film.

Erté's response to this situation was abrupt; he resigned on November 4 amid a storm of headlines, criticizing the studio's impossible schedules and equally impossible stars. At one point, he even advised Constance Bennett to go on a "milk diet" in order to add needed pounds.

Yet a short article, sans headline and hidden away in the back pages of the November 11 issue of *Variety,* was probably closer to the real story behind the designer's sudden departure: "Romain de Tirtoff (Erté), French fashion designer, whom MGM imported nine months ago to head its costume department at Culver City, is through. He will shortly return to his native land. It seems as though during the past two months Erté has not been getting along too well with the studio's officials. They did not seem to care for the manner in which he did his work as it was not performed in the speedy way required of their various department heads."

Moreover, Erté could not adapt to the effect film had on color. The orthochromatic film that was in general use before 1928 distorted certain hues; reds and yellows often came out unnaturally dark, and pure blues faded to white. Costume designing for motion pictures called for special skills, which Erté, quite simply, was not interested in learning.

Thalberg had been displeased enough to hire Joseph Rapf (producer Harry Rapf's brother) as business head of the wardrobe department, two months before Erté resigned. Rapf, thirty-nine, brought three new designers to the studio: Clement Andre-Ani, Kathleen Kay, and Maude Marsh. Kay and Marsh were a team who had owned a modiste shop in Los Angeles, and they generally worked together as Andre-Ani's

MGM, Coulter had spent fifty years making trick and character costumes for stage performers such as Weber and Fields and Marie Dressler. She once designed a pair of pants for an elephant and on another occasion, a sweater for a white mouse.

*One of the costumes for* La Bohème *designed by Max Rée, who MGM brought in to replace the temperamental Erté.*

assistants. They were signed to a contract at the suggestion of Mae Murray, who often used their services for her personal wardrobe. Before 1926 was out, they would be joined by David Cox and Gilbert Clark from New York.

Rapf's real coup, however, was signing Bennett Nathan to organize and head up a department of fabric decoration. Rapf had seen Nathan's handiwork on a trip to New York, when he attended the *Greenwich Village Follies,* a musical revue. Nathan had made elaborate shawls for the Sicilian Ballet troupe, who were performing in the show. A graduate of the Parsons School of Design in New York and the recipient of several medals from the National Academy of Fine Arts, Bennett Nathan already had fifty patents to his name, the first of which was for a process to adhere silver and gold leaf to chiffon fabric. For his first assignment at MGM, Nathan showed how economical his method could be with a pair of sleeves that were

part of an Erté-designed costume for *The Mystic.* One of the sleeves had such an intricate pattern that it would have taken six seamstresses two weeks to embroider it. Using Nathan's processes, it took only fifteen hours.

With Erté's departure, a triumvirate soon arose in the MGM wardrobe department, consisting of Gilbert Clark, David Cox, and Clement Andre-Ani. These three men, along with occasional freelance designers such as Rene Hubert, Max Rée, and Howard Greer (after he left Paramount) designed the costumes for several classic movies during the final flowering of silent film at MGM: Andre-Ani created the wardrobes for *The Wind* and *Annie Laurie,* both with Lillian Gish, and for King Vidor's *The Crowd* (all 1928); Gilbert Clark was responsible for *Man, Woman and Sin* with John Gilbert and Jeanne Eagels, and *The Actress* with Norma Shearer (both 1927), as well as *The Patsy* with Marion Davies (1928); David Cox dressed Joan Crawford for her breakthrough role in *Our Dancing Daughters* (1928).

Problems, however, persisted. In the spring of 1928, Gilbert Clark walked off the lot after Greta Garbo refused to wear one of the costumes he had created for her role as a spy in *The Mysterious Lady.* Clark was working for the studio on a film-by-film freelance agreement, and the incident was reported by Jack Jamison in *Modern Screen* magazine. Garbo had stayed locked in her dressing room for over three hours, until she was given permission to wear something other than the low-cut gown Clark had designed. The delay must have cost at least as much as the dress.

Andre-Ani had also had difficulty with Garbo. In an interview he has described designing for the newly arrived star in three of her first four films, *The Temptress* (1926), *Flesh and the Devil* (1927), and *Love* (1927): "She is very difficult to do things for. She has a very difficult figure; she has very set ideas and very foreign ones. She has innumerable dislikes. She will wear nothing that has fur, absolutely nothing! She will wear no laces, no velvets. She goes in for flaunting bizarre collars and cuffs. She likes short skirts when she should wear longer ones." And in 1927 he was quoted in *Motion Picture* magazine regarding his distaste for directors who criticized his designs.

MGM art director Preston Ames remembers that an ability to get along with people was very important at the studio: "You have to have the patience of Job. You don't fight the director. You work with him." Knowingly or unknowingly, Andre-Ani had violated a cardinal rule at Metro-Goldwyn-Mayer.

According to Robert Riley, a former professor at the

manager M. E. Greenwood on June 7 to loan Adrian to Metro. Adrian's contract with DeMille did not expire until July 26, and so his salary, $450 a week, would be issued to DeMille's payroll for the first seven weeks of his tenure at MGM.

Adrian's initial independent agreement with Metro-Goldwyn-Mayer, and his first signed contract with the studio, was dated July 27, 1928, and ran for one year, with two options of one year each. MGM raised his salary to $500 a week, where it would remain until 1931 when, if everything went according to plan, a new contract would be negotiated. The contract itself was unusual in that it had a proviso that allowed Adrian to make a trip to New York once a year, all expenses paid, with an agreement to provide him with "not less than a compartment" onboard the train east. This was a perk unprecedented in Metro's agreements with its costume designers. In addition, the contract contained a clause which stated that, as per a verbal agreement, MGM promised Adrian "a certain amount of dignified publicity. Also, we agreed with him that it is considered more appropriate to show billing as 'Gowns by' instead of 'Wardrobe.'"

The contract reflected the studio's faith in its new designer, and the two one-year options were merely a legal formality, with a convenient "out" if things didn't go as planned. And there were big plans in the works. After much consultation with DeMille, the powers at MGM—Mayer, Thalberg, and wardrobe supervisor Rapf—were convinced they had found the right person for the job. Within months after Gilbert Adrian's arrival at the studio, they began to plan a campaign that went far beyond "a certain amount of dignified publicity." A massive promotional operation was put into effect to make Gilbert Adrian the most important costume designer in all Hollywood.

Fashion Institute of Technology in New York and a co-author of the book *American Fashion,* "David Cox, Andre-Ani, and Gilbert Clark were not really respected at MGM or anywhere. They ran a higgledy-piggledy operation, and Clark and Ani, especially, were prima donnas. They didn't want to have a working relationship with the actresses. They felt their word was law."

But Mayer's word was the only law recognized on the MGM lot, and on the heels of Gilbert Clark's walkout, he accelerated negotiations with a young designer at the DeMille Studios to replace him. Gilbert Adrian had been prepared to join Cecil B. DeMille when the director signed a three-picture deal at MGM in August. With DeMille's consent, however, Adrian reported for his first day's work at Metro-Goldwyn-Mayer in June of 1928.

W. C. Hutchinson, the business manager at the DeMille Studios, had agreed in a verbal agreement with MGM studio

# The Advent of Adrian at MGM

O n the morning of Monday, June 11, 1928, Gilbert Adrian was met in front of the MGM studio gate on Washington Boulevard by Pete Smith, the head of publicity for the studio, his assistant, Howard Strickling, and Joseph Rapf.

Adrian was awestruck. His experience at the tiny DeMille Studios had left him unprepared for this giant, self-contained municipality devoted exclusively to the making of motion pictures. Dozens of extras, many in elaborate costumes, roamed the paved streets. The soundstages were the size of airplane hangars, with mammoth doors that, as George Hurrell would later note, "looked like giant gaping mouths" when they were flung open. Adrian took immediately to his new assignment, if not to his new quarters: a small alcove office on the third floor of the wardrobe building. If Louis B. Mayer did not herald the arrival of his new designer with a luncheon at the Beverly Hills Hotel, as he had Erté, one reason may have been because there wasn't a minute to spare. Adrian was put to work almost immediately.

In retrospect, the first films Adrian was assigned at his new studio seem deliberately chosen to test the young designer's mettle. *The Masks of the Devil* was a John Gilbert vehicle, to be directed by Victor Sjöström. *Dream of Love* featured Aileen Pringle, MGM's resident clotheshorse in the late 1920s, as well as a young starlet named Joan Crawford. Both productions contained potential pitfalls for an unsuspecting—and untested—twenty-four-year-old designer.

*Eva von Berne wearing an Adrian costume of petit point lace in* The Masks of the Devil *(1928).*

*An Adrian costume sketch — one of his first at MGM — for Alma Rubens in* The Masks of the Devil. *The dress, which Adrian called the "peacock gown," was made of black chiffon velvet. The long train extending from the left shoulder was decorated with a pattern of peacock feathers embroidered in sequins.*

Opposite: *Alma Rubens wearing the peacock gown in the film. The dress is cut along a severe, straight line. As with many Adrian costumes, the viewer's eye is drawn to one defining feature.*

Sjöström, a meticulous craftsman with a restrained, solemn, somewhat ponderous style, had been signed by the Goldwyn company in 1923 and had stayed on the payroll when the studio merged into MGM the following year. He quickly became one of the studio's most prestigious and successful directors, responsible for a number of major hits, including *He Who Gets Slapped* with Lon Chaney and *The Scarlet Letter* with Lillian Gish. He shot many of his films at least partly on location — a rarity in the studio era — and had clashed more than once with costume designers on the lot. During production on *The Wind* earlier in the year, Sjöström had sent Andre-Ani back to revise costumes on two separate occasions, claiming that his designs were not realistic enough for a hardscrabble woman living on the prairie.

*The Masks of the Devil* (1928) was a Ruritanian romance, with Gilbert as an unscrupulous baron who plots to steal his best friend's fiancée. Two weeks after production began on 23 June, Thalberg decided to cast eighteen-year-old Eva von Berne as Gilbert's leading lady. He had discovered the young actress in Vienna during his honeymoon with Norma Shearer.

As with so many films of the 1920s and 1930s, *The Masks of the Devil* featured a scene set in a dressmaker's shop, which afforded the opportunity for a fashion show attended by members of the baron's immediate circle. Even at this early stage of his MGM career, the differences between Adrian's designs and those of his peers at the studio are readily apparent. His use of black-and-white materials complements and even seems to complete the creamy Cedric Gibbons set. Most of his clothes are cut along a severe, straight line, with a minimum of decoration. Again and again, the viewer's eye is drawn to one

overriding, sometimes startling, feature: a bow, a length of fringe, or a ripple of sequins cascading down the length of a dress or across the bodice. This "focus" would become one of the hallmarks of Adrian's costume designs. As he explained to a reporter from *Ladies' Home Journal* in 1933: "Every costume should have one note. Concentration on that one note emphasizes it and makes it interesting. When you start to concentrate on more than one note, then you detract from the main idea and merely have a conglomeration. Sound one note truly; then it will have a definite value."

For Von Berne, Adrian created a series of light, frothy gowns, made of lace and cotton crepe, that served to heighten her innocence and naiveté when compared to the worldly members of Gilbert's inner circle.

Production on *The Masks of the Devil* concluded on July 25, after a shooting schedule of four weeks, without incident between one of MGM's most important directors and the studio's new costume designer. The first test had been passed.

*Adrian supervises a last-minute costume fitting for Josephine DeVorak, left, and Renee Torres on the set of* The Masks of the Devil.

RIGHT: *Alma Rubens visits a dress shop in* The Masks of the Devil. *There was a natural collaboration between the look of Adrian's costume designs and Cedric Gibbons's sets. Unfortunately, still pictures are all that remain of* The Masks of the Devil, *one of MGM's lost silent films.*

Aileen Pringle was an entirely different hurdle for Adrian. Widely publicized in the late 1920s as one of the best-dressed women on the screen, Pringle was particular about what she would and would not wear. The actress had made her screen debut in 1919, and had achieved instant fame after appearing as an exotic siren in two productions, *Three Weeks* and *His Hour* (both 1924), which were written by Elinor Glyn. At the time they were considered daring for their sexual frankness.

Pringle herself was no less frank. She once received a message from Louis B. Mayer after he watched her film a scene from *His Hour* in a diaphanous gown that left little to the imagination. The note read that he wanted to see the gown in

his offices at the end of the day. "I knew, of course, what the old goat wanted," she said many years later. Blunt, cynical, and with a wicked tongue, Pringle sent the gown to Mayer's office when filming had concluded for the day. The card attached to the white box read: "Dear Mr. Mayer. Here is the gown you wanted to see. I hope it fits!"

Aileen Pringle had worked with many of the top designers of the day at MGM, including Erté on *The Mystic* in 1925, but antics like the one on the set of *His Hour* had caused her

star to dim considerably in the front office. (In 1926 Mayer gave the newly-arrived Greta Garbo two films, *Torrent* and *The Temptress,* that he had previously promised to Pringle, a fact that she still fumed over six decades later.) Her role in *Dream of Love* (1928) was essentially a supporting one; Joan Crawford's role might not have been larger than Pringle's but the plot hinged on the fate of her character—a strolling guitar player who meets Nils Asther, a European crown prince, and opens his eyes to the joys of true love. Asther jilts her on the grounds

that he could never marry a commoner, but is then deposed in a coup and becomes involved with a duchess, played by Aileen Pringle, who schemes to win back the throne for him. Crawford, however, exacts her revenge: she becomes a wildly successful cabaret performer, is reunited with her prince, and manages to save her country from a military takeover as well. The road Crawford travels—from impoverished player to glittering celebrity—is similar to the path she would take as a post-Depression Cinderella in a few years.

Although Pringle was not nominally the star of *Dream of Love*, and did not walk into the sunset with Nils Asther before the final credits, she still resented the fact that MGM had assigned a new and, in her eyes, untried designer to create her wardrobe. The resentment grew on a hot day in early July when Pringle climbed the stairs to Adrian's office for her first meeting with her new designer. Puffing on one of her monogrammed cigarettes, Pringle made a grand entrance and announced to the startled Adrian that she wanted sequin and rhinestone decorations on one of her dresses. "I remember he frowned," she said. "He started to say, 'I'm not sure whether . . .' but I cut him off. 'This [story] is supposed to be laid in a mythical kingdom, isn't it?' I asked him. 'How do you know whether I should have decorations or not? How does anybody know?'"

Adrian tried to explain that he felt rhinestones and brilliants were fine for a cabaret performer, but not for a member of royalty, mythical kingdom or not. But Pringle remained adamant, and Adrian, undoubtedly remembering his experience with DeMille on *The Volga Boatman*, realized it would be unwise to butt heads with an MGM star. So Pringle's duchess got her decorations, in an over-the-top gown Adrian dubbed "Crystal Magnolia."

Aileen Pringle was so pleased with this gown and the rest of her wardrobe that she requested Adrian for her next film, *A Single Man* (1929), the sixth feature to star Miss Pringle and Lew Cody, a comic who had honed his talents in vaudeville before entering silent films. The film offered a change of pace for the star. Billed as "the flaming youth comedy," Pringle was cast as the dowdy personal secretary of a best-selling author (Cody) who makes a fool of himself when he falls in love with a young flapper. The battle between the secretary and the flapper for the author's attention forms the basis of the comedy. In the end, Miss Pringle transforms herself, appearing in a gown that so changes her appearance Mr. Cody can barely believe his eyes. Elements of this basic plot would be recycled some forty years later in the hit Broadway comedy *Cactus Flower*.

Adrian saw the transformation in symbolic terms and designed appropriate costumes: "Throughout the picture Miss Pringle depicts the efficient, capable business girl, giving more attention to her mental capacities than to her physical charms. Drab colors in severe lines envelop her body and mind. Then, awakened by love, she sees beauty and reaches to express it. This was the expression I had to work on. I visualized her as a cocoon working in the dark, and then I pictured her as a

butterfly casting aside her shell and blossoming out in sheer loveliness. I sketched a butterfly costume and fashioned it in delicate, filmy white soufflé."

The costume took nine seamstresses fifteen days to make and at $850 was also publicized as the most expensive gown ever made at MGM up to that time—a debatable point, but it made for good publicity. Aileen Pringle was so enchanted with the dress that she bought it when filming was over. Years later, she remembered how astonished she had felt when she met with Adrian to go over the costumes for her role as secretary Mary Hazeltine. "He presented me with a series of sketches, and then asked me which ones I preferred. I had never had this experience with a designer before. We then discussed the character I was going to play, and he explained to me how he saw her transformation, sketching all the while. He created four new sketches during our conversation! I remember one of the gowns he created for the secretary, which I eventually wore, had a series of scarves around the neck."

Pringle's delight would soon be shared by other MGM actresses. "When we were working on a film together," remembers Anita Page, "[Adrian] would always say 'What do you think of this?' or 'How do you feel about that?' His creations were so wonderfully designed for both the film as well as the star, I always felt I could depend on whatever he gave me." And after her unfortunate experience with Gilbert Clark on *The Mysterious Lady*, Greta Garbo found working with Adrian much more to her liking. Years after she left MGM, she told the Swedish journalist Sven Broman, "I have always liked wearing clothes up to my throat. That is where I think men are cleverer than women. Adrian, who made many of the clothes I wore in films, understood my wishes. And he went to great lengths to help me avoid anything too low-cut."

After his initial encounter with Aileen Pringle, Adrian learned very quickly that a satisfied customer meant a return customer. Once he discovered the proclivities of the stars he was to dress, Adrian always attempted to incorporate their likes and dislikes into his designs. Over time, this led to a growing trust between star and designer that gave him a great deal of autonomy in the wardrobe department. He was also shrewd enough to use this information to his advantage; for example,

*Warner Oland, left, and Aileen Pringle in* Dream of Love, *with Pringle in Adrian's "Crystal Magnolia" gown. Pringle, who had insisted that the designer give her lots of brilliants, got them in spades: the dress was made of white velvet encrusted in a solid embroidery of bugle beads and mirrors, with a two-tiered collar.*

knowing Joan Crawford's preference for the color blue, Adrian would often present the actress with a sketch for a dress that *he* preferred in *her* favorite hue.

The "butterfly gown" Adrian designed for *A Single Man* enchanted not only Aileen Pringle, but also Irving Thalberg. The studio's vice-president left little to chance, and before the Pasadena preview of *A Single Man* he had audience reaction cards printed that specifically asked for opinions on Miss Pringle's costumes in the film. Response was overwhelmingly favorable, with high marks for the "butterfly gown." As a result, Thalberg instructed Pete Smith to make arrangements to have the gown featured as part of a photo essay in the August 15 issue of *Hollywood* magazine.

Shortly after the *Hollywood* article hit the stands, Adrian's worth to MGM was fully ascertained when the studio arranged to have him write a series of monthly articles for *Screenland* magazine. As fashion editor, Adrian analyzed the clothes problems of a particular type—the flapper, the debutante—as personified by an MGM star. Introduced to *Screenland* readers as MGM's "fashion authority," he was thus able to solidify the images the studio sought to create for its female stars. In one issue, timed to the release of *A Single Man*, Adrian dealt with the smart sophisticate as embodied by Aileen Pringle:

There are not many Aileen Pringles in the world—even the world of fashion, so there will not be a host of women who will find their clothes problems solved in the study of her wardrobe; but there are many who border on that type and they should find helpful ideas in analyzing the frame she provides her personality by means of her dress, accessories and adornments.

The Pringle type should not adopt the same general *motiff* [sic] for all her costumes. Some women can; they find a basic style that is becoming, that is a perfect frame, and they build a wardrobe for all occasions upon that one fundamental style. But not the Pringle type. Hers is a multi-faceted personality, kaleidoscopic in its changing impressions, and her clothing should be as varied. For instance, one costume as austere as a nunnery, the next as gay, as flashing as the fountains of Versailles. But all must be extreme.

I do not advise the average woman to

*Aileen Pringle wearing the "butterfly" costume in* A Single Man. *The garment had a large circular cape that, when posed over the back of the dress, created the effect of butterfly wings. Shirred to the bodice, the skirt falls in soft circular folds and extends just below the knee in front, while in back it barely clears the floor. The exaggerated hemline is cut in scallops, giving irregular dips to the silhouette. Women's clothes of the 1920s favored shirring over more rigid clothing; by this time even coats and blazers were soft and unconstructed.*

OPPOSITE: *Aileen Pringle as overworked secretary Mary Hazeltine in* A Single Man. *The many hem-length scarves Adrian looped around her neck literally weighed down the actress, giving the impression that her character was symbolically caught in a noose—which indeed she was.*

try to copy Miss Pringle, but if they want to get a thrill I do advise them to see her as she always stages a very spectacular show. She brings a quality of reality to the most artificial of clothes.

Adrian would also go on to write about Greta Garbo, Joan Crawford, Norma Shearer, and Anita Page in *Screenland*'s pages. Early in 1929, Thalberg bestowed another vote of confidence in Adrian when he elected to move him into Erté's old office in the MGM wardrobe building.

Almost three years after Erté's departure, Louis B. Mayer still keenly felt the loss of the French designer, despite the problems he had created at the studio. According to Mayer biographer Charles Higham, the studio chief had been fascinated with Erté, who had often reported for work in rose and gray crepe de chine or crimson and black brocaded coats and gold pants. When Erté decided to return to France, Mayer gave him a car as a parting gift.

Thalberg, however, had never had much use for Erté. Maintaining personal—and professional—self-control was important to Thalberg, and a trait he valued in the executives who comprised his inner circle. In Adrian, Thalberg had

found a kindred spirit. The two men had taken to each other at first meeting, and in fact had much in common with one another. Both Jewish, with dark, ascetic features, they were contemporaries in age (Thalberg was four years older than his new designer) and shared a quiet, contemplative nature. They each favored dark business suits for office attire, and Adrian had an air of New England self-control about him, a look, as Robert Riley described it, of "austere simplicity" that complemented what writer Jim Tully described as Thalberg's "gentle, dreamy" air.

The changes that Adrian would soon instigate in the wardrobe department would justify Thalberg's faith in him. And unlike his temperamental predecessors, Adrian loved jokes—his friend, writer Leonard Gershe, recalls that he would sometimes assume a convincing Chinese accent, and then trap unsuspecting friends in telephone adventures that involved absurd tales of smuggled gems and international intrigue. One April Fool's Day some members of Adrian's staff turned the tables on their boss and arranged with the studio commissary chef to serve him a salad of artificial leaves. Rather than pitch a fit, Adrian ate it with relish, down to the last shiny green olive.

# A New Beginning

*1929–1930*

**A**drian moved into his new quarters in the wardrobe department in March 1929, but not before making several sweeping changes to the overall design of the three-room suite. After conferring with and receiving budgetary approval from Joseph Rapf, Adrian finally decided on a neutral color scheme because he didn't want anything in the room to detract from the clothes. Both walls and carpets were done up in a soft oyster white, which offered a stark contrast to the red, ivory, and black shades preferred by Erté, and even the bright green and gold colors that had decorated Adrian's offices at the DeMille Studio.

A row of windows to the left of the entrance was shielded from the glare of the California sun by Venetian blinds and off-white chintz drapes. A large quilted sofa was flanked on both sides by tall stands supporting flat bowls of growing ivy. Faint sepia murals of a jungle scene, drawn by Adrian himself, ran along the baseboard, and one wall was solid with mirrors. A platform in front of this wall was crowned with spotlights so that the gown being fitted could be lit as it would be seen by the camera.

At the end of the fitting room, before louvered doors that revealed a small library, was a comfortable yellow chintz chair and a drawing board where Adrian produced the 50 to 75 sketches he created during an average work day.

*An Adrian drawing of Joan Crawford wearing a costume for* This Modern Age *(1931).*
*Opposite, the costume worn by the actress in the finished film.*

*Adrian in his studio at MGM.*

BELOW: *For actresses such as Ann Rutherford, the wardrobe department under Adrian became the center of the MGM lot: "It wasn't just
floor after floor of clothes. It was ringed with a cast-iron balcony so
that you could stand there and look at these marvelous racks brim-
ming with costumes." Here the racks hold Adrian's costumes for the
munchkins in* The Wizard of Oz *(1939).*

MGM wardrobe workroom, Robert Riley maintains, "he hired
good people who had training—not because somebody's sister
or brother needed a job. He insisted, for example, on not dying
fabrics from somebody's relatives' operation but going to a
professional dyer."

And to a professional dry cleaner as well. Makeup is very
hard on clothing, and Adrian arranged to have each costume
spotted when filming had concluded for the day. If necessary, it
was sent out for dry cleaning on special order. A truck from
Malone Studio Service came each night at 7 P.M. and collected
the wardrobe that would have to be cleaned, pressed, and
returned to the studio by 7 A.M. the next morning. Clothing
worn by the stars at MGM was hand-cleaned at night by Marie
Wharton, whom Adrian hired in 1929. In the mid-1930s, the
MGM cleaning bill came to almost $40,000 a year. By 1941, the
year Adrian left MGM, the racks in the studio's wardrobe department held over 250,000 costumes inventoried at $1,500,000.
Cyanide was used four times a year to prevent moths and other
pests from inflicting damage on the sartorial glory that had once
belonged to Garbo, Shearer, Crawford, Harlow, and MacDonald.

Adrian was also instrumental in hiring a number of
professional beaders from Getson's Eastern Embroidery, a bead
shop in downtown Los Angeles. "They brought their lunch in
brown bags and never went out on the lot," recalls MGM publi-

To actress Ann Rutherford, who began working at MGM
in 1937, Adrian's fitting room was "nirvana. . . . He had white art
deco sofas and marvelous sketches on the walls, rugs deep as the
middle of the ocean, and he served tea and things. There was a
maid in uniform to help you in and out of your clothes."

In the summer of 1929, after he had finished redecorating
his new office and fitting room, Adrian turned his attention to
reorganizing the entire costume department. "He was extremely
well organized," recalls Robert Riley. "He demanded promptness.
He had to, as he was often juggling as many as five productions
at one time. He wouldn't wait for anyone. If a star was late for a
fitting, he would often cancel the appointment,
and she would have to reschedule it."

This worked to Adrian's advantage for
another reason, as Leonard Gershe remembers. "Adrian once told me that the stars
would get very angry if they found their scheduled time was being appropriated by another
actress whose appointment had run into overtime. They all made one exception, however,
and that was for Garbo. They were all a little
bit in awe of her—even Norma Shearer—and
no one ever complained if Garbo's fitting took
longer than expected."

As Adrian took steps to overhaul the

*Long bands of silver lace, spangled by hand in the MGM workroom, circa 1938, are created for this costume worn by Norma Shearer in* Marie Antoinette *(1938).*

cist Ann Straus. "They just sat and beaded and embroidered all these beautiful costumes. They never knew the people for whom they were doing the work. They just knew it was production number 1420 and that was all." When journalist Frank Nugent visited the wardrobe department in the early 1940s he marveled at these expert craftspeople: "At one table several middle-aged women were working at what looked like embroidery frames. One was scissoring tiny snips off a spool of pure-gold wire and sewing each minute fragment to a band of heavy silk. Others were working with beads and sequins of precious metals. They were expert craftsmen, patient, painstaking, utterly absorbed in their metallic designs. I asked one how long she had been working on a gleaming gold-and-silver border two inches wide, a foot long. 'One week,' she said."

Georgina Grant, who worked in MGM's costume department for 30 years, could still remember the intimidation she felt sixty years after her initial interview with Adrian in the mid-1930s. Adrian had a single-minded approach in his pursuit of excellence, and he wasted little time: "He lined about seven or eight of us up in a row, and he handed us each an appliqué—white satin with braid on it—and told us to sew it to a backing. He'd pick them up and say, 'You go. You stay.' And when he came to me, he said, 'Is that the best you can do?' I said, 'No, but I thought you wanted it in a hurry.' He handed me another one and said, 'Do this one and give me your best work.' So I did and he said, 'You stay.'"

Adrian's insistence on fine workmanship became a hallmark of his designs, and stemmed primarily from his lack of control over how his costumes were to be filmed. He knew that a close-up magnifies everything in a film approximately eight times; machine embroidery, cheap fabric, or bad workmanship would stand out pitifully, unless the role the actress was playing called for her to be dressed in such a fashion.

Adrian applied the same no-nonsense approach he used in

*The Joan Crawford mannequin fitted with the
burlesque costume she wore in* Dancing Lady *(1933).*

organizing his workroom to the actual process of designing, which became streamlined under his guidance. He was instrumental in breaking the MGM costume department and its employees into two sub-departments: those who worked to manufacture the clothes and those who dealt with the finished costumes. The people in manufacturing included beaders, milliners, cutters, fitters, tailors, figure makers, shoemakers, and drapers. These were the people who were responsible for transforming Adrian's sketches into finished garments, and he insisted that they have proven experience. A select group in manufacturing also analyzed scripts ready for production for costume requirements, and purchased bolts of fabric from retail and wholesale operations on Adrian's recommendations.

Once the gowns were completed, Adrian had costumers who were responsible for insuring that the right dress was on the right actress at the right time. It was also part of their job to maintain accurate records as to which actress wore which costume in which scene. Lucia Coulter, who had assisted Lillian Gish with her costumes for *La Bohème* in 1926, was in charge of period costumes at MGM in the early 1930s.

When a script was finished and had been approved by the producer, a breakdown artist from the script department would make a "costume script," which was simply a list of all the different scenes and locations in the film, along with a plot synopsis and a description of each character. Adrian rarely requested a complete script. He knew the star, so he chose to conceive then and there what she would look like, for example, in a railroad station alighting from a train, or in a drawing room before dinner.

Once Adrian received the costume script, his first task was to make pencil sketches of costume ideas—a silhouette, or "body line," upon which the costume would be developed. When this was completed, a conference with the star was called, and if she had suggestions, an attempt was made to incorporate them. For a beaded or sequined design, Adrian would make a rough sketch of what he wanted and send it to Mrs. Cluett, the head of the beading department. Her staff would make a swatch, and would then create their own designs based on what Adrian had roughly sketched out. These samples would then be sent to Adrian, and all he had to do was pick the one he wanted.

This method was in sharp contrast to the working habits of Andre-Ani and David Cox, who began designing for each film by reading the entire script and then taking notes on the costumes that would be needed. Sketches, before they were approved by the director and producer, were complete in every detail, including color and incidental jewelry, shoes and hosiery. If the sketch wasn't approved, days of work had been wasted. Adrian's approach saved time and money.

When the sketch was approved by the star, the director, and the producer, Adrian then recreated it in watercolors in the approximate tones in which the costume would appear on the screen. Swatches of the fabrics to be used were often attached to the finished sketches so that texture and color contrast could be easily visualized. The actual gown was created by one of the cutters in the wardrobe department in unbleached muslin, and then the star was called in for a fitting. She walked, turned, and posed in the muslin copy of the dress before the mirrors, and on the pedestal in the spotlight, making it possible to view the costume line from every angle.

All necessary alterations were made on the muslin, and in doing so Adrian was adopting, perhaps unwittingly, one of the methods utilized by the French couture. This was a practice that couturieres such as Chanel and Vionnet had used since 1918. It saved money in the long run, as muslin was relatively inexpensive. If a beaded or appliqué design was to appear on the costume, it was drawn in pencil on the muslin, so that there would be no question about how it would fall on the figure.

Like Chanel, who worked directly on her mannequins and had them swing their arms and legs for hours until she was sure how a fabric worked in motion, Adrian watched the actress intently during the fitting. He was interested not only in the static visual aspect of his work, as were most Hollywood designers, but in the physical performance of his creations as well. After this final inspection, every seam was adjusted by a fitter working under Adrian's direction. Only after the fitting was the dress actually cut and made in the fabric and colors that would be used in the film. By the mid-1930s, there were eight cutters and fitters working under Adrian and each of these professionals had a staff of ten people.

This first fitting with the actress was also the last until the costume was completed. At the final fitting Adrian improved on Cecil B. DeMille's method of staging a fashion show before production began. Instead, he would often film the actress with a small home-movie camera so he could look at the dress later and better determine how the lines moved on film, making any final adjustments that he deemed necessary. This method also gave him an opportunity to deduce which fabrics worked best on film, and how they could be used to underscore or heighten a certain mood: the ripple of lamé under a direct key light, the transparency of organza, the vibrations of gingham, the stiffness of taffeta.

Although designers such as Chanel put their mannequins through an endurance test, making them stand for an exhausting six or seven hours while they fitted a dress, Adrian realized that an actress's schedule—not to mention temperament— would not accommodate a fitting that went on for hours. In addition to using the home-movie camera as a time-saving device, in 1930 Adrian instituted the practice of using dress dummies for each actress, padded to exact measurements. Actual fittings were done on these models, leaving the actress free until production on the film began. Upon completion, the wardrobe was kept in a glass case, labeled with the name and number of the production. Often, four or even six identical outfits were made, in case the original was damaged in a scene that required multiple takes.

Many years after Adrian had left MGM, Edith Head would exclaim to her biographer, Paddy Calistro, that her greatest career anxieties came when she had viewed Adrian's latest film costumes: "I often felt pangs of inadequacy when I watched Garbo slink across the screen in one of his perfectly engineered gowns."

So accomplished were Adrian and his cutters and fitters that they were capable of near-miracles of "engineering." In 1931, actress Madge Evans was signed to a long-term contract at MGM; her first assignment was the feminine lead opposite Ramon Novarro in *Son of India*. The contract Evans signed, however, had one stipulation: she did not have to report for work at the studio until the play she was appearing in on Broadway had ended its run.

The play ran longer than expected, and finally it was necessary to start the picture. Much to Adrian's dismay, he was unable to locate a couturier in New York who would be willing to take Ms. Evans's measurements for a wardrobe that would be made by another designer. The day Madge Evans finally arrived in California, the last scene that could be shot without her had been filmed. If she could not go to work immediately, the entire company would be idle, resulting in a terrible financial loss for the studio.

Arriving at 5:45 P.M. on the 20th Century-Limited, Evans was whisked to the studio's wardrobe and makeup departments. Her costumes fit perfectly. They had been designed and made with only one guide: a yardstick placed against a photograph of Evans, that had been taken in New York. Solely through the use of this comparison Adrian's wardrobe department created costumes that required only slight alterations at the shoulder. Evans declared herself to be "thrilled" with her costumes, and "astounded" by the expertise of the MGM wardrobe department.

For Adrian, all of this effort and precision was in the service of two goals: revealing character through costume, and presenting each of the MGM actresses he designed for at her best. "Designers in real life seldom worry about dramatic values," he said in 1936, "for they know little about the events in the life of the individual wearing their creation. . . . On the other hand, a designer for the screen knows, before he starts his sketch, every experience the wearer of the gown will have. It is his business to dress his character in a manner that will intensify, to an audience, the mood of the scene."

In *Riptide* (1934), for example, Norma Shearer played a young American woman, married to an English lord, who has a fling with an American playboy. Discussing the modern wardrobe he created for Shearer, Adrian wrote, "I gave her moulded lines with a long-leg line to make her look taller. Bouffant clothes and fussy jewelry are out, because her curly hair in this film is adornment enough. The other adornment she must get from the details of her clothes, the cut, the buttons, the sleeves, the trimmings, and, of course, the materials. . . . A clever designer can substitute a single costume for whole scenes through the mere expedient of making clothes talk. In *Riptide* I achieved this explanatory short cut by introducing the slit skirt and other dramatic deviations, which as Miss Shearer first flashed on screen, said, wholly without words, 'I am a woman of fashion, young, beautiful, gay and just a little reckless.' It is sketching a character by virtue of scissors, needle, [and] thread."

Modern Hollywood costumes, like those in *Riptide,* represented a special subdivision in the world of 1930s haute couture fashion. Throughout the twenties and thirties, designers such as Vionnet, Schiaparelli, Patou, and Chanel expanded on Charles Worth's concept of the mutable silhouette, and with it the concept of the "new" in fashion. They created a modern vocabulary of forms, achieved primarily through contrasts of fabric texture, color, and plasticity of line. While Hollywood designers adhered to similar principles in designing costumes, they also had to enhance the studio-constructed images of the stars and, as Adrian explained, fulfill the narrative demands of the screenplay.

The Hollywood designer of this time also had to work

*With just a yardstick and a photograph as a stand-in for the actress Madge Evans, who was unavailable, Adrian was able to make costumes for Evans that required the most minimal of final adjustments. In the dress seen here that Evans wore in the film* Son of India *(1931), fluted ruffles outline the neck and similar ruffles form a peplum at the hips, with flared panels that form the bouffant skirt. With Evans are Marjorie Rambeau, at left, and Ramon Novarro.*

*Emphasis above the table:*
*An Adrian costume for Greta*
*Garbo from* Inspiration *(1931).*

OPPOSITE: *Norma Shearer in*
Riptide *(1934), in which she*
*plays the young wife of an*
*English lord who dallies with*
*playboy Robert Montgomery.*
*The long skirt Shearer wears*
*is silk crepe. The velvet jacket*
*has dolman sleeves shirred to*
*fit the arm closely. The cord*
*loop fastening at the throat,*
*accented with silver buttons,*
*is repeated at the waist.*

within the confines of black-and-white film. As early as 1929 Adrian had begun to avoid middle grays as much as possible, contrasting black and white because he realized that these colors would create the greatest impact on monochromatic film. In 1931, Peggy Hamilton gave a showing of costumes from Adrian's films. Almost every single one was black-and-white.

In addition, the inherent building blocks of film—long and medium shots, close-ups and tracking shots—dictated how fashion was presented on-screen. "Emphasis above the table" was Adrian's own phrase to describe his propensity for detail that was designed to rivet the viewer's eyes around the neck with tucks, flaps, beading, or unusually shaped collars and bows. This was hardly an accident of design or a capricious whim. Adrian knew that during the course of a film there might be only a few long shots to show-case an entire gown. And films—not to mention stars—were built around close-ups. Accents in sequins, fur, and bugle beads around the neck not only lent a certain cachet to a close-up shot but also called attention to the flamboyance and imagination of the designer. The torso and head thus became the focus of many of Adrian's designs, and the skirts were used to provide a shape to fill out the overall effect.

"There is no question that Hollywood has a great influence on the spread of style ideas," Adrian said in 1936, "but Paris remains the great center of style." The great triumph of Holly-wood was its ability to spread established fashions over a wider range of social groups in a shorter time than was ever possible before the ascendance of the motion picture. In addition, by associating certain style ideas with actresses whose images best typified them—the "conservative" Norma Shearer in *Riptide;* the "exotic" Greta Garbo or Marlene Dietrich—Hollywood could market and sell a trend with a finesse that caught Paris up short.

The concept of costume (Hollywood) vs. fashion (Paris), and the tendency of studio publicity departments to pounce on the sensational and the spectacular, and promote them as high style, would often become a thorn in Adrian's side. "Motion picture style designers cannot give the effect of good work as can the designers of Paris for this reason: American women receive well-edited versions of the styles of Paris," Adrian told a reporter in the mid-1930s. "In the motion pictures they are conscious, perhaps, of some charming dresses, some mediocre dresses, and some distressing dresses. The result is confusion: the feeling that there is some good,

*Wallace Beery (left) and Jean Harlow arrive for* Dinner at Eight *(1933), with Harlow in the new dress designed to "knock their eye out."*

OPPOSITE: *Jean Harlow as Kitty Packard in* Dinner at Eight, *wearing Adrian's beaded negligee cuffed in 22-inch ostrich fronds. This negligee became one of Harlow's most famous costumes, and was heavily promoted as a "Hollywood style," much to Adrian's distress.*

some bad, but no standard. Some of the styles which I design are not at all suited to general wear. Sometimes a part requires that an actress dress in bad taste: the character which she portrays demands this."

Two gowns designed for Jean Harlow in her role as Kitty Packard, the tarty wife of a nouveau riche tycoon (Wallace Beery) in *Dinner at Eight* (1933) were singled out by Adrian years after the film was released. "The ostrich-feathered negligee," he told reporter Elaine St. Maur, "was publicized as a 'Hollywood style' when it was far too extreme, having been designed to aid (Harlow's) characterization. The really style-setting gowns (in the film) were overlooked by the vast majority." For Adrian, costume always took precedence over fashion, and the ostrich feathers, which slice the air as Kitty dices her parvenu husband with a tirade of insults, punctuate each outrage while never failing to underscore her femininity. They also serve to add a larger physical dimension to Harlow's slight frame, allowing her to hold the screen against the hulking presence of Wallace Beery.

Harlow's evening gown in the film, which she wears to a Park Avenue dinner party, was introduced in the script itself as an utterly impractical style: "Once in our life we get asked out to a classy house, and I gotta new dress that'll knock their eye out, and we're goin'!" Kitty shrieks at her husband. The dress—a silver satin gown cut on the bias and trimmed with fur—became one of Harlow's most famous costumes, and it did indeed knock everyone's eye out. But it was designed for theatrical effect and not as a style for the fashion-conscious American woman.

Sometimes, however, Adrian was able to carry out his effects with a subtle wink at the audience. Katharine Hepburn still remembers one accessory for a costume in *The Philadelphia Story* (1940): a tight-fitting knitted cap with a long tassel that topped off a striped, cream-colored summer suit. "I wore it in the scene in the library with Jimmy [Stewart]. Tracy Lord went to the library, you see, to find this book that he had written. She was very impressed with his writing." As a result, Stewart's character, reporter Macaulay Connor, changes his original impression of Tracy as "the young, rich, rapacious American female" and begins to fall in love.

"When Adrian showed me the sketch, I laughed," remembers Hepburn. "It looked like a hat for a very young girl, and it didn't seem to go with the suit. Then he explained to me how he saw Tracy's character. She comes on, you know, and she wants to be running the show. Very bossy. She wants to defy convention, and she won't take advice from anyone. But inside there's a frightened young girl. He thought the hat would help show that

Tracy wasn't as stiff as she seemed on the surface, and also give a glimpse of that girl inside. Well, I loved it, you know. Very smart!"

*The Philadelphia Story,* which went before the cameras in the summer of 1940, shows Adrian near the end of his career at MGM. Yet Hepburn's experience with him on this film and two others, *Woman of the Year* and *Keeper of the Flame* (both 1942), were enough to make her a fan for life. "Adrian was my favorite designer," she told Calvin Klein in the late 1970s. "He and I had the same sense of 'smell' about what clothes should do and what they should say."

*Almost as odd as the funnel-shaped hat that Garbo wears in* Ninotchka *(1939), is this tasseled knit cap, opposite, that Adrian designed for Katharine Hepburn's Tracy Lord in* The Philadelphia Story. *More remarkable is that Adrian convinced Hepburn to wear it, considering that Hepburn generally eschewed whimsy or cuteness, both on screen and off.*

ABOVE: *Katharine Hepburn wearing both the hat and suit in* The Philadelphia Story *with James Stewart.*

*"Ten thousand yards of pleated chiffon . . . one million tiny blue sequins. . . 12 yards of curled white ostrich plumes . . . 55 dozen Chinese pheasant tails . . . these were a few of the items needed for the magnificent costumes designed by Adrian for* The Great Ziegfeld.
— Souvenir program for *The Great Ziegfeld*, 1936

# The Spectacle Films

## "Stepping into a Dream"

When designing wardrobe for the stage revues, costume parties, and fantasy sequences that took up a considerable amount of running time in films such as *The Great Ziegfeld* (1936), *Madam Satan* (1930), and *The Wizard of Oz* (1939), Adrian was able to design costumes that were divorced from overt narrative concerns. Some of the extravagant apparel he created for these productions has never been equaled, and it is difficult to believe that they could even be created today. Sheila O'Brien, who eventually became organizer and head of the Costume Designer's Guild in the 1970s, remembers working for Adrian on *The Great Ziegfeld* in 1936: "He had no assistants—he designed for all players. He had marvelous cutters and tailors, beaders, milliners. He had a crew that was unbelievable. . . . In *Ziegfeld* Adrian had to design thousands of costumes. You couldn't do that show today. First of all I don't know where you would get those things made. I don't know where you would get all those marvelous helpers; they have all faded out of the industry."

Adrian found inspiration for many of his *Great Ziegfeld* designs in the actual costumes the legendary showman had used for his *Midnight Frolics* revues on the roof of the New Amsterdam Theater in New York. But Adrian's conceptual approach to the project was influenced by the work of his old boss, Hassard Short. With a generous

*Weighing 100 tons, the set for this production number in* The Great Ziegfeld *was a massive spiral volute built of structural steel on a revolving stage 70 feet in diameter. The structure contained 75 steps that led up to the apex. The cyclorama partially surrounding this amazing set was 80 feet high and 300 feet in length, with 6000 blinking lights making up the star-studded sky. Adrian's costumes, drawing on his Broadway revue background, found inspiration from such diverse sources as the Orient, ancient Egypt, and the circus.*

budge and every resource of the stage at his command in the early 1920s, Short devised many novel features for Irving Berlin's *Music Box Revues* that left Ziegfeld himself, according to the *New York Sun*, "green with envy."

For sheer lavishness, however, Adrian was able to create costumes for *The Great Ziegfeld* that Short could never have imagined in his wildest dreams. He had the resources of the world's largest and most successful movie studio at his disposal, and he taxed it to the limit not only to re-create, but augment and exceed, the elaborate and extravagant era of the Broadway revue.

To start, it took more than a year to obtain the various materials. One thousand people were employed for over three months on *The Great Ziegfeld*. It took 250 people more than six months just to complete the costumes. Two months before actual production got underway, Adrian hired 100 extra seamstresses who worked in shifts around the clock. Exceptionally, all the costumes were fashioned completely by hand. The peculiar design and cut of many of the garments made this necessary in order to obtain the effect Adrian sought. Some of the gowns weighed more than 100 pounds and were equipped with special shoulder pads to relieve the weight. Similar padding was also used in several of the huge headdresses. Virginia Bruce, who played showgirl Audrey Dane in the film, wore one gown with a glass headpiece that weighed 22 pounds. It took three men to carry her up the steps of one of the sets.

In an unprecedented move, one of the largest soundstages at Metro-Goldwyn-Mayer was turned into a workroom for Adrian's army of embroiderers, beaders, feather workers, jewel craftsmen, and seamstresses. The creations were so elaborate and depended so much upon their effect in motion that Adrian, for the first and only time during his tenure at MGM, decided to use live models instead of tailor's dummies for costume fittings. Each model tried on an average of 12 different costumes a day.

The costumes Adrian designed for the two revues that anchor *The Great Ziegfeld* required 50 pounds of silver sequins in various sizes, 1 million tiny blue sequins, 300 crystal drops that had to be ground to a uniform size, 10,000 yards of pleated chiffon, 12 yards of curled white ostrich plumes, 55 dozen Chinese pheasant tails, and more than 75 pounds of costume jewels, including pearls.

The film itself purports to trace the career of impresario Florenz Ziegfeld, Jr. (William Powell) from its inception, when he managed Sandow the Strong Man at the Chicago World's Fair of 1893, through his various financial crises, stage successes, and his relationships with his two wives—the willful and temperamental Anna Held (Luise Rainer) and the more compliant Billie Burke (Myrna Loy).

Despite the glossy treatment of its subject, *The Great Ziegfeld* garnered seven Academy Award nominations at year's end, winning Oscars for Best Picture and Best Actress (Luise Rainer). Dance director Seymour Felix won an Oscar for his direction of the "Pretty Girl Is Like a Melody" production number.

Critical reaction to the film, however, ranged from Clive Hirschhorn's appraisal that it was "the classiest biopic ever to emerge from Hollywood, and one of the most successful in its recreation of the period in which Ziegfeld flourished" to Graham Greene's scathing indictment: "This huge inflated gas-blown object bobs into the critical view as irrelevantly as an airship advertising somebody's toothpaste at a south coast resort."

The truth may lie somewhere between these two assessments. Viewed today, the film, with a running time of three hours, does seem ponderous and tedious. Directed by

*The Grand Finale in* The Great Ziegfeld.

OPPOSITE: *Another dreamy name by Adrian for his creations, this one "White Flight." Essentially an enormous wing, it is composed of curled ostrich wings and pheasant tails; sequins cover the long train and covering. The costume is worn by Margaret Lynam. Photograph, Clarence Sinclair Bull*

Robert Z. Leonard—a tried-and-true MGM workhorse who dabbled in everything from adaptations of literary works (*Pride and Prejudice, Strange Interlude*) to soggy melodramas (*Susan Lenox*) and operettas (*Maytime*)—*The Great Ziegfeld* needed a more daring, visionary touch, the kind that Hassard Short had introduced onstage in the 1920s, when his performers seemed to provoke the laws of gravity. When Adrian's quixotically gowned showgirls each make their grand entrance, Leonard's camera obediently follows them around the stage like a dog carrying a newspaper in its mouth. In the costumes he created,

Adrian captured the wonder that showmen such as Ziegfeld and George White had once induced in their *Follies* and *Scandals* revues; Adrian needed the vigor of a Busby Berkeley, with his swooping crane shots and impeccable rhythmic cutting, to match his dazzling costume designs.

Still, there is one sequence that never fails to elicit a gasp from the audience. As showgirls Margaret Lynam, Diane Cook, Lorna Lowe, Clarissa Sherry, and Mary Jane Halsey parade on stage in creations Adrian dubbed "White Flight," "Paradise Shower," "Sequin Fountain," "Silver Pheasant," and "Silver Mirage," a curtain behind them slowly parts to reveal Virginia Bruce at the top of a moving cyclorama wearing a sequined dress festooned with five incredible ostrich-plume trains that nearly stretch the entire length of the stage. In this one brief, awe-inspiring moment, Adrian succeeds in bringing the gaudy, enchanted, preposterous, and theatrical world of Ziegfeld to life.

*The sequins on this tight-fitting garment, which Adrian called "Silver Mirage" and was worn in* The Great Ziegfeld *by Mary Jane Halsey, were all handsewn. Photograph, Clarence Sinclair Bull*

Worn by Diane Cook, this Great Ziegfeld costume, which Adrian called "Paradise Shower," has 27 bird of paradise feathers in the headdress and on the sleeves. Adding to the indulgence are long strands of silver beads and mirrors.

Lorna Lowe's dress is aptly named "Sequin Fountain." The crepe sheath underpinning has been embroidered with a solid mass of silver sequins with sequin tabs of varying lengths along the arms and the tall headpiece. Pearls interspersed throughout add a shimmering effect. Photograph, Clarence Sinclair Bull

# The Wizard of Oz

*The Wizard of Oz* had been Adrian's favorite book as a child growing up in Naugatuck, Connecticut. So clearly were the various characters in the novel impressed on his mind that one of his frequent occupations after he came home from school was to make sketches in his schoolbooks of the imaginary characters that inhabited Frank Baum's fantasy world. "I remember the Munchkins all had long mustachios which shaded from yellow to blue-green," he said many years later, "and the Quadlings were extremely proud of the golden cages which grew from their heads and contained strange animals."

As preparation for work on the costumes in *The Wizard of Oz* began in the late spring of 1938, Adrian wired his sister Beatrice in Connecticut and arranged to have a box of his old schoolbooks shipped post-haste to Culver City. Studying the drawings he had made almost thirty years earlier, Adrian then scanned the entire series of Oz books for costume ideas. He began to sketch early in the summer, and by August preliminary wardrobe tests were underway in his studio in the wardrobe building. Actual work on the costumes commenced in September.

Adrian made 3,210 individual sketches for the costumes in *The Wizard of Oz,* all hand-tinted to match early technicolor requirements. Practically every costume was fancifully colorful, and before any work was actually undertaken, director of photography Harold Rosson had to work out a list of "relative color values" that filled six typewritten pages. Adrian and Jack Dawn used these notes to guide them in creating both makeup and costumes. Every garment was custom made since nothing that might be appropriate for the Land of Oz could be found anywhere in stock in the wardrobe department.

While working on the film, Adrian

*Fred Ritter in his costume as one of the Munchkin fiddlers in* The Wizard of Oz.

reported to Hedda Hopper that he was "having more fun over *Oz* than a trip to Europe," and when the picture was completed he concluded that "it was the greatest fun I have ever had in film work." Without having to do historical research or bend to any realistic checks on his designs, Adrian was free to indulge his imagination. His personal touch was on every costume. For example, desiring a doll-like effect for the 120 Munchkins, Adrian designed dozens of tiny vests, jackets, slippers, bonnets and dresses, and accessorized them with a range of oversized buttons, bows, and belts that accentuated their tiny stature. Very early on, he decided to use felt as the primary material in the construction of the Munchkins' costumes, thus enhancing their doll-like quality. Felt was also added to the soles of the Munchkins' shoes (as well as Judy Garland's ruby slippers) so they would not make noise during the musical numbers.

As a final touch, Adrian added hundreds of individually made felt flowers to scores of costumes. They grew on metal wires extending from the toes of shoes; they crept up the backs of bonnets, and sprouted from button holes. The Munchkinland set was surrounded by shrubbery, and since some of the Munchkins even slept within flowers, and used the bushes and plants as hiding places, Adrian wanted to connect them to their environment. "A full picture of Munchkinland, with the midgets in costume, should look like a flower garden," he said.

None of the 120 performers who played the Munchkins had individual costume fittings with Adrian, remembers Margaret Pellegrini, who played one of the "sleepyheads." "We came into the fitting room, and we were given a costume to try on. It was fitted on each of us by one of the wardrobe people. Then we were given a number for the costume, and each day we had to present that number to somebody in wardrobe, who would then go and fetch the costume for us."

The MGM wardrobe department was under tremendous pressure as the deadline

for actual filming loomed. A combined total of approximately a thousand extras were to appear in the four different scenes set in the Emerald City, and construction for the costumes in these sequences could not begin until the wardrobe for the 120 Munchkins had been completed. "Green shoes, green stockings, green dresses, green coats," wardrobe supervisor Vera Mordaunt remembers. "We could buy some of the material, but we had to dye the rest. We dyed all the stockings. You can't get emerald green in cotton hose. Emerald green can only be done successfully on silk materials or wool. And you couldn't buy green shoes, so we had to dye all the shoes."

A metal spray-dying room on the second floor of the wardrobe department, and a second room with a gigantic vat used for water-based dyes became the center of *Oz* costume construction a month before shooting began. At the same time, in another room on the second floor, which housed Mrs. Cluett's beading department, the famous ruby slippers were being made. At first, a pair of patent leather shoes was spray-painted red, but Adrian wanted something that was more visually exciting. Red sequins were then hand-sewn onto a piece of very fine pink chiffon, which was in turn sewn onto the shoe. The effect was perfect.

The wings on the flying monkeys were first constructed out of cloth, but again, Adrian wasn't happy with the effect. He

*One of the Munchkin heralds in* The Wizard of Oz. *Rather than just complement the garden setting, Adrian's costumes were metaphors for the floral abundance of Munchkinland.*

had modeled the wings after those of the South American condor. Finally, it was decided that for long shots of the monkeys in flight, cloth would do, but for close-ups real feathers had to be used. MGM contacted zoos around the country, and zookeepers who agreed to cooperate collected molted feathers in their aviaries—primarily from condors, but also from eagles and even vultures—and shipped them to MGM.

The Hussar-like costumes and arms for the witch's guards—the Winkies—weighed more than 125 pounds each, and before the film was released Adrian contemplated adapting the design he used on the guards' jackets for a line of women's winter clothing. He also felt that the fantastic and colorful use of flowers, tassels, appliqués, capes, and cloth jewelry for the Munchkins and other habitués of Oz might start a new feminine mode of fashion. "None can be adopted in its entirety," he said, "but in small details adaptation will be widespread."

While films such as *The Great Ziegfeld* and *The Wizard of Oz* allowed Adrian's imagination to work overtime (both films remained among his favorites long after he left MGM), they also created a conundrum for him within the international fashion community. Since the very nature of the costumes in these movies breathed excess they were not publicized by MGM for their stylistic innovations, but rather as inventories of extravagance: a carload of ostrich feathers imported from Australia for one gown; a million silver sequins sewed to the bodice of another. Suffused with an aura of the fantastic, these costumes necessarily worked against the broader image Adrian was trying to establish for himself as one of the arbiters of American style. Only the more astute viewer could see that regardless of the level of fantasia, Adrian was always working to reveal character through costume.

# Madam Satan

Cecil B. DeMille's *Madam Satan,* released in 1930, is a prime example of a spectacle that offers up outrageous images of elegance and at the same time offers new ideas for couture design. On September 21, 1930, a week

before the film's premiere, the *Los Angeles Herald-Examiner* contained this headline on one of its Art and Entertainment pages: "Garment Hits World Record In Cloth Used: Actress' Costume To Be Sent To Paris Air Mail to Show Ateliers Ingenuity of Americans." The article went on to describe a costume Adrian had created for *Madam Satan* that supposedly had more cloth in it than "any so far made in all the world." He called the gown "Confusion," and it was to be packed up and shipped to Paris, where it was scheduled for display in several fashion ateliers as an example of what Americans can do in the way of extreme novelties. "I was anxious to see just how much material we could get into a single costume," said Adrian, "and I think Paris will find it a little bit hard to beat our record—a mile and a quarter!"

"Confusion" was designed by Adrian for extra Marie Valli, who wears it during a costume ball sequence in the film. Perhaps the most interesting thing about the gown is the fact

*Watercolor sketch from the 1930 film* Madam Satan.

RIGHT: *A costume sketch for one of the partygoers in* Madam Satan.

OPPOSITE: *Marie Valli in Adrian's "Confusion" costume for the costume ball in* Madam Satan.

chasing loosened pink balls around the boudoir, and under the bed. It was conceived purely as a novelty, and I hope Paris will get as much amusement in seeing it as we did in the making. . . ."

Marie Valli's costume was just one of a number of sensational designs Adrian devised for the costume party in *Madam Satan*, which takes place on a moored zeppelin. The screenplay, by Elsie Janis, Jeanie Macpherson, and Gladys Unger, offered Adrian innumerable comic suggestions for costumes. At one point, extra Lotus Thompson makes her entrance in a scanty ensemble with an elaborate beaded headdress: "I am the spirit of innocent pride," she announces to the assembled partygoers, "and I'm proud of the fact that I've nothing to hide!" Another guest, introduced as "Miss Movie Fan," is attired in 25 open Japanese paper fans.

Spectacle aside, however, the plot of *Madam Satan* is as simple as a story can get: Angela (Kay Johnson), a society wife, discovers her husband Bob (Reginald Denny) is having an affair with a chorus girl named Trixie (Lillian Roth). Angela confronts her rival at the apartment of a friend, then decides to beat her at her own game: "He likes 'em hot, does he?" Angela says when she gets a good look at the woman her husband has been seeing behind her back.

that Miss Valli is by no means overdressed. The dress is fashioned from 2,000 yards of silk net, one of the lightest materials known, fastened into 200 balls. Each ball required 30 feet, or 10 yards of material. The balls are arranged to billow around Miss Valli more or less like an airy pink cloud, now hiding, now revealing the wearer—hence, *confusion*. "It is not a gown which will be generally copied," Adrian said, "else husbands of wives who wore it would spend half their time

"I'll give him a volcano! They'll have to call out the whole fire department to put me out!" This brings a snort of derision from Trixie as she takes in the gown Angela wears in this scene: "What?! In *that* Mother Hubbard?! You've got a lot to learn!"

Throughout this early part of the film, Adrian dresses Johnson in formal, graceful tea gowns fashioned in sweeping lines from the draped collar and sleeves to the train line finish. On board the zeppelin, however, the audience finds that while

*Lotus Thompson as "The Spirit of Innocent Pride" for the Zeppelin masked ball sequence in* Madam Satan. *Innocence was more tongue-in-cheek than actual, for with the exception of her fabulous headdress, Thompson's costume was more than a little naughty.*

Angela might have had a lot to learn, she learned it all rather quickly. Now masked and costumed as the title character, Madam Satan, Angela makes her entrance at the ball in a bias-cut silk sheath and matching cape. A dragon's head and body are boldly outlined on the cape in silver and blood-red sequins. In contrast, Adrian dresses Lillian Roth's Trixie for the party as an overreaching chorus cutie, in short panties and a bra accented in sequins and covered with flashy, oversized pheasant feathers. Trixie is a walking billboard for 1920s frivolity.

*Madam Satan* went into production just as the first effects of the Depression were beginning to alter the national mood. When the zeppelin breaks in two after it is struck by lightning, the event can be seen as symbolic: the Jazz Age of carefree parties is over. But Adrian, through deft use of costume, makes the point clear before the first lightning bolt streaks across the sky. At one point, when Trixie initiates a "kissing game" with Bob and the other male guests, Madam Satan/Angela suddenly appears at her side to break up the fun: "Come, come! Enough of these baby games!" she admonishes. Then, looking out at the men gathered around her with a

come-hither smile, she brandishes her sequined cape and offers a new proposition for entertainment: "Who wants to go to hell with Madam Satan?!"

Madeleine Vionnet may have developed the bias cut in Paris in the late 1920s, but it was Adrian who celebrated and endorsed it to the world on-screen. With this short scene, one can almost see the 1920s morph into the 1930s: Kay Johnson's silk sheath is more sophisticated, less obvious, and sports an elegant new line. Adrian's ingenious designs were not lost on Paul Poiret, who had visited the *Madam Satan* set. "Before motion pictures, the public never anticipated Paris," the couturier said. "We could hold a style for six months or a year with perfect safety. Today, however, you are putting so many pretty gowns in your American pictures, striving so hard to make your pictures novel in their costumes, that we must keep on the alert to stay ahead of you!"

Adrian designed more than a hundred costumes for *Madam Satan*. The successful completion of these garments, like so many that were made during his tenure at MGM, required miracles of tailoring. For example, as all of the silk net balls in the "Confusion" costume had to be symmetrical, they were made by one person in the wardrobe department, who worked three-plus weeks on this one garment.

All of this effort was not lost on Adrian. Once, just before *The Great Ziegfeld* had its premiere in September of 1936, he had the MGM publicity department take out full-page ads in both the *Hollywood Reporter* and *Motion Picture Herald,* officially expressing his gratitude for the hard work that went into the making of the costumes for the film. While space did not allow him to list everyone who worked on the production by name, the head supervisors "and their staffs" were praised for their work. Shortly afterward, a wardrobe supervisor made a sign and hung it in one of the wardrobe workrooms: "It can't be done. But here it is." The motto later also appeared in the MGM art department.

This motto neatly sums up the enormous effort that went into the great MGM spectacles. But maybe Judy Garland, as Dorothy Gale in *The Wizard of Oz,* summed it up even better. In the middle of a makeover by a trio of beauty technicians in the Emerald City—a fantasy metropolis to which MGM was sometimes compared—she is astonished at the skill and expertise of the three women attending to her every need. "Can you even dye my eyes to match my gown?" she asks them. When the answer is affirmative, she grins in wonder and exclaims, "jolly old town!"

*Adrian with Kay Johnson and his sketch for her costume as the notorious "Madam Satan."*

BELOW: *Two views of Kay Johnson as Madam Satan.*

OPPOSITE: *Lillian Roth, left, and Kay Johnson at the Zeppelin masked ball in* Madam Satan. *Johnson's gown, floor-length and cut on the bias, is a harbinger of the future. Roth's costume, with an excess of bared flesh, is pointed squarely into the past.*

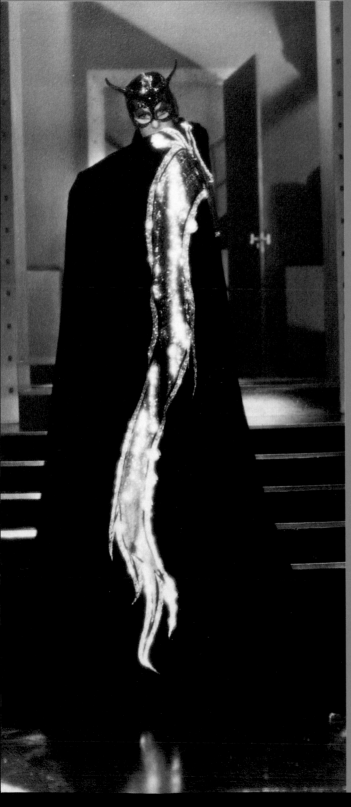

*"Paris is still fashion dictator of the world on paper. But Paris must get Hollywood to accept and use its fashions if it wants to make a dent on young America. Garbo, of course, isn't the only actress who sets styles by what she wears. But the Garbo influence goes deeper and is more comprehensive than that of the rest. Not a copy of one of her dresses nor all of them is the point. It's an attempt to get the same mood that Garbo expresses."*
                                          —Virginia Schmitz, *New Movie*, March 1933

# Greta Garbo
## *Expecting the Unexpected*

"Garbo wears the unexpected," Adrian told a reporter for the *Ladies' Home Journal* in 1932. "It is out of the unexpected that style is born, and the influence comes."

Greta Garbo's fashion influence on American women, however, was virtually nonexistent in her first films at Metro-Goldwyn-Mayer. She arrived at Culver City from her native Sweden in September 1925, and the first two films on her initial three-year contract, *The Torrent* (1926) and *The Temptress*, were for Cosmopolitan, William Randolph Hearst's production company, which released its films through MGM. Three days before *Torrent* premiered in New York on February 21, 1926, Hearst's *New York Evening Journal* launched a publicity onslaught that focused on Garbo's costumes in the film: "Gowns worn by Sembrich and Gadski have been reproduced in what has been regarded as one of the most elaborate wardrobes ever assembled for a screen star," the newspaper noted. "The wardrobe will be worn by Greta Garbo, noted Swedish star of Ibanez' *Torrent*. As an opera star in the picture, Miss Garbo will be shown in triumphs in Paris, Milan, and Madrid. Max Rée, famous Danish costume creator, outfitted her."

Marcella Sembrich and Johanna Gadski were both divas of the operatic stage, born in Eastern Europe, who reached their greatest vogue in the United States around the turn of the century. By 1926, Gadski was

*For their first film together, Adrian designed Garbo's trench coat in A Woman of Affairs (1928), seen in this sketch and opposite.*

preparing for a comeback tour of the states, while Sembrich had
been in retirement for nine years. Many of Sembrich's most
famous opera costumes, including one known as "Queen of the
Night," a floor-length midnight-blue ball gown embroidered
with sequins and five-point stars, were lovingly displayed at the
Marcella Sembrich Opera Museum in Lake George, New York.

By the mid-1920s, however, the new sporty flapper style
embodied by Clara Bow and Colleen Moore was all the rage
onscreen, and the frippery and elaborate veils Rée designed in
homage to Gadski and Sembrich were not the calling cards that
drew audiences to Garbo in her initial American feature, despite
the relentless promotion of the Hearst press. More to the point,
Garbo was being noticed just for being Garbo. As the critic for
the *New York Post* wrote, "Miss Garbo, as it happens, is dark,
beautiful, and rather exhilarating to look upon. She possesses, so
it would seem, some of the vibrant personality of a Pola Negri,
and lobby talk at the Capitol likewise mentioned her in the same
breath with Carol Dempster, nicely confusing anyone who has
yet to see the lady herself upon the screen. The truth of the
matter, of course, is that Miss Garbo is a separate and distinct
being, quite unlike anything else on earth. Once seen, she will
not be soon forgotten."

While Garbo's countenance fascinated American audiences, it was her body, and the way she used it, that immediately
struck moviegoers as exotic and unfamiliar. Here was a female
star who did not mince or swish or undulate seductively, but
who strode across the screen with an assured manner, display-
ing a liberated, confident will. And while *Flesh and the Devil*
(1927) is remembered today as the film in which Garbo and
John Gilbert incited passion with their horizontal love scenes,
*The Torrent* features the supine Ricardo Cortez with his head
in Garbo's lap, creating, as Alexander Walker has written, a
moment of "great sensual tension," with the man as the passive
partner. It was an image that would be repeated again and again
in both Garbo's silent and sound films.

MGM's new star was creating a different kind of tension
off the set, however. She very quickly came to hate costume
fittings, and by her second film, *The Temptress*, had become the

bane of the wardrobe department. "Dresses!" Garbo exclaimed in one of her rare early interviews. "I wish they were all bags, and all alike, to jump into quick!" On *Flesh and the Devil* Garbo attempted to select a wardrobe of her own in a less "vampy" style than the one that had been designed for her, and was severely rebuked for her efforts by Louis B. Mayer. This action did little to endear her to the wardrobe's designer, Andre-Ani, who proceeded to bad-mouth Garbo at every opportunity. "She has foreign ideas about clothes that do not go well in American pictures," he told an interviewer in 1927. "And her figure— it is difficult to dress."

In an effort to find out just *how* her growing public wanted to see her dressed onscreen, the marketing department at MGM suggested that exhibitors hold a contest when *Flesh and the Devil* made the rounds of the Loew's circuit in January 1927: "Every-one remembers Greta Garbo in *The Temptress,* a siren role which she again portrays in *Flesh and the Devil.* Instead of presenting the usual fashion designing contest, order this cut or mat [a paper doll figurine of Garbo] from your exchange, print it on cheap news stock, and distribute in circular form with a cash offer of first prizes and admission tickets creating and drawing the type of gown or dress which, in their opinion, not only enhances her beauty but helps her characterization in this type of siren portrayal."

The results of these contests were then sent to MGM, although their effect on Andre-Ani and his designs was, for the most part, completely negligible. Andre-Ani hated incorporating suggestions from directors and the actresses themselves; he was not about to start taking orders from the moviegoing masses. When the tension between Garbo and Andre-Ani had reached a crescendo during the making of *Love* (1927), their third film together, MGM assigned Gilbert Clark to design Garbo's cos-tumes for *The Divine Woman* (1928), a thinly disguised retelling of Sarah Bernhardt's life that is the only film of Garbo's to be lost. It was also the only film she made with her countryman, Swedish director Victor Sjöström. Perhaps Garbo was mollified to be working with a fellow Swede after her mentor, Mauritz Stiller, had been summarily fired from directing her in *The Temptress,* for any fireworks with Clark were postponed until their subsequent film together, *The Mysterious Lady* (1928). In the middle of that production Clark literally walked out of the studio when Garbo refused to wear one of his revealing costumes for her role as a female spy.

Adrian, who had arrived at MGM only weeks after Clark's walkout, had been hired by Mayer and Thalberg as Clark's replacement. As a result, Adrian must have known that he would soon be called upon to design for Garbo. Their first film together, *A Woman of Affairs* (1929), would bring a new Garbo to the screen. It also began a screen partnership that would last until Garbo left MGM in 1941.

# A Woman of Affairs

*"She was tall, not very tall, but as tall as becomes a woman. Her hair, in the shadow of her hat, may have been any colour, but I dared swear that there was a tawny whisper to it. . . . Her hands were thrust into the pockets of a light brown leather jacket—pour le sport—which shone quite defiantly in the lamplight: it was wide open at the throat and had a high collar of some fur of a few minks. One small red elephant marched across what I could see of her dress, which was dark and not pour le sport."*
—a description of Iris March, the heroine of Michael Arlen's *The Green Hat,* 1924

In 1924 a new sort of heroine took the literary world by storm when Armenian novelist and society bon vivant Michael Arlen published his best-selling novel *The Green Hat.* The book became a *succès de scandale,* and its heroine, Iris March—a young flapper who has countless affairs and wears men's clothing—a role model for millions of young women. All over Europe and the United States they set out to imitate Iris's style, and of course they wanted defiant, liberated, and slightly androgynous clothes to match: *pour le sport.* By 1924, too, designers such as Jean Patou and Coco Chanel had established this distinctive look for real sports clothes. In the early 1920s Chanel began to borrow many details from menswear, and her suits featured boxy cardigan jackets as well as straight, knee-length skirts with pleats. And although the majority of Patou's clients did not play tennis or golf, by 1924 the mood was such that they wanted to look as if they did. Patou was developing the language of pure sporting clothes into almost every area of women's apparel, including full evening dress, and in 1925 he opened Le Coin des Sports, a boutique devoted to women's sportswear. The designs of Patou and Chanel, along with the arrival of Michael Arlen on the best-seller lists, created a synergy that could not be ignored.

MGM paid $50,250—an awesome amount in 1927—for the screen rights to Arlen's novel, cleansed the plot of its more unsavory elements (embezzlement charges replaced venereal disease as a reason for one character's suicide) and retitled it *A Woman of Affairs,* a move which fooled no one, and elicited a humorous commentary on the editorial pages of the *New York Times*: "They could not use *The Green Hat* in name, so they decided to retitle it. *A Woman of Affairs* was suggested by someone who realized that Babbitdom would flock to see a picture with such a name. *The Green Hat* would not be a nice title to inflict on our butter-and-egg men, their families and their friends, but *A Woman of Affairs* would be perfectly all right."

Just to be safe, executives at MGM also renamed the main character, and Iris March became Diana Merrick in the film. The screenplay, by Bess Meredyth, opens with the following title card: "the story of a gallant lady—a lady who was perhaps foolish and reckless beyond need—but withal a very gallant lady." With this, Garbo then bursts onto the screen as Diana, "foolish and reckless beyond need," clutching the wheel of her Hispano-Suiza. She narrowly avoids hitting a hay truck, and then proceeds to scare the wits out of a group of men digging a ditch along the side of a country road while her lover, Neville Holderness (John Gilbert), shouts warnings to no avail.

It is a Garbo entrance like no other, quickly followed by another surprise. Stopping at an old oak tree that she and Neville used to frequent as children, Garbo hops out of the car, wearing a costume unlike any she has yet worn on the screen: a loosely belted trench coat, lined in bold plaid wool. After the costumes she had worn in her six previous films at MGM, it is completely unexpected and, as Adrian noted earlier, it is out of the unexpected that style is born.

This style, however, had a very difficult delivery, as both the film's director, Clarence Brown, and studio head Louis B. Mayer were dead set against it. "They feared she would lose all her allure if she came down to earth," Adrian remembered years after the film's release. "In *A Woman of Affairs* I put (Garbo) in sport clothes, and so amazingly beautiful is her face, she is just as intriguing in a sweater. . . . She is frankly delighted with clothes that have 'line' as their most important factor."

It was Garbo's delight that led Brown and Mayer to acquiesce, finally approving Adrian's costumes for the film. For the first time, Garbo's onscreen moods were perfectly complemented by her wardrobe. In truth, Adrian simply followed Michael Arlen's lead, and used the author's descriptions of his heroine's clothes as a starting point for Garbo's costumes.

As melodrama, *A Woman of Affairs* has some similarities to many of the "madcap youth" films Hollywood churned out in the mid- and late 1920s. Neville Holderness's father, Morton, objects to his romance with Diana not because of any inherent class difference (the film is set in England) but because of her

seemingly wanton lifestyle and loose reputation. When Morton separates the lovers, Diana drifts through a series of affairs until she finally marries David Furness (John Mack Brown), a friend from childhood. David has been labeled decent early in the film but on their wedding day he commits suicide rather than face arrest for embezzlement. David's suicide perplexes all who knew him, but when Diana discovers the truth behind his death, she keeps quiet rather than besmirch his reputation: "David died for decency," she tells the police at the official inquest, with Neville and his father in attendance. But David's best friend Jeffry (Douglas Fairbanks, Jr.), who also happens to be Diana's brother, has other ideas: "I suppose you told David what you had been before he married you—and he couldn't stand it!"

Diana's activities in the years following David's death are represented onscreen in a series of news photographs. Once again, sorrow, the sublimation of her desire for Neville, and now her need to pay back David's debts takes the form of social activity, as Diana embarks on a string of affairs with men of power and wealth. She returns to England seven years after David's suicide to see Jeffry, who has become an alcoholic and is ill.

For her trip through the foggy London streets, Adrian dresses Garbo in a gray skirt with roomy kick pleats, a three-quarter length suede jacket with a turned-up collar, and a snugly fitted cloche hat. A silk scarf is casually knotted around her neck. She interrupts Neville's pre-wedding dinner with his fiancée, Constance (Dorothy Sebastian), to summon a family friend, Hugh Trevelyan (Lewis Stone), to come to Jeffry's assistance. Word of Diana's arrival soon brings the meal to a halt.

"Oh, I must see that fascinating woman!" Constance exclaims. "I've heard so much about her!" She leads the way to the window, where her face suffuses with fascination as she catches a glimpse of Diana. But a glimpse of what? Diana's hat obscures the details of her face and hair; all that's left for Constance to react to is an image, an attitude, which is communicated solely through Diana's attire, and stands in sharp contrast to the image Constance herself presents. Diana strides purposely out to the car, hands stuffed in the pockets of her coat, and settles herself behind the steering wheel with little assistance from Hugh. She is firmly in charge. In this short scene, lasting only a few seconds onscreen, Garbo's fashion icon is born: "her natural aloofness and the manner of her bearing," Adrian wrote shortly after the release of *A Woman of Affairs*, "make it possible for her to put meaning into simple clothes." Nor did her clothes distract the audience from her performance—rather they helped to define it.

*In* A Woman of Affairs, *Garbo confronts Morton Holderness (Hobart Bosworth) wearing an unassuming cloche hat and suede jacket.*

BELOW: *Constance (Dorothy Sebastian) does her best to get Holderness's dinner guests to tell her anything off-color about Diana Merrick. In pointed contrast to Garbo, Adrian dresses Sebastian in virginal white, with frills, ribbons, and furbelows that flounce around her like excited puppies when she walks.*

The cloche hat, too, takes on a special meaning here and in subsequent scenes. Until after World War II, women's hats had symbolic as well as protective functions. As Alison Lurie points out in *The Language of Clothes,* when a middle-class woman left her house, she always put on a hat or bonnet. She thus shielded her pure and private thoughts, covering them with a conventional representation of public femininity. Garbo's cloche, pulled low over her brow, almost obscuring her eyes, is the literal "green hat" of the novel's title, and it serves to protect the secrets she carries with her: her love for Neville and the real reason behind David's suicide.

Later, when Diana and Neville are alone at his house, she continues to wear her hat up until the moment she admits her

love for Neville. At this point, she tellingly removes the cloche and as such lifts the veil on her private thoughts. It is a perfect partnership of costume and character.

Much later, Neville visits Hugh, unaware that Diana is staying with him. As the two men talk downstairs, Hugh discloses to Neville Diana's second "secret," while Brown's camera cuts to Diana upstairs on the veranda, pacing back and forth in a white chiffon dress, whose skirt extends just below the knee in front and barely glances the floor in back. The color alone—white—indicates that Diana has given up her secrets, at least to Hugh and Neville, and appears "cleansed" before those present. The hemline is cut in scallops, giving irregular dips to the silhouette. As Diana paces in agitation, the dress, caught by the breeze, creates its own life around her, further accentuating her unease. Adrian would use this device again and again during his MGM career, most notably with Joan Crawford in *Letty Lynton* (1932).

But Diana is, above all, independent both in attitude and in fashion. So Adrian returns Diana to her forthright self in the closing scenes, dressed once again in her cloche hat, suede jacket, and gray skirt. In the film's final moments, Diana sends Neville back to Constance with the misinformation that Constance is carrying his child. Constance reveals this to be untrue, and the resulting confusion lasts just long enough for Diana to escape; she crashes her car into the tree that she and Neville visited in the opening scenes. The final image in the film is telling: Hugh gingerly picks up Diana's cloche, which has been thrown from her head by the impact of the crash, and fondles it gently. Diana has finally given up all of her secrets.

# Wild Orchids

*In fashion—as in everything else—there is a danger of carrying eccentricity too far. Just a word of warning about that. Eccentricity—in its extreme form—is never beautiful. You will notice that very few beautiful women dress in an eccentric manner. Those who do merely try to shine in some way and wear bizarre clothes with which to attract attention. If you are the typical American girl I suggest you make a fad of sports clothes—how attractive and smart they are!—and the nice part about them is that they may be worn all during the day. One even notices them at luncheons and teas.*

—Greta Garbo, quoted in the exhibitor pressbook for *Wild Orchids,* 1929

For some fans, Garbo's costumes in *Wild Orchids* were more than a disappointment—they made Garbo seem hard, less

conventionally feminine. But Garbo was happy with Adrian's onscreen wardrobe for her.

In *Wild Orchids,* released only two months after *A Woman of Affairs,* Garbo played the much younger wife of Lewis Stone, who seems oblivious to his wife's charms, and acts more like her father than her lover. When the couple meet a Javanese prince (Nils Asther) on a cruise, he soon attempts to seduce Garbo, who remains true to her husband. It was Garbo's first wholly sympathetic role, and in designing her costumes Adrian built upon his work in *A Woman of Affairs* with clothes that went beyond the cutting edge. Near the end of the film, accompanying her husband on a safari with the prince, Adrian outfits Garbo in jodhpurs, a man's shirt, and tie. The costume was created two months before *Vogue* heralded a new look from the house of Bernard et Cie in Paris in its issue of January 19, 1929: a checked woolen suit, leather belted jacket, man's tie and "shirt blouse."

By late 1929, with the release of her last two silent films, *The Single Standard* and *The Kiss,* the plots of Garbo's films began to pander to what MGM's screenwriters perceived the audience knew—or thought they knew—about her private proclivities. She is the independent woman who walks alone. As Arden Stuart in *The Single Standard,* we first get a glimpse of her on the veranda of a grand house, having left the party taking place inside, which is filled with philandering husbands and gossipy wives. "I'm sick of cards and hypocrites!" she tells one of her potential beaus, nodding at the guests in the drawing room. "I want life to be honest—and exciting!" Later, walking alone in the rain, she tells a middle-aged gentleman who accosts her, "I am walking alone because I want to *be* alone." And when she summons her chauffeur to get the car ("Let's go for a drive—I feel like doing seventy!") it is Garbo who gets behind the wheel.

As in *A Woman of Affairs,* she is firmly in charge, and Adrian's sports clothes reflect her liberated spirit. Later in the film, with very little prodding, Arden impulsively accepts painter Packy Cannon's (Nils Asther again) invitation to join him aboard his Windjammer (named, not coincidentally, the "All Alone"). Adrian dresses her for the cruise in a loose woolen robe, canvas shoes, and a regulation yachting cap. Yet his designs for the film reveal not only his sensitivity to Garbo and the character she is playing, but to one of her female co-stars as well, as he explained shortly after the film was released:

The tall girl accentuates the great difference between dressing a woman for the screen and dressing her for private life. Take, for example, our dress problems with Miss Garbo in her new picture *The Single Standard*. Dorothy Sebastian, who is in the same picture, is several inches shorter and as they have several important scenes together Miss Garbo's clothes must not have too much length of line.

Fortunately, in this picture, the type Miss Garbo is playing—an athletic, youthful, outdoor type—makes possible the horizontal line that counteracts her height. Applied to other types of dresses, this would ruin the unadulterated line that is so charming on a tall girl.

Her sport jackets are cut square as are the skirts and even her flat-heeled shoes. There is even an abruptness to the line of her hat, which makes a series of cross-cut lines. This makes the eye falter on the way down from her head to her feet, giving the illusion of a much shorter person.

# The Kiss

Garbo's independent mien continued in *The Kiss* (1929), the last silent film made at MGM. The film is a drama of French society in which Garbo plays Irene, a married woman having an affair with a young lawyer (Conrad Nagel), but who inadvertently becomes the object of affection of a young college boy (Lew Ayres). When he innocently asks for a kiss before he returns to school, Garbo's husband surprises them, and proceeds to strangle the young man in a fit of jealous rage. Garbo, attempting to restrain his assault, kills her husband and is then tried not once, but twice—in a courtroom and in the court of public opinion.

There are echoes of *A Woman of Affairs* in this tale of thwarted passion, and in the first scene Irene meets her lawyer-lover in a museum, wrapped heavily in furs and a close-fitting cloche: this is a woman of means, trapped in a loveless marrriage to a wealthy man. During the film's conclusion, at her trial, Adrian dresses Garbo in a floor-length black mourning dress and a black tricorn hat with veil. She stands defiantly in the witness chair like Napoleon in exile while director Jacques Feyder's camera cuts away from her to show two middle-aged women in the courtroom, giving their opinion of Irene's hat and veil, and gesturing disapprovingly. But Garbo remains undaunted, not only in front of her fashion critics, but also before the judge, who disparages her by asking if her marriage had been a love match: "It's been said you did not take your marriage vows too seriously. . . ." Garbo pulls herself up to her full height and

*Garbo faces her accusers in* The Kiss *(1929). Adrian's tricorn hat and black cape amplify her character's defiant nature.*

surveys the courtroom with barely concealed disdain. She announces that she has nothing to be ashamed of and that she is indifferent to public opinion. Those present are visibly shocked.

But public opinion, in movie palaces all across America, was beginning to shift in Garbo's favor. A month before the release of *The Kiss, Photoplay* ran an article criticizing Garbo, her aloofness, and her "bizarre" fashion sense, both onscreen and off. The magazine received an avalanche of mail denouncing the article, and one reader, Leonard Hall, summed up the feelings of millions of "Garbomaniacs" in his letter: "Garbo can dress as she darn well pleases, and does. If she wants to wear 20 yards of opaque cheesecloth to a formal gathering, it's quite all right with us. In the greatest scene Garbo ever played—the renunciation scene in *A Woman of Affairs*—she wore a slouchy old tweed suit and a squashy felt hat. She never looked more mysterious, more alluring, and she never acted with greater authority or arrogant power."

Fashion arrogance was increasingly seen as the divine right of a queen by 1930. Early that year, the Hollywood columnist for the *New York Evening World* issued the following summation of the Garbo mystique:

Greta Garbo strolls around the lot [at MGM] in duck sailor trousers these days. As her rivals become more and more feminine, with ankle length frocks, the Norse mystery goes to the other extreme. Her severe bathrobes, her unrelenting

use of a navy blue beret, her adherence to the roughneck sweater and tailored skirt of flannel, her simple belted tweed coats and mannish felt hats are characteristic of her working hours.

Her evening frocks are simple. Often in need of a pressing. Never characteristic of a recent mode. But always revealing some individualistic taste. She is the enigma of moviedom—and because of these things, as much as through her acting genius, she is the most glamorous name in Hollywood today.

Finally, in 1931, *Variety* gave credit where credit was due:

Garbo is a mighty fortunate person, having in Adrian, the MGM designer, an artist who so subtly understands her individuality. He designs for her costumes that capitalize her slouch and lazy bearing. Nothing he creates for her could possibly be worn by anyone else, they are so completely for her, and her alone. Her broad shoulders he has the wisdom to emphasize with yokes, raglan, or kimono sleeves. Necklines are either round and shallow, extending well toward the shoulders, or round and close to her neck. Adrian fears no severity for Garbo; he knows severity brings to a climax her strange personality. Huge, preciously careless sports coats, prodigally lavish with long-haired furs. Tiny little mites of hats, utterly simple. Pajamas of rich fabrics, worked in restraint, all line. However difficult it may be to find stories to suit Garbo, there is always the joy of knowing her clothes will do rightly by the glorious creature she is.

# "Gimme a visky": Garbo's Talkie Debut

MGM had delayed Garbo's talkie debut for almost a full year, in order to give the actress time to practice her English. Though Garbo had expressed an interest in playing Joan of Arc in her first talking picture, Irving Thalberg chose Eugene O'Neill's *Anna Christie*, in part because its heroine was Swedish. It also offered some insurance: the play was a venerable stage and screen property, first as a vehicle for Pauline Lord on Broadway, and then as a silent film success for Blanche Sweet in 1923. Clarence Brown, a Garbo favorite who had been behind the camera on *A Woman of Affairs*, was chosen to direct.

*Garbo's entrance in* Anna Christie *(1930), wearing clothes that Adrian purchased from local stores in Los Angeles.*

OPPOSITE: *Anna, in a fisherman's sweater, makes peace with her father, Chris Christofferson (George Marion).*

*Anna Christie* proved to be a fortuitous choice. As critic Andrew Sarris has observed, while John Gilbert became a "cautionary legend" with his fevered, high-pitched exclamation "I love you, I love you, I love you, I love you" in his talkie debut, *His Glorious Night* (1929), Garbo was more fortunate in that her first words onscreen, slow and dolorous, came from O'Neill: "Gimme a visky," she sighs to the waiter in a waterfront dive, "ginger ale on the side. An' don' be stingy, ba-bee."

How fitting that Garbo's first talkie, and her first film to be released after the Crash, should be set in the grubby barroom, dockside, and tugboat of a port city's lower depths. And that her first costume in the sound era should be so much shabbier than anything she ever wore in the silent era.

After *Anna Christie*, Garbo would spend much of the rest of her career (thirteen films in eleven years) in period costumes or chic contemporary outfits. But for that pivotal moment in film history represented by *Anna Christie*, Garbo sank low enough in social status to rise in public esteem. Garbo's Anna rose as well from the bedraggled bravado of her lurid entrance to the redemptive romance with Charles Bickford's brawling knight of the open road and the purifying sea. Now provocatively respectable in a warm sweater, Garbo gave audiences a fair share of the sublime stillness that was supposed to have gone out with the onset of the squawky talkies.

Eschewing any designs he himself might have created for the character of O'Neill's prostitute, Adrian took Garbo shopping in the discount stores and thrift shops of downtown Los Angeles, and together they selected her costumes off-the-rack. As Adrian said in the early 1930s, "Until the arrival of talking pictures, it was not wise to accept the movie capital as the focal point for fashions. But, with their advent, they have caused truer, more authentic modes of living to be represented." In her first appearance in the film, a barroom waiter goes to answer the

buzzer. Brown cleverly cuts to a medium shot so that when the waiter opens the door his body will block our view of Garbo. He stands to one side to let her in, and suddenly there she is, in a medium-close shot that gives the audience a chance to see her entire costume. She is wearing a nondescript black skirt, a dark, solid-color low-cut blouse, and a battered cloche hat. Viewers with sharp eyes can discern two drop earrings dangling from her earlobes. Garbo gazes around the room apprehensively and then, with a slight shrug of her shoulders, walks into the bar.

She's been traveling a day and a half on a train, she explains to Marthy (Marie Dressler), an old waterfront barfly who occupies an adjoining table: "Had to sit up all night in the dirty coach, too. . . I guess I do look rotten."

Rotten? Not by half, but Adrian knew that any costume Garbo wore in this scene had to accomplish two things: establish her character, and at the same time offer few if any distractions from what the audience had come to experience: her voice. He succeeds admirably on all counts, although he had to supply a bit of persuasion to get Garbo to wear the blouse, because she hated clothes that were low-cut.

*Anna Christie* was a great success for all concerned, but even in 1930 there was a feeling that something had been irrevocably lost when Garbo crossed the sound barrier. Perhaps because, with the exception of Chaplin, she was the last star to talk onscreen, it even prompted an editorial by film critic Mordaunt Hall in the *New York Times:*

> The old gods go, and with them the young goddesses. The talking screen has taken its last and greatest toll from the glamorous personalities of the silent screen. It has taken Greta Garbo, the incomparable, indescribable, inscrutable enchantress, run her through its mills, and turned out a good screen actress.
>
> While the passing of the original Garbo is one of the saddest blows ever suffered by the screen, it is softened somewhat by the debut of the new and wholly different personality presented by the Garbo of *Anna Christie*. Here is an actress with infinite possibilities: a young woman with beauty, poise, grace, and a striking, melodious voice. Here is a star who need not be cast to type, who can play most any sort of role with understanding and conviction. But (and this is the most doleful "but" that ever lifted its hesitant head from these typewriter keys) she is not the glamorous, mysterious, tragically beautiful girl who played in *A Woman of Affairs*.

It is a tribute to Adrian, as much as to Garbo, that Hall singled out her performance as Diana Merrick above all her other silent roles, for in *A Woman of Affairs* her costumes at once defined and enhanced her mysterious, glamorous appeal. And the importance of Garbo's costumes in continuing to define that appeal in the sound era was not lost on the *Times*. Hall enthused over the fact that Garbo was already working on her second talkie, a version of the stage drama *Romance,* which was set in the late 1860s: "Imagine the alluring Miss Garbo . . . in the gowns of yesteryear, especially after seeing her in the clothes of *Anna Christie!*"

Hall was writing in the spring of 1930, and he felt that this old Doris Keane stage vehicle would give Garbo a dramatic opportunity surpassing the drab O'Neill drama, which hardly gave Garbo an opportunity to wear head-turning costumes. If *Romance* is remembered at all today, however, it is not because of its "gowns of yesteryear," but on account of a hat Garbo wore in the film, which started a fashion craze that would surpass even the cloche. It was a fad that Adrian would find puzzling and, ultimately, most disconcerting.

# Beautiful, Aloof, and Foreign

According to Garbo biographer Karen Swenson, Irving Thalberg was well aware that Garbo's sound debut in *Anna Christie* had somewhat altered her onscreen personality, and he wanted to remind moviegoers of the star's "ethereal side." *Romance,* in which Garbo plays Rita Cavillini, a nineteenth-century Italian soprano, would present her in lavish period gowns and hairstyles. Adrian outdid himself, but after the film's release, all the public could remember was a hat that Garbo wore in the middle of the film, a complement to a magnificent costume of black-and-white velvet. Seven years after the release of *Romance,* Helena Rubinstein wrote an encomium to Adrian's hat design for *Cinema Arts* magazine: "A pert, audacious hat which Greta Garbo wore in a picture called *Romance* left the women in the audience gasping with astonishment. This little hat was perched on one side of her head. How it was held on only Heaven knew, probably by main will power. But instead of being in the accepted deep and substantial tradition, covering hair and ears, it sat saucily and flatly aslant her head, while in front it was pulled down provocatively over one eye. It unashamedly revealed hair and ears. In fact, it served to establish once and for all the oft-disputed question that women had ears."

A number of factors led to the popularity of Garbo's hat in *Romance,* which was dubbed the "Empress Eugénie" or "the Eugénie hat" by the fashion press, in part because the style harked back to an era sixty years earlier when Eugénie, Empress of France, set fashion trends for all of Europe during her reign as Napoleon III's consort (1853–70). Adrian's design also built on a new style heralded by *Vogue* early in 1929, when the magazine featured a variation on the cloche that extended to a wide-shaped wing at one side. The "Eugénie" was also worn to one side, but its frivolousness was exemplified by the feathers that sprouted from its brim and the fact that it did not completely cover the head, making it somewhat impractical when compared to the cloche. These features were ideally in keeping with Garbo's character, a woman who, if not of loose moral character, was at least impractical when it came to matters of the heart.

The hat is never mentioned overtly in the script, but it receives, nevertheless, a buildup worthy of Madison Avenue. After initiating an affair with the director of a church, Rita Cavillini comes to call on him at the rectory. Her entrance is preceded by comments from the man's sister, who is appalled that she has been asked to stay and greet the singer: "That woman! I won't see her! There ought to be a law against such women. Why I'd sooner have a hungry tigress come in the room . . ."

And right on cue Garbo sweeps in, taking over the room— and the screen—wearing a magnificent black-and-white velvet gown with matching jacket. With an edging of ermine, and a rippled flare extending from a fitted waistline, it resembles a modernized version of a mid-nineteenth-century ball gown. A wrap collar deflects all the light in the room to Garbo's face and, of course, to that hat. For women starved for a completely new style six months after the Crash, which signaled the end of the flapper era, the "Eugénie" was a breath of fresh air. Even better, when wearing it, a person adopted the subtlest veneer of notoriety by virtue of the scene in which it appeared.

Headwear inspired by the "Eugénie" hat hit small boutiques and department stores almost overnight following the release of *Romance,* partially because the hat industry had moved toward mass production by the end of the 1920s. Machines that could construct, block, and trim hats were now in use, and as a result prices came down and availability expanded coast-to-coast. In lean economic times, too, a hat was a relatively inexpensive commodity when compared to a dress or suit, and could add a dash of spice to an outfit that was beginning to turn stale in the eyes of its owner.

Privately, however, Adrian was astonished at the popularity of this hat, a design for a costume picture that he never intended to be adapted for street wear. In more than one interview in the early 1930s, Adrian cautioned women to be "very careful" when wearing the "Eugénie style", emphasizing that it should be worn only on "very formal" occasions. The source for some of his irritation over the vogue created by the "Eugénie" no doubt came

*Garbo as Italian opera diva Rita Cavillini in* Romance *(1930) wearing Adrian's fantastic black-and-white velvet gown, topped off with the "Empress Eugénie" hat.*

with becoming the unpaid designer for the wholesale fashion houses of the country, since a hat is a relatively easy design to pirate. Three years after *Romance* was released, Adrian commented to a reporter for the *Los Angeles Times* that "the French designers can sell their models for huge prices, but ours are just pirated. Look what happened when we designed the Eugénie hat for Garbo in *Romance* . . . ugh!"

Garbo's head, however, and what Adrian placed on it throughout the 1930s, would become of prime importance to thousands of women who sought new and exciting accessories in lieu of a new dress that might place undue strain on a tight clothing budget. This headwear would also become a major marketing tool for MGM when selling Garbo's films. The "Empress Eugénie" was something new under the fashion sun, and it reflected Adrian's desire to use Garbo as a muse for his most daring designs. "I want to create a style for Garbo which continues to be individual in spite of styles," Adrian said in 1932. "I never take any notice of prevailing modes when I create a costume for her."

The pillbox hat, which he created for *As You Desire Me* (1932), was worn in one brief scene, when Garbo hurries through a crowded European train station to meet an Italian army captain who may or may not be her long-lost husband. The hat initially drew titters from audiences, and the director, George Fitzmaurice, had been dead set against using it. Adrian used his friend Hedda Hopper, who had a small role in the film, to help him prevail upon Fitzmaurice, and he was not above hatching a somewhat devious plot to advance his agenda. Hopper played Garbo's sister in the film, and for one scene Adrian designed a hat for Hopper that, in her own words, looked like a "giant, overgrown, over-sexed artichoke, made entirely of blue ribbon." As she recalled in her memoirs:

That hat was part of the plot. When I appeared in it before director George Fitzmaurice, who had approval of all clothes, he screeched, "Oh, no! You can't wear that!"

"And why not?"

"Because no one would see anything else on the screen."

"Is that bad?"

Again, Adrian uses one primary feature — in this case a hat — to enhance character. Moreover, the hats display the couturier aspect of Adrian's duties at MGM. As Katrin in The Painted Veil (1934), Garbo wears three different hats that each define her role. As later described by MGM's publicity department, they are, clockwise from the far left, the "Oriental brimless hat," the "shovel hat," and "twisted turban."

"You're not the star. They must look at Garbo."

"Oh, come now, can't I have some crumbs of glory?"

"Not in that hat, you can't," he assured me.

At that moment, as Adrian and I had planned, in walked Garbo wearing the pillbox tied under her chin. Now even George Fitzmaurice couldn't damn two hats in a minute and a half. He gave her a sick stare, looked at me, then said, "Change your hat, Hopper, we'll get on with the scene." The plot worked as planned. I got the oversexed artichoke for my collection, and Garbo wore the pillbox.

Fitzmaurice's concerns aside, the hat achieved the objective the director had sought: the audience did indeed look at Garbo. Adrian had known what he was doing all along. In a train station crowded with extras, where Garbo would be photographed in a number of long and medium-shots, the hat was sure to stand out and thereby draw attention to the star. He would never have used such an accessory for a tense dramatic scene with a number of sustained close-ups. Initially, the pillbox may have drawn startled titters from audiences, but once again the unexpected set the style pace, and less than thirty years later Halston would reinvent Adrian's design for Jacqueline Onassis.

In *The Painted Veil,* an adaptation of Somerset Maugham's novel released in 1934, Garbo played Katrin, a young Austrian woman who marries a bacteriologist (Herbert Marshall) for reasons other than love: his assignment in China ignites her passion for travel and new experiences. "What more do you want than a good husband, I'd like to know," Katrin's mother asks her early in the film. "Must he be good, mother?" Katrin replies. "Not very exciting to be good . . ."

Garbo's Katrin, it turns out, may not be overtly reckless and hedonistic in her pursuit of excitement, but Adrian's hat designs for *The Painted Veil* immediately set her apart from the "respectable" European ladies traveling with their husbands through the Far East in their enormous, wide-brimmed, ostentatious picture hats. Three of his designs stood out: a hat with a brim of medium width that turned sharply off from the head at each side and at the back; a turban of white faille, which Garbo wore in the final scenes of the film, giving her a look of unsullied redemption when she returns to her husband after a brief affair and assists him during a cholera epidemic; and finally, a small brimless hat, fashioned from row after row of white silk

*At the conclusion of* The Painted Veil, *Garbo's Katrin finds redemption in Adrian's nunlike head covering.*

cording. The top of the crown is slightly rounded, with an ornament of carved jade set in a rim of antique silver placed directly in the center of the top.

In these three designs for *The Painted Veil* Adrian was asserting the couturier side of his professional duties, recalling Charles Worth's concept of the mutable silhouette that followed the birth of French couture. For each of these hats, in fact, was a variation on designs Adrian had already created for Garbo, and the marketing and publicity departments at MGM dubbed them the "shovel hat" (which bore a resemblance to the Empress Eugénie), the "twisted turban," and the "Oriental brimless hat" in their exploitation plan for the film: "The noted Adrian once more scores another style scoop on the fashion world!" read a headline in the exhibitor's pressbook. "Women are dazzled by anything that savors of foreign influence and in that weakness you have a lot of theatre and store style strength!"

Along with the promotion hyperbole, however, came a warning for exhibitors seeking a fashion tie-in with local department stores: "Beware of overdoing the Chinese fashion influence. These photos of Chinese-influenced fashions are sufficiently style-exciting by themselves and WILL NOT give your public the possible adverse effect of thinking the picture has a Chinese locale, provided you do not permit merchants to dress their windows with a lot of unnecessary Chinese 'atmosphere.' WATCH THIS!"

Of course, much of the film *was* set in China, but this warning reflected a growing concern that Garbo's box office, stronger than ever among more urban, sophisticated moviegoers, was

beginning to dwindle by the mid-1930s in parts of the South and Midwest, where homegrown stars such as Fred Astaire and Ginger Rogers, Clark Gable, and Shirley Temple were packing them in at the box office, and pictures with overt foreign locales (the Venice of *Top Hat* looked more like Coney Island than any city found in Europe) were often summarily dismissed.

In addition, Adrian's costumes for the film, according to the *Omaha News*, were considered "so—well—distinctive" that at one point the audience "burst into gales of laughter upon (Garbo's) entrance." This would never happen at a revival showing today, but in 1934 Adrian's designs for Garbo were pushing the envelope in startling and surprising ways, and the publicity department at MGM was undoubtedly afraid that he was on the verge of losing rural audiences. In fact, memories of the headwear he designed for *The Painted Veil* would be recalled years later in one of his most sublime comic creations—the hat purchased by comrade Nina Ivanona Yakushova in *Ninotchka*.

## The Mata Hari Mystique

Adrian's costumes for Garbo in her early sound films and in the historical dramas she made in the mid- and late 1930s, reflected his unique appreciation of Garbo's singularity as well as his extraordinary gift for interpreting character through clothes. "(Garbo) must never create situations," Irving Thalberg once said of MGM's most prestigious star. "She must be thrust into them. The drama comes in how she rides them out." And in many of her sound films—*Mata Hari, Susan Lenox, As You Desire Me, Queen Christina, Anna Karenina, Camille*—the drama reaches a climax when Garbo's character finds herself thrust into situations that leave her stranded between two worlds.

*Mata Hari*, released in 1932, was loosely based on the life of Margaretha Geertruida MacLeod, née Zelle, a dancer and courtesan whose name has become a synonym for the seductive female spy. She was shot by the French on charges of spying for Germany during World War I, although the nature and extent of her espionage activities remain uncertain. The daughter of a prosperous hatter, Margaretha began to dance professionally in Paris in 1905. She soon called herself Mata Hari, said to be a Malay expression for the sun (literally, "eye of the day"). Superficially acquainted with East Indian dances, and willing to appear virtually nude in public, the real Mata Hari was an instant success in Paris and other large cities. Throughout her life she had numerous lovers, many of them military officers.

As directed by George Fitzmaurice, the film takes great liberties with Margaretha's story (she is seen working for a spy syndicate), and it has none of the style and polish Josef von Sternberg had brought to a similar story in *Dishonored* a year earlier. It does, however, have Adrian's costumes, and they lend a sheen to the production that still shimmers after seventy years.

For her first scenes in the film, when Mata Hari meets and bewitches Alexis Rosanoff, a Russian aviator (Ramon Novarro), Adrian wraps Garbo in a masterwork of design, enveloping her from head to toe in gold braid and sequins. Bejeweled, dolman-shaped sleeves, gathered at the wrist, anchor the eye as Garbo toys with a cigarette. A slightly raised collar and a jeweled turban focus attention on her exquisite face, which, caressed by William Daniels's camera, resembles a pearl resting on top of an elaborate brooch. The skirt, of gold braid, is split open at the front, revealing legs that have been poured into the same glittering material. Here is a femme fatale few men could resist.

Early in the film, Mata Hari's superior Andriani (Lewis Stone) chastises another agent for not picking up on the development of the tank, a new British weapon. Shortly afterward, Mata walks into Andriani's office for her latest instructions, and the elaborately embroidered V-shaped bodice of her costume, cut from shoulder to waist, gives her an attitude of impenetrability very similar to armor—or, looked at another way, an armored tank. Here, then, is Andriani's answer to Britain's new implement of war: Mata Hari, secret weapon of the Central Powers. And when Garbo walks across the room, or nonchalantly crosses her legs, the material glistens as the light deflects the motion of her body, and the oily sheen of the fabric lends her the aspect of an athlete in the prime of condition, ready to take on any challenge.

Adrian's inspiration for this and many of the other *Mata Hari* costume designs came from the mania for "all things Oriental" that had reached its peak early in the twentieth century. This trend was inspired by a nostalgia for the tales of the Middle East—Scheherezade and the stories of "a thousand and one nights"—as well as the Paris debut of Serge Diaghilev's Ballets Russes in 1909. The set and costume designs for the ballet, by Russian artist Leon Bakst, had inspired Paul Poiret and Jeanne Paquin to

— Mata Hari —

*Garbo in gold brocade, the secret weapon of the Central Powers in* Mata Hari *(1931).*

ABOVE: *Adrian's sketch for Garbo's* Mata Hari *costume.*

experiment with opulent decorative elements: turbans topped with aigrette or ostrich plumes, elaborate jeweled ornaments added to simple velvet sheaths. Just prior to the outbreak of World War I, when Mata Hari was the sensation of Paris, the Parisian socialite Rita de Acosta Lydig worked with couturiers such as Marie Callot Gerber of the House of Callot Soeurs to create Orientalist designs. They introduced elaborate vests and one-piece garments that were made like pants rather than skirts—much like Garbo's costume of gold braid.

Toward the end of the film, when Garbo as Mata Hari renounces her espionage work after falling in love with Rosanoff ("What do I care for your orders?" she lashes out at Andriani, "You can't frighten me. I'm Mata Hari and my own master!"), Adrian dispenses with glitter, enveloping Garbo completely in black at her trial. With her hair swept back from her forehead, or covered in a tight black skullcap, she bears a striking resemblance to the Madonna icon that hangs on the wall in her lover's quarters.

When Mata Hari first sees the icon, she asks Rosanoff, "What is it supposed to do? Bring you luck?" "Oh no," he replies, "it guards you from evil." And so, too, does Mata Hari-as-Madonna finally protect her lover from the knowledge that would surely destroy him—that she is to face a firing squad after their final meeting, and not a surgeon's scalpel, as she has led him to believe.

Most of the clothes for *Mata Hari*, with their straight, severe lines and touches of Orientalism, were not easily adapted to the American sportswear market in the early 1930s. Yet once again, Garbo's headgear became the rage, and imitation-jeweled skullcaps swept the nation.

Not long after the film's release, however, the studio assembly line that had been manufacturing Garbo vehicles at the rate of two and even three films a year since 1925 was abruptly halted when Garbo's seven-year contract expired in the spring of 1932. By the following year, and her return to MGM following an eight-month hiatus in Sweden, each new Garbo appearance on the screen was heralded as an event. As the decade grew to a close, one and even two years between films became the norm. In addition, beginning with *Queen Christina* in 1933, when MGM's biggest star did grace the nation's screens more likely than not it was in a film with a historical setting.

*Adrian found his inspiration for many of Garbo's* Mata Hari *costumes in the opulent decorative elements that were in vogue when Margaretha Geertruida MacLeod was a sensation in Paris.*

# The Period Films: *Queen Christina, Anna Karenina, Camille*

Christina of Sweden came to the throne at the age of six, in 1632, and abdicated her crown twenty-two years later in favor of her cousin, Karl Gustav. As early as 1927, her life story was seen by MGM as the source of a possible Garbo vehicle. The romantic angle that provides the impetus for the queen's eventual abdication in the MGM version of events, however, was actually due to her eventual conversion to Catholicism in a country that was rigidly Protestant. And just as MGM's screenwriters took liberties with the facts of Christina's life and reign, so Adrian favored dramatic interpretation over adherence to historical accuracy.

"The costuming in *Queen Christina* presented numerous problems since there were several instances where sheer authenticity—that is, literal reproduction from a plate—would in no way have achieved the dramatic quality sought," Adrian said soon after the film was finished. "In one instance, Miss Garbo wears a gown of ivory velvet adorned with bands of silver thread and bits of cut steel and square diamonds. As far as is known, the queen never possessed such a costume, but gowns on this order were then in fashion in the court, and as a sheer picture it struck both designer and director as conveying a dramatic credibility within the particular scene."

This court gown, which Garbo wore when Christina received the Spanish ambassador Don Antonio de la Prada (John Gilbert), was the costliest gown made at MGM up to that time. Fifteen seamstresses toiled for six weeks to hand-sew the small diamonds and bits of cut steel to the velvet fabric. "By modification of Sweden's exorbitant styles for women at the time," Adrian said, "and aided by authentic reproductions from other countries of the period, I believe we have clothed Queen Christina more faithfully than any other agency of the present era could do."

Garbo had done a great deal of research on the period during her sojourn in Sweden, and she consulted with Adrian on every step of the design process. Aside from Christina's court dress, most of the other costumes and uniforms in the film actually were inspired by paintings from the period. John Gilbert's costumes were based on a series of portraits by Velásquez that are housed at the Prado in Madrid. His costume for his first audience with the queen is almost an exact copy of one worn by the brother of Philip IV of Spain. It was made from black hand-loomed cut velvet embroidered in gold thread and studded with amber.

The luxurious materials, as well as the undergarments that were required to go with them, had an unforeseen consequence on the set: they were incredibly heavy. At her first fitting for the completed court gown, Adrian asked Garbo to take a few steps in it under the lights. She tried, but she could not move. She seemed to be anchored to the floor. Adrian thought about removing some of the brilliants in the lower panels of the dress in an attempt to lighten it, but soon realized this would have little effect. Elizabeth Young, who played Christina's lady-in-waiting Countess Ebba, recounted how difficult it was to learn how to move in the heavy velvet gowns:

> [Director Rouben] Mamoulian kept impressing on me that I had to float through the picture. . . . But the first time I tried on one of my costumes I told him nobody could "float" in such clothes. They were frightfully heavy. Even Garbo couldn't take a step in them without tottering. In fact, that first day we each went around clutching a bottle of smelling salts. But Mamoulian insisted that "float" I must and every time a new man came on the set and I asked who he was, Mamoulian would reply, "He's your new floating instructor." Garbo thought it was a great joke.

Beyond the parameters of historical accuracy, however, there remains the visual significance of Adrian's designs within the context of the drama that serves as his comment on seventeenth-century sexuality, power, and the royal ties that bind. Garbo wears ten costumes in *Queen Christina*, and each of them plays with the idea of stiffness—the royal raiments signify uncompromising allegiance to God, country, and duty. Her release from her obligations is conveyed by the softness of the trousers and traveling cloak she wears when she finally escapes from her duties and travels incognito to a country inn. In her first appearance, riding swiftly toward the palace on horseback for a meeting with her ministers, Garbo wears velvet riding pants and a stiff white collar that draws attention to her face, but which also gives the subtle impression that her head is being offered up on a plate. Later, this same costume subtly evokes the queen's ambiguous sexuality, as she greets her lady-in-waiting Ebba with a passionate kiss, and promises that she will not let her official duties interfere with their plans to go on a sleigh ride.

This idea of royal sacrifice will be replayed throughout the film. Preparing for an audience with the Spanish ambassador,

Garbo in Queen Christina's court gown, receiving the Spanish ambassador Don Antonio de la Prada played by John Gilbert, right.

LEFT: *Here a collar as both symbol and metaphor in* Queen Christina *(1933). And what better vehicle than Garbo's nearly implacable face?*

*As Queen Christina, Garbo's shoulders may have been bared, but her otherwise heavy gown still conveys the gravity of her position.*

BELOW: *Adrian's militaristic costume for Garbo's Queen Christina gives her exactly the ammunition she needs to prove her might to her subjects.*

Don Antonio, Garbo, wearing her court gown, is surrounded by attendants and the material appears to be so heavy and unyielding that it looks as if it might stand up by itself. Contrast this with the velvet gown she wears in her private audience with Antonio, her shoulders bared, vulnerable, and quivering in a rare (for Garbo) exposed V-neck, with huge voluminous sleeves arranged in a series of puffs, and a fitted waist that evokes connotations of a straitjacket. For even in her own chambers Christina is not at ease, and must contend with the prying eyes and ears of her courtiers. Later in the film, when her subjects invade the castle in objection to her liaison with "the Spaniard," Adrian dresses Garbo in a fitted black coat with militaristic, horizontal gold braid adorning the sleeves, bodice, and skirt. With a high back collar and black fur hat, any background is blotted out as Mamoulian's camera slowly glides in for a close-up of Garbo's face: Christina proceeds to stare her subjects into submission. Finally, an ostrich plume adds a touch of femininity to the hat that completes the velvet traveling costume she wears when she leaves Sweden at the end of the film.

*Anna Karenina*, released in 1935, and *Camille*, which followed in 1937, offered different challenges for Adrian. These literary classics were both written—and set—in the nineteenth century, but neither dealt with historical personages. Much of Tolstoy's work, however, reveals an almost obsessive concern for clothes, and *Anna Karenina* is no exception. The novel offered a wealth of costume suggestions. Tolstoy's descriptions of attire are not only clues to his character's traits, but also a way of judging them; when Oblonsky, the unrepentant adulterer, awakens in the opening pages of *Anna Karenina*, Tolstoy describes his toilette in detail, down to the gray dressing gown with blue silk lining he dons upon rising. Here is a man who is not only unfaithful, the author seems to be saying, but self-indulgent and very particular as well.

At the ball where Anna formally meets Count Vronsky, Tolstoy offers an almost itemized description of Anna's dress: a black velvet, low-cut gown completely trimmed in Venetian lace. In her hair she wears a small garland of pansies, which are also present in the black band of her sash, entwined through the white lace. The following paragraph from the novel, in which the young Kitty Shcherbatsky describes her reaction to Anna's gown, must have brought a smile to Adrian's face: "Kitty had been seeing Anna every day . . . and invariably imagined her in lilac.

*Adrian surprises Garbo with a birthday gift on the set of* Camille *(1937), September 1936.*

OPPOSITE: *Garbo, as Anna Karenina, wearing Adrian's black ball gown.*

But now, when she saw her in black, she felt she had never realized her full charm before. She saw her now as something completely new and unexpected. Now she realized that Anna could never be in lilac, and that her charm consisted of just that—she always stood out from her dress; it was never conspicuous."

Something completely new and unexpected—Adrian's own by-law when designing for Garbo, who wore his designs with such authority that they never seemed conspicuous. Adrian followed Tolstoy's description to the letter in creating this ball gown for the film, except that he eschewed the white lace, opting to create a more severe line for the camera. But Garbo in black, amid the whirling white and pink tulles of the Russian nobility, created an arresting image that foreshadowed the tragedy to come, and was true to the spirit of the novel.

*Camille,* from a novel and play by Alexandre Dumas fils, offered little in the way of costume descriptions in its original text. Further, the occupation of the main character— a Parisian courtesan who, according to the film, "lived on the quicksands of popularity," made research an unrewarding chore: "At first we had difficulty in finding data about the demi-mondaine of the period," Adrian told *Vogue* in 1936. "You see, all the prints of that day show us very proper young ladies. Practically the only artist who perpetuated the florid tempestuousness of Marie Duplessis, Camille's original, was Constantin Guys, who made a series of drawings of "the Lioness," as she was called at the time."

In designing the costumes for Garbo's role as Marguerite Gautier, the Lady of the Camellias, Adrian used Guys's portraits as a starting point, but he also relied on a tried-and-true visual device that he had used successfully many times before in modern dress productions, specifically with Jean Harlow in *Dinner at Eight* and Joan Crawford in *Possessed:* the "kept woman" who can be spotted straight away by her extravagance. It was Adrian's idea for Garbo to wear ornate jewelry in *Camille;* she

argued with him over this decision, maintaining that in Sweden during this period no woman—including a courtesan—would wear such ostentatious gems. But Sweden was Sweden and France was something else entirely. The script for *Camille,* by Frances Marion, Zoë Akins, and James Hilton, supported Adrian's conceptualization of the role: "Of course, I buy too many hats and too many dresses and too many everything," Marguerite says in the opening scene. "But I want them!" When Garbo as Marguerite is torn between her feelings for Armand Duval and the financial necessity of continuing her relationship with the Baron de Varville, Adrian dresses Garbo in elaborate, lavish, yet burdensome fur-trimmed coats and dresses. The designs work to make her a prisoner of her own existence.

As an article in the exhibitor's pressbook for the film made clear, "Adrian's glamorous costumes for Garbo follow the period but are dramatized to the needs of modern film techniques. In other words, he used the period costumes as suggestions for dramatized versions rather than attempting a mere duplication. 'Period costumes, as such,' Adrian said, 'may be historically accurate and still lack drama. It is the designer's province not to reconstruct or duplicate but to dramatize the garb of a period.'"

And dramatize he does with three decorative and, at the same time, touching gowns that reiterate a slightly ominous message each time. When Armand attends Marguerite's party early in the film, she wears a gown of white tulle sprinkled with gold stars, creating, in her lover's eyes, a luminescent vision of untarnished beauty that could only truly be realized in the imagination of the besotted. In the dark recesses of her bed chamber, the iridescent fabric creates its own light around Marguerite, the object of Armand's devotion as he finally expresses his love.

This gown has its complement later in *Camille*. Having left Armand at the request of his father, Marguerite returns to the Baron de Varville, only to encounter her lover at the opening of a new gambling club in Paris. As she walks slowly down the stairs on the Baron's arm the sight of Armand causes her to stumble and drop her fan. Adrian created a dress of shimmering black net, embroidered with sequins, for Garbo to wear in this scene. The design suggests a number of ideas simultaneously: the gleam of the brilliants at once identifies Marguerite as the prize trophy of a vain and supercilious nobleman, while the color black, and the netting that creates the effect of a dark aureole around her head, imparts the look of a woman in mourning for her lost life. Finally, the gold stars so securely locked in the firmament of her white dress have been replaced by shooting, or falling, stars on the black gown.

At the end of the film, Garbo is seen wearing a plain white dressing gown as Marguerite's spirit slowly slips away. The lack of embroidery on the garment, along with the hint of a monk's cowl in the fabric gathered about her neck, gives the gown an ecclesiastical feel, and lends to the scene an added spirituality.

If *Camille* was Garbo's high point at MGM, it was also one for Adrian, for again his instincts were correct. Seen today, Garbo's noble, ironic performance— Marguerite is painfully aware of the contradictions in her character —is beautifully underscored by the

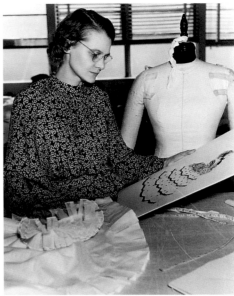

*The process of making one of the costumes for* Camille. *First, Hannah Lindfors, in the MGM wardrobe workroom, studies Adrian's sketch. Behind her is Garbo's dress dummy, padded to her exact measurements. The careful measuring and cutting required a high degree of workmanship. Garbo in the completed costume, at left.*

lavish furs, glittering gems, and vulnerable dotted-Swiss cotton used to dramatize her dissension.

Later that year, Garbo starred opposite Charles Boyer as Napoleon's mistress Marie Walewska in *Conquest,* an expensive re-creation of history that would be the only film Garbo made at MGM to lose money. Upon its completion, she left the studio for over a year. When she returned to the United States after an extended holiday abroad, she found herself, amazingly, under fire from both the film industry and the popular press.

On May 8, 1938, Harry Brandt, president of the Independent Theater Owners of America, placed a notorious advertisement in *Motion Picture Herald* and several other industry publications, labeling Garbo "box-office poison" along with,

among others, Joan Crawford, Fred Astaire, Marlene Dietrich, and Katharine Hepburn. Movie grosses were in a late Depression slump, and Brandt's purpose was not so much to destroy the star system as to start a public debate about the wisdom of "block booking": the habit of studios to force-feed small theater owners expensive, prestige "product" if they wanted to show the pictures that were more popular with rural audiences, such as the new Andy Hardy series. *Conquest* lost over $1 million, and with the threat of war looming in Europe, MGM could no longer count on European receipts to lift Garbo's films out of red ink.

Even more alarming, however, were the personal attacks on Garbo in newspapers and magazines. On October 21, 1938, Gertrude Bailey, the society and women's editor for the *New York*

*When Garbo, as Marguerite Gautier, becomes torn between her feelings for Armand and the financial necessity of continuing her relationship with the Baron de Varville, Adrian dresses Garbo in elaborate — and constricting — garments. Beauty comes at a price.*

OPPOSITE: *Two costume sketches for* Camille.

*World-Telegram,* led the charge with the following appeal:

We're getting sick and tired of hearing, "of course, Garbo can get away with it." How long can she go on wearing that mannish suit, that dreadful straggly bob, those heavy stockings, and flat heels, and no makeup, and still remain the screen's No. 1 glamour girl?

Where's the justice in a fashion world that keeps the rest of us girls breaking our necks to get the right-colored lipstick for each dress, then have to change the nail polish to match it? To bake our curls under a dryer and wax our wisps? Keep an extra pair of hose in our lockers so we won't be caught with that terrible embarrassment of a run in our stockings? . . . We love the beautiful costumes you wear on the screen, Miss Garbo. Those fragile ruffles around your throat and wrist in *Camille.* Your hair in fringes and soft curls in *Anna Karenina.* Your smart postilion hat in *Conquest.* Must we credit them only to Adrian? Come, Miss Garbo, don't disillusion us. Don't you really give a damn how you look?

Ten years had passed since the release of *A Woman of Affairs,* and Garbo's inimitable, classic style was, for the moment, thought to be passé by those "in the know," or who at least made their living by professing to counsel others on such matters. There were a number of reasons for this, not the least of which was the fact that by late 1938 Garbo had not appeared onscreen in modern dress for almost five years.

When *Queen Christina* was released in 1933, the marketing department at MGM, encouraged by the furor Adrian had created the previous year with his designs for Joan Crawford in *Letty Lynton,* engineered a mammoth campaign to market the "Christina look" to consumers. On December 27, 1933, *Women's Wear Daily* carried a feature story on the Christina designs, focusing on the variety of collars in Garbo's costumes.

Starched white fabric worn with a soft black velvet frock was seen as "an unusual and interesting development" by the publication's editors. Newspaper ads placed by stores

*Adrian makes sure that Armand "sees stars" when he comes across Garbo in this magnificent gown, casting her in an aura of peerless and pure beauty.*

OPPOSITE: *Garbo in Adrian's dress of shimmering black net for* Camille.

such as Joseph Horne and Company in Pittsburgh ("Visit our Hollywood Shop—where the creations of the American Paris find a Pittsburgh outlet") and Macy's in New York went even further, announcing the birth of a new silhouette: "boyish yet exquisitely feminine, which follows the basque line with a slightly pulled-in waist; an enchanting sleeve unlike any bishop sleeve ever seen before, and withal an ascetic, ecclesiastic 17th century glamour." In its Cinema Shop, Macy's offered a three-quarter suit jacket of ribbed tweed, priced at $58.75, which was adapted from the velvet swagger coat that Garbo wore in *Queen Christina* during the scenes at the inn.

On the heels of the bright, airy *Letty Lynton* look, however, the dark-hued ecclesiastical feel of the Christina-inspired ready-to-wear line failed to create much excitement among consumers anxious to escape the gray reality of the Depression. The publicity department at MGM concentrated its marketing efforts on the headgear in Garbo's subsequent film *The Painted Veil*, and then completely dropped all fashion merchandising in their promotional campaigns for *Anna Karenina, Camille,* and *Conquest.*

Adrian, however, had found his own outlets to draw attention to his designs in these last three films. In March of 1934 independent agent Clark H. Getts had approached MGM about engaging Adrian for a series of personal appearances: "I have in mind," Getts wrote to Howard Strickling, the head of publicity for the studio, "presenting him on radio for a woman's hour coast-to-coast, or speaking to women's clubs, with up to $1500 to $2500 a week gross." Getts managed such illustrious celebrities as Eva Le Gallienne, Alice Roosevelt Longworth, and, closer to home, Pola Negri and Mary Pickford, for similar speaking engagements. Adrian was eager for this kind of exposure, as it granted him a measure of autonomy over which of his styles were promoted to the ticket-buying public.

On July 25, 1935, Getts arranged for Adrian to speak to the press section of New York's Fashion Group at a luncheon at the Town Hall Club. During his address, Adrian hazarded a guess that the frilly, frothy feminine garments worn by Garbo in *Anna Karenina,* with their preponderance of bows and lace, might start a vogue for such clothes next spring. His efforts were ultimately self-defeating, however, for the modern-dress films that Adrian designed in 1935—Joan Crawford's two annual productions, as well as *After Office Hours* with Constance Bennett, *Reckless* and *China Seas* with Jean Harlow, and *Biography of a Bachelor Girl* with Ann Harding—offered wholesale manufacturers and female consumers more immediate ideas that were sympathetic with contemporary wardrobes. In *After Office Hours,* for example, Adrian used what he called "butterfly bows"—frivolous bits of material and ribbon—to ornament a shoulder on one of Constance Bennett's costumes or to trim a cuff with a nonchalant touch.

# Ninotchka:
# No Longer Alone

*Ninotchka* in 1939 was not only Garbo's first comedy, it was also her first modern-dress picture since *The Painted Veil*. Because Garbo had been left behind by the fashion mavens of America, Adrian had to tread a fine line between what was considered "fashion" in 1939 America, and Garbo's own inimitable style. A period of five years had elapsed between *The Painted Veil* and *Ninotchka,* during which Garbo had appeared dressed in the furbelows of history. In the words of Garbo biographer Alexander Walker, *Ninotchka* "did the last thing left to do to the Garbo myth—it debunked it."

When *Ninotchka* is viewed today, the fashion subtext of the film becomes overwhelming; it not only provides a visual accompaniment to Nina Yakushova's transformation from communist to capitalist, but it takes on an almost universal symbolic importance as the very essence of capitalism itself. Playing a Soviet commissar who travels to Paris in an attempt to ameliorate a tense situation involving three of her male comrades and the sale of some royal jewels, the script calls for Garbo to laugh, but it also spoofed her humorless style and legendary private proclivities. "Do you want to be alone, comrade?" Commissar Iranoff asks Garbo at one point. "No!" she replies bluntly, and a decade-old publicity story is given a comic spin. Strolling through a Parisian hotel lobby soon after her arrival, she spies an odd, funnel-shaped hat in a shop window and stops dead in her tracks.

By 1939, Elsa Schiaparelli's collaborations with Salvador Dalí had come to the attention of the fashionably dressed in America. Throughout the early and mid-1930s, they had dazzled Paris with a succession of crazy, flattering, fanciful headwear, adorned with cunning absurdities and little jokes. There were pie-shaped hats strewn with calla lilies made out of silk, and hats made out of layers of pleated organza that were meant to resemble sea shells. Adrian's idea for the hat in *Ninotchka* (which, after all, was set in Paris) took its cue from some of his own whimsical sketches of the past, as well as Schiaparelli and Dalí's designs, most specifically the high hats Schiaparelli called the "Russian Crown" and the "Breton Sailor."

"How can such a civilization survive which permits their women to put things like that on their heads?" Ninotchka asks her comrades Buljanoff, Iranoff, and Kopalski as she stares at the shop window. "It won't be long now, comrades."

The revolution will have to wait, however, for it isn't long

before Count Leon d'Algout (Melvyn Douglas) provokes a laugh out of dour Comrade Yakushova, initiating a transformation in her personality that commences with one of the most graceful sequences in any of the twenty-four films Garbo made at Metro-Goldwyn-Mayer. Ushering her comrades out the door, Garbo stays two steps ahead of Ernst Lubitsch's camera as she sweeps through the enormous hotel suite, locking one door after another. Finally alone, she glides onto the floor in front of an ornate credenza and quickly produces a key, opening the bottom drawer. Raising up the hat she spied in the shop window and furtively purchased, she backs away from it slightly and regards it for a brief moment like a scientist studying a specimen jar. She then walks slowly to a full-length mirror—never once taking her eyes off the hat—until she catches sight of her reflection in the glass. She studies herself, in a nondescript pencil-thin gray skirt and matching blouse, and then slowly places the hat on her head, facing the mirror like a condemned man confronting a firing squad. In one long, slow, uninterrupted movement she sinks to a divan in front of the mirror, cups her head in her hand, and stares at herself. As Adrian's hat—an object of irresistible farce—meets Garbo's immovable persona, the surface calm of Garbo's face throughout the sequence recalls Buster Keaton's countenance at his most deadpan. It is a sublime, sweetly comic moment.

"It's a little bit of a hat—a crazy little hat," Adrian explained when the film was released. "She wears it in a lot of sequences in the picture but I hope women generally don't adopt it because it wouldn't look good on them. In fact, it wouldn't look good on anybody but Garbo. It's tailored to her character and individuality. There are plenty of Garbo gowns that can safely become the fashion. But *not* the hat."

Adrian was no doubt thinking of practicality more than the actual shape of the hat, for it is open at the top, and would certainly not offer the wearer much protection. But how perfect it is, and how inspired for the scene in which it appears. Not a Schiaparelli hat that draws attention to its ingenious, imaginative motifs, but a confection as light and bubbly as the champagne that will later break down all of Ninotchka's defenses.

When Ninotchka returns to Moscow after her trip to Paris, her roommate Anna finds a silk slip hanging on the communal laundry line. She questions her friend about it, which leads to a discussion of Western fashion. After some prodding, Ninotchka admits that she also had a hat and an evening gown in Paris:

"An evening gown?" Anna asks in astonishment.

*Garbo in* Ninotchka *(1939) wearing Adrian's "crazy little hat."*

Right: *When ice melts: the transformation of Ninotchka as portrayed strategically through costume.*

*Adrian's version of a coming-out party dress in* Ninotchka.

"Yes, it's a dress you wear in the evening."

"What do you wear in the morning?"

"When you get up you wear a negligee, then you change into a morning frock."

"You mean to tell me you wear a different dress for different times of the day?"

"Yes."

"Now, Ninotchka, you are exaggerating!"

"No, it's true. That's how they live in the other world. Here we dress to cover up our bodies . . . to keep warm."

"And there?"

"Sometimes they're not completely covered but . . . uh . . . they don't freeze."

By this time Ninotchka has traveled all over Paris, stayed in a world-class hotel, visited the Eiffel Tower, and yet her experiences with the "other world" are boiled down to a silk slip. And while she might have worn a different dress for different times of the day, Adrian's designs for Garbo in the film always stress line over ornamentation as their most important component. Just as surely as screenwriters Charles Brackett, Billy Wilder, and Walter Reisch play free and easy with the history of Garbo's onscreen image, Adrian presents the audience with a parade of legendary Garbo fashions in the first part of the film.

Arriving at the train station in Paris, she wears a variation of the famous cloche, which is replaced by a beret in her first encounter with Count Leon d'Algout. The "straggly bob" remains untouched by a permanent wave, and there is not a bow or ribbon in sight on Garbo's severe, mannish suits, as Adrian appears to be thumbing his nose at Gertrude Bailey and her brethren. Removing her jacket at Leon's home, Ninotchka reveals a mimimally tailored Russian peasant blouse.

Then comes the onset of Ninotchka's transformation: Leon makes her laugh, and icy idealism is converted into a tentative, searching, bourgeois affability. "I don't look too foolish?" Ninotchka asks, visiting Leon's apartment for the second time in a narrow, pleated suit with broad shoulders. Two large beige buttons are arranged on each side of the yoke top, and the same note is repeated on the five-inch-wide belt. The only accessory is a small silk scarf knotted around Garbo's neck.

Leon is enchanted: "If this dress were walking down the boulevard all by itself," he tells her, "I'd follow it from one end of Paris to the other. And when I caught up with it I'd say 'Wait a moment, you charming little dress. I want you to meet Ninotchka. You two were meant for each other.'" And so they are. Adrian's

costume displays a Ninotchka still very unsure of herself and her new-found feelings, but on the verge of opening up to new ideas. A small accessory here and a tiny, unnecessary detail there, and suddenly clothes are not just for keeping warm anymore.

Ninotchka's transformation is completed in the next scene when Leon takes her to Café de Lucesse, and she wears Adrian's version of a coming-out party dress: white chiffon, light as a cloud, accented with a jeweled belt and a bodice trimmed with sequins. The effectiveness of the gown can be measured in the reaction it provokes from the Grand Duchess Swana (Ina Claire), Ninotchka's rival for Leon's affections, and the original owner of the confiscated jewels Ninotchka has come to sell in Paris. "One gets the wrong impression of the new Russia," Swana drips with utter condescension. "It must be charming. I assume this is what the factory workers wear at their dances?"

"Exactly," responds Ninotchka without missing a beat. "You see, it would have been very embarrassing for people of my sort to wear low cut gowns in the old Russia. The lashes of the Cossacks across our backs were not very becoming, and you know how vain women are."

# Two-Faced Woman

Vanity notwithstanding, *Ninotchka* was a triumph for both Garbo and Adrian; it was also their last fully realized collaboration. Following the release of the Lubitsch film, executives at MGM began looking for another romantic comedy in which Garbo might appear, but it would be two years before a property was chosen. *Two-Faced Woman,* which would ultimately become Garbo's last film, was based on a story by Ludwig Fulda called *The Twin Sister,* a simple tale about an uncomplicated woman who masquerades as her nonexistent, more outgoing and aggressive twin sister in order to try to win back her wandering husband. The story had already been used as the basis for a silent comedy, *Her Sister from Paris,* with Constance Talmadge. Oddly enough, this was one of the first films Adrian worked on when he came to Hollywood in 1925. It had already been remade once as an early talkie with Constance Bennett, who would play a supporting role in the new version in 1941.

The part of Karen and her twin sister Katherine was a saucy, flirtatious role in a farce for which Garbo felt little empathy. It was a part that might have suited Constance Bennett, Marion Davies, or perhaps even Norma Shearer, but not an ethereal presence like Garbo. The problems on the film began early, in the wardrobe department. In Hedda Hopper's *Los*

*Angeles Times* column dated July 27, 1941, Adrian described some of the fashions he had designed for Garbo to wear in the film: "One gown, which she wanted to wear but the Hays office banned, is so beautiful. It's made of suntan soufflé over the same shade of lining, gathered skirt, gold-lace belt with lace coming up the front."

This was a reference to the 1934 Hays Code of movie censorship. Just when it seemed that Hollywood designers could get away with almost anything, the 1934 Hays Code—named after Will Hays, the former Postmaster General, who was head of the Motion Picture Producers and Distributors of America, Inc.—imposed rules that banned certain language, subjects, and behavior from the screen. The Code also contained a provision that banned revealing dresses and gowns cut low in the front. The objections of the Hays Office precipitated a conflict between Adrian and the film's producer, Bernard Hyman, who wanted to eliminate the glamour and bring Garbo "down to earth." Hyman was supported by director George Cukor and, when matters came to a head, by Louis B. Mayer also. In 1941, with the European market cut off to American filmmakers, austerity was becoming the order of the day. Mayer felt that Adrian's original designs were simply too expensive. In the final film, Garbo wound up wearing several ensembles that had originally been designed for another—unidentified—actress, and a bathing suit by the New York couturiere Valentina.

The debacle of *Two-Faced Woman* ("It's like seeing Sarah Bernhardt swatted with a bladder," concluded the critic for *Time* magazine) was a contributing factor in Adrian's decision to leave MGM at the end of 1941. According to biographer Barry Paris, on his last day at the studio Adrian went to Garbo to bid her a final farewell. As he later told Irene Selznick, he was astounded at Garbo's parting words: "I'm very sorry that you're leaving," she told Adrian, "but, you know, I never really liked most of the clothes you made me wear."

Was she being disingenuous, or was Adrian simply naive? Garbo being Garbo, he should have realized that a statement like this should not have been taken at face value. The truth is that Garbo reacted emotionally to the costumes of each film she worked on, and she relied heavily on Adrian to help her interpret her roles. Further, she could also be counted on to assist him whenever he encountered a problem with a costume. During

*An anxious Garbo waits as a wardrobe supervisor makes a last-minute adjustment on the set of* Two-Faced Woman *(1941), her last film. The dress was not originally made for Garbo.*

pre-production for *Camille,* for example, Garbo spent countless hours with Adrian to perfect a taffeta silencer for screen use. Together they found that the desired effect could be attained by using a thin layer of silk beneath the material, thereby eliminating the swishing sound so objectionable to the microphone.

To sum up this most unique partnership between two extraordinarily gifted individuals, the old cliché "actions speak louder than words" may be apt. Two separate incidents, decades apart, reveal more about the Garbo/Adrian professional relationship than anything either one of them ever said about it. One of the few mementos Garbo kept from her Hollywood career was a pair of mauve kid gloves she had worn as Marguerite Gautier. Adrian had sent them to her when filming had concluded, and they contained an inimitable Adrian touch: each glove was adorned with motifs of flowering vines executed in seed pearls and miniscule steel beads. Upon close examination, the delicate tendrils intertwined to form the initials "GG."

Thirty-eight years after the release of *Camille,* Diana Vreeland gave Garbo a private tour of the "Romantic and Glamorous Hollywood Design" exhibit at the Metropolitan Museum of Art in New York. As she examined the gowns on display, Garbo was moved to lightly touch the cream-colored silk faille ball gown she had worn as the Lady of the Camellias, and a wistful smile spread slowly across her face.

*"From Boston to Budapest to Bali they copy the way Joan Crawford walks, the way she dresses, the way she does her hair—trains her brow—paints her lips."*

—Dorothy Spensely, *Motion Picture,* May 1937

*"If I'm copied, it's because of my clothes and Adrian designs those. He is responsible for all of that."*

—Joan Crawford

# Joan Crawford

## *The Most Copied Girl in the World*

"Who would have thought," Adrian exclaimed in 1941, "That my entire reputation as a designer would rest on Joan Crawford's shoulders!"

Throughout the 1930s, Adrian reserved many of his most extreme fashion statements for Crawford, whose visual appearance was an overstatement all by itself: enormous eyes, a jutting, defiant jaw, and a large mouth made larger through a generous application of lipstick. Her long waist, short legs, and broad shoulders would have been a challenge to any designer, but these physical characteristics, when coupled with the often fierce intensity of her characterizations, tended to overwhelm conventional clothes.

Adrian's historic fashion partnership with Joan Crawford began in 1929, when he became the star's exclusive designer at MGM, and his decision to accentuate Crawford's shoulders and cinch her waist in the spring of 1932 created a ripple on the surface of American style that soon turned into a tidal wave. No less an authority on Hollywood fashion than Edith Head has proclaimed that the broad-shouldered look Adrian gave Joan Crawford in the 1930s was Hollywood's single most important influence on American fashion.

The fashion angle that was to play such a vital part in Crawford's stardom, however, was actually set in her earliest days at the studio. Joan Crawford was signed to a contract at MGM in January 1925, and as a starlet eager for publicity few chances were lost to capitalize on a dressy fad or a flirtatious, attention-getting bit of fashion business.

OPPOSITE: *A close-up of the wool crepe suit from* No More Ladies *(1935), as photographed by Hurrell.*

What was missing in these early days was a uniform look, a distinct point of view. Any novelty would do, as long as it garnered attention, and Crawford dressed the Sunday newspaper supplements attired as Hamlet, in gypsy raiment, in the new "ready-rolled" stockings favored by flappers of the era, even as a lady pirate! When the release of *Our Dancing Daughters* in 1928 finally provided Crawford with an identifiable star image as the headstrong yet carefree "flapper" Diana Medford, it also supplied her with something even more marketable: a distinct fashion viewpoint, one that helped establish her as a fashion arbiter for the younger generation. Six days before the film had its world premiere in New York on 6 October, an article appeared in the *New York Evening Journal* that was ostensibly written by Joan Crawford herself. More likely, it was the creation of an anonymous writer in the publicity department. In either case, this article, widely reprinted across the country, goes a long way toward establishing an image for the actress that would reverberate throughout her career at MGM:

> Something new has entered the world of clothes and personal adornment. It is not just a change in fashion, a new style. It is a concrete, tangible thing. A spirit. The spirit of modernity.
>
> The spirit finds an expression of itself in the clothes we wear. They are modern. They are startling. They do not blend; they contrast. They do not conceal; they expose. They do not rustle; they swing. They do not curve; they angle.
>
> Perhaps this new feeling in the dress finds its first and most definite expression in the motion picture world. We are the first to exploit a style. The modern clothes spirit I am talking about is abundantly typified in the picture *Our Dancing Daughters*. My own wardrobe, and the wardrobe worn by Dorothy Sebastian and Anita Page, breathe the very essence of restless activity. . . . The costumes of that particular production are the costumes of my own personal wardrobe.

This article was one of the final pieces of publicity in an exploitation onslaught that made *Our Dancing Daughters* a watershed film for the marketing and publicity departments at Metro-Goldwyn-Mayer. Produced under the aegis of Hearst's Cosmopolitan Productions (it was based on a short story by Josephine Lovett that had appeared in Hearst's *Cosmopolitan* magazine), the film is a morality play of the late 1920s that dramatizes the era's clash between a puritanical heritage and the postwar urge toward a new attitude of sexual freedom and hedonism. With the emergence of the flapper in the early 20s, stars such as Colleen Moore and Clara Bow had acted out various manifestations of the energetic and youthful new American woman in films such as *Orchids and Ermine* and *It*. These new heroines might be shopgirls or co-eds, but their main preoccupation was a search for romance. More often than not, they discovered that success was simply a matter of choosing the right dress. As a result, class became less fixed, and modern romance and modern fashion became inseparable.

There was nothing very new about this theme by 1928. What made *Our Dancing Daughters* the apotheosis of what might be called, for lack of a better term, the "flapper film," is the fact that it was a movie purposely designed—and marketed—to amuse us with the very latest in home and personal adornment. The Hearst press did not have a star to promote while the film was in production, and so the innumerable newspapers Hearst owned discussed the costumes and sets at length. Months before the movie reached the nation's screens in October, photographs of the settings were reproduced in Hearst magazines. Although this kind of advance publicity is common today, it was almost unheard of in 1928, when newspaper and magazine publicity for a movie generally started the month it was released.

Many of the sets created by Cedric Gibbons, with their nude walls and geometric abstraction of stairs, arches, and fireplaces, were influenced by the 1925 Exposition des Arts Décoratifs et Industriels Modernes in Paris. Nothing like them had ever been seen on the screen before. In addition, *Our Dancing Daughters* was the first film at MGM to be accompanied by sound effects. The studio had gone to work quietly, determined that its initial excursion into sound would have none of the hit-or-miss qualities of the first impetuous displays by other studios. A major innovation was the sounding device that accompanied the film. Piano notes, strings, and other instruments were audible as never before; human voices were astonishingly lifelike.

The "Crawford Romp," a new dance craze supposedly originated by Joan herself, broke across the country at the end of September. During the film's initial showing in Dallas late that autumn, the management of the Melba Theater engaged a local dancer, Mary Nick Lovelace, to introduce the new dance onstage between showings of the film.

When the film finally had its world premiere in New

York, the lines in front of the Capitol Theater on Broadway that balmy October evening stretched for blocks. Disregarding fire regulations, people stood five deep behind the last row of seats in an auditorium that accommodated 5,300 people.

And what did they see?

The film tells the story of three young socialites (Anita Page, Dorothy Sebastian, and Crawford) and their differing relationships with friends, parents, and various boyfriends. Crawford plays "Dangerous Diana" Medford, a headstrong young deb noted for her love of wild parties, yet at heart a good sport—true and incapable of lying. Flirting is her hobby; kissing boys her avocation.

Crawford later recalled that "none of us was starred in the picture, but theater owners, sensing the audience response, 'starred' me. My name went up on their marquees." But if there was ever a star-making role in the history of American film, it was Diana Medford. Attending an all-night party at a yacht club as the film opens, Crawford is carried by an admirer through a throng of gyrating young people as balloons cascade from the ceiling. Deposited on a table, she proceeds to do the Charleston, and as the fringe on her dress churns like a pinwheel, Crawford's star is born.

Hearst's publicity machine worked overtime in the weeks after the film's release, and on October 12 the final piece of publicity in MGM's four-month campaign appeared in the arts section of the *New York Journal American*.

Not only was *Our Dancing Daughters* a manifesto for the younger generation, it was also one for MGM (at a time when the top ticket price was 75 cents, the film grossed $95,000 its first week at the Capitol in New York, and $100,000 the second). *Our Dancing Daughters,* more than any other film in MGM's formative years, helped to establish and consolidate the studio's house style. For while Irving Thalberg might indulge directors such as King Vidor with personal projects from time to time, and would sometimes seek out top directors such as Rouben Mamoulian or Ernst Lubitsch for special films, the four most important participants on any MGM production were always the producer, the star, the set designer, and the costume designer. The last three were the primary selling tools of each film's marketing campaign.

In the spring of 1929 Crawford began production on *Our Modern Maidens*, the sequel to *Our Dancing Daughters*. It was

*Joan Crawford wearing her David Cox-designed Charleston dress in* Our Dancing Daughters *(1928).*

her first starring feature, and when publicizing *Maidens* upon its release in the late summer of 1929, MGM went to special lengths to focus attention on its new designer, Gilbert Adrian. Publicity photos were released across the country showing Adrian posing with Crawford while she holds a costume sketch from the film. David Cox didn't leave MGM until 1930, but the handwriting was already on the wall when the studio did not assign him to design the costumes for the sequel.

Crawford would later remember *Our Modern Maidens* as "the first [film] that gave the wardrobe department a chance to go all out and make Crawford a clotheshorse," but Adrian was already locked in to promoting Crawford's image as a flapper. Much of the film was already familiar in the manner of most

*A sketch for a car coat, designed for Joan Crawford in* Our Modern Maidens *(1929). Adrian's use of geometric lines in this design was an attempt to liberate Crawford from her flapper frills.*

sequels. In some ways, though, *Our Modern Maidens* was already the end of one kind of road. It was Crawford's last silent film, and the stock market crash in October would sound the death knell for the flapper. In the spring of 1930, the third and last "sequel" to *Our Dancing Daughters* went into production, and it was in *Our Blushing Brides* that Depression-era realities began to seep into the screenplays of Crawford's films.

# Our Blushing Brides

*Our Blushing Brides* reunited the three dancing daughters—Crawford, Page, and Sebastian. Instead of being fun-loving types straight out of the social register, they share a tenement flat and have to earn their keep holding down jobs at Jardine's, a big department store in New York. ("America's dancing daughters go to work!" was one catch-line MGM used to publicize the film.) Just two years earlier the opening shot of *Daughters* had shown an emblematic figurine, high-stepping to celebrate the spirit of the Jazz Age. *Brides,* made by the same director, Harry Beaumont, opens with a close-up of a time clock as a bevy of shopgirls arrive at Jardine's to start a new workday. Beaumont's camera then tracks Crawford, Page, and Sebastian as they walk through a dank, overcrowded employee locker room.

Connie (Anita Page) works in ladies' perfume, and Franky (Dorothy Sebastian) toils in the blanket department ("I may as well be buried back here, where there isn't a male customer in a carload.") But Jerry (Crawford) works as a mannequin in the store's "Salon Française," modeling high-fashion creations for the store's elite customers. The fashion show first used in *Our Blushing Brides* and later in *Mannequin* (1938) and *The Women* (1939) serves several purposes in a Crawford film, not the least of which is showing styles that viewers might want to purchase or make for themselves. Its most important purpose, however, is to make a none-too-subtle point that will run through a great many of Crawford's 1930s films like a hymn: *we* (the working class) are as good as *them* (the rich) if only we can obtain the right clothes. Jerry's position at Jardine's not only allows her to appear in the latest fashions, but it also gives her an opportunity to be romanced by young Tony Jardine (Robert Montgomery) wearing the appropriate "uniform"—and ultimately sustaining the idea that she is his social equal. Indeed, Jardine first spots Jerry at a fashion show in the store, and their initial exchange neatly encapsulates the aspirations of thousands of shopgirls circa 1930:

> "Miss March, where did you learn to wear clothes so well?"
>
> "In Simpkinsville, New York. A lovely place—to leave."
>
> "Well, I'm glad you left, for the sake of the store. Anyone with such beautiful carriage and poise would be wasted in Simpkinsville."

RIGHT: *Crawford as Jerry March, participating in a fashion show at Jardine's department store in* Our Blushing Brides *(1930), the third and final sequel to* Our Dancing Daughters.

LEFT: *An Adrian-designed evening gown from a fashion show in* Our Blushing Brides.

Jerry seizes her opportunity for romance with the scion of the Jardine fortune when the store throws a fashion show to publicize the creations of a visiting French designer, Monsieur Pantois, at the Jardine Oyster Bay estate. Producer Hunt Stromberg gave Adrian leeway in designing the show, and he bowed to the influence of designer Jean Patou, who in 1924 began showing his collections for sportswear and daywear first, with evening gowns shown after an intermission. Adrian also decided to divide the fashions in his show into three separate themes: creations for winter sports, summer sports, and wraps and gowns for evening wear. The decisions Adrian made regarding individual designs, however, resulted in his first direct challenge to both Paris and the dictums of the New York fashion magazines. In the winter of 1929 Jean Patou had initiated a bold style change by raising the waistline from the hips back to its natural level and dropping the hemline to the floor for evening clothes. It was the first salvo in what was to become a barrage: the knee, the erotic focus of twenties style, became invisible, and would not be seen again for ten years.

This departure from the current vogue transformed fashion virtually overnight, and MGM, along with most of the other studios, was left with recently completed movies featuring short-skirted actresses. By January 1930, *Vogue* was so confident of this new long, waisted look that they published a drawing by Cecil Beaton showing a group of women in the shortest of all possible skirts, and the same women, three months later, wearing long, clinging dresses. The editors were also able to give readers a "checklist" of the new fashion: a generally accepted level was ten inches off the ground for daywear, and clear to the ankle for dining and dancing in the evening. For a really grand occasion, the hem might go right down to the toes.

Considering these new changes, Adrian realized that intense fashion slavery was ill-advised. In a move that was oddly prescient, he predicted in 1930 that standard fashion would soon be a thing of the past: "Beginning with this season, the swing toward originality is already being stressed in a marked degree, which spells the end of uniform fashions. Carrying out this idea in the dresses I have designed for Joan Crawford in *Our Blushing Brides*, I have originated costumes which resemble each other only in the skirt lengths." As if following his cue, couturiers across the Atlantic began to express their own ideas in the wake of Patou's influence. Skirt lengths may have been fixed for the time being, but in the 1931 spring collections Molyneux dropped the waistline to the hips, while Schiaparelli raised it to just under the bust. Worth and Lanvin left it in its natural position. With help from the formidable MGM publicity department, Adrian began in 1930 to concentrate on his own brand of classicism—albeit with a decidedly flamboyant touch—rather than attempt to keep abreast of all the latest modes.

One of the "latest modes" that continued to sweep Seventh Avenue that year was the little print dress, which began to be offered by both East and West Coast manufacturers in the new synthetic silk as well as in real silk, making it less expensive and wildly popular. The style was eagerly promoted by

both *Vogue* and *Harper's Bazaar*. Its waistline was placed at the natural waist and given little emphasis, following Patou's dictum, and the prints were smaller and more delicate than the patterns of the previous decade, often featuring small polka dots or fragile blooms.

On film, however, these blooms were much too small. Adrian knew that minute prints would be lost in a fashion show that was shot almost completely in long and medium shots. When designing the show for *Our Blushing Brides,* he chose instead to utilize bold, geometric stripes for many of the designs so they would register vividly on screen. Today the sportswear in this sequence looks almost surprisingly modern.

*Joan Crawford, front and center, in the winter sportswear finale from the fashion show in* Our Blushing Brides. *Adrian's canny sense of what would read on-screen is in evidence here: eschewing the delicate prints so popular at the time, he chose patterns that would appear bold.*

Significantly, too, the dress chosen to spotlight the advertising campaign for the picture was not one of the fantastic creations Crawford wore in the fashion shows at Jardine's, but rather a dress from her ordinary life as a working girl.

"The idea of false economy is past," reads one article in the pressbook for the picture, "and with it has gone the absurd idea of hoarding one's best dress while wearing one's second and third best until the best one becomes out of date. . . . Rather than fill their wardrobes with all sorts of clothes, the [modern girls] stock up on a select few that will serve them for every occasion throughout the day and evening. Some of the patterns that answer for these modern engagements can be viewed in *Our Blushing Brides.*"

Adrian was leading the campaign to make Hollywood a style center for all women, not just to certain women, as Paris had been for years. The division between rich and poor was growing wider every day in 1930, but as Michael Harrington points out in his book *The Other America,* economic depression has historically encouraged mass-produced fashion. Mass manufacturing blurs class distinctions and so performs an ideological function: it maintains the appearance of equality. A style executed onscreen in silk could always be copied in cotton or crepe. And thirties Hollywood was eager to exploit this new trend in the themes and plots of the motion pictures it created.

# A New Crawford Emerges: *Possessed*

*Possessed,* which was released at the end of 1931, can be seen as a 1930s fashion primer and it is in this film that Joan Crawford's new Depression-burnished fashion image is fully realized.

At one hour and 17 minutes, Possessed is a short film even by early talkie standards. It wastes little time in making its salient points. Crawford exits a paper-box factory in a small northeastern community at the end of a hot, tiring day, and director Clarence Brown frames the desperation of millions of working-class filmgoers in a few neat phrases. "What do you want, anyway?" asks her factory beau as the two walk together through a dilapidated shanty town. "I don't know," replies Crawford. "I only know I won't find it here."

She finds it minutes later at a railroad crossing, in the windows of a passing private railroad car. The train windows are lit from within, and Crawford watches them pass, her back to the camera, her head snapping back and forth like a marionette as one image succeeds another: A maid caresses a silk slip with an iron; a pre-dinner cocktail is fastidiously shaken in a gleaming silver canister; a couple in tuxedo and evening gown glide and dip to the rickety strains of a portable phonograph. Although this juxtaposition perfectly delineates America's class struggle in film terms, it is almost too self-conscious as Crawford assumes the role of thousands of her acolytes, yearning for images that shimmer just out of reach.

When the train stops on the observation platform, Crawford is startled to find herself facing a middle-aged Manhattan millionaire pouring himself a glass of champagne, which he promptly shares. "Off to the big city to be done wrong?" he asks. "To be done right," she replies. For this scene Adrian dresses Crawford in a simple polka-dotted cotton shift with matching white collar and cuffs. Before the film is over, she will travel to penthouse and back, and the audience will discover which clothes Adrian deems *right*.

The millionaire offers his business card, and the champagne soon does its work. Tipsy but emboldened, Crawford makes a decision she might otherwise have buried as a wistful regret. Returning to the shack she shares with her mother, Crawford erupts when her boyfriend ridicules her sudden plan to move to New York: "If I were a man, you'd think it was right for me to go out and get everything I could get out of life. Why should men be so different? All they've got are the brains, and

they're not afraid to use them. Well, *neither am I!*"

It is a searing indictment that reverberates through hundreds of movie palaces across the heartland. This is a woman who knows exactly what she wants and will resist compromise at every turn. Indeed, the drama and tension of *Possessed* arise out of the compromise Crawford eventually does have to make.

But initially, Crawford's rise is swift. On her first day in the big city, she meets Mark Whitney (Clark Gable), a divorced lawyer, and promptly becomes his mistress, assuming the name "Mrs. Moreland" so that the unsuspecting will think her money comes from her deceased "husband," and not from Gable's wallet. In a montage sequence to denote the passing of time, a feminine hand languidly tears the years off a wall calendar. 1928 . . . 1929 . . . 1930 . . . and finally 1931. With each year another bracelet is added to the extended arm; by 1931 it is festooned with glittering gems.

Crawford is preparing a dinner party for Gable as the film glides into the present. She is wearing a black satin bias-cut evening gown, belted with a white cloth orchid hugging her waist. The flared shoulders are the only accents. Midway through the evening, Gable receives a telephone call from an associate, and Crawford, taking the receiver Gable hands her, invites Horace Travers (Frank Conroy) to join the festivities. He's bringing his wife, she tells Gable as she hangs up the phone.

> "Really? Oh, that is nice. You know, I've always hoped you might meet her."
> "What's she like?"
> "Oh, terribly conservative, strait-laced. Her family settled New York and have stood still ever since."
> "Maybe she won't like me."
> "She has good taste as well as good family, my dear."

Crawford may be encouraged, but she is not yet convinced. She heads straight for the bedroom, where she studies herself intently in a mirror, examining her dress. Then she sits down at her makeup table. Smoothing out her lipstick, she makes her mouth wider. She slicks down her flyaway eyebrows. Then she stands and hitches up her bodice so that the fabric will cover her shoulders. Casting a worried look in the direction of the closed door, she hurriedly takes off several bracelets, leaving only one. A quick final examination in the mirror, and she rejoins the party.

The scene serves a twofold purpose: The audience is made aware that Crawford's character recognizes the subtleties of wardrobe and the inappropriate message that can be transmitted by an incorrect accessory. But the dress—the dress works. Crawford's approval endorses the rightness of Adrian's design before the camera. The social ramifications are driven home in the next scene, however, for Horace Travers does not arrive with his wife. He arrives with Vernice Laverne (Marjorie White), a short blond with a bad perm who is wearing a lumpy gray suit with ostentatious cat fur on the lapels and cuffs.

She is also wearing a knock-off of the Empress Eugénie hat that Adrian had designed for Garbo in 1930. The costume touch is Adrian's little joke; in an issue of *Ladies' Home Journal* that reached newsstands the month that *Possessed* was released, he urged women to be "terribly careful" about wearing the Eugénie only at the right time and the right place; it was his opinion that "plumed hats should be worn only with formal costumes and on very formal occasions."

All wide-eyed in the entrance foyer, Vernice steps away from her hosts and leans into the living room, hands on hips, to take a peek at the assembled guests. Clarence Brown's camera pulls back to reveal the entire set, the guests impervious to her presence. The shot serves to drive home just how out of place Miss Laverne is in this setting.

> "I thought you were bringing your wife," says Gable.
>
> "My wife?" replies Travers. "I couldn't bring my wife here." Then, sensing Gable's anger, he whispers, "You've got your sweetie here and I've got mine. What's the difference between them?"

No one sitting in the audience needs to be told. Slowly, almost unselfconsciously,

*Crawford wearing a bias-cut, black evening gown for the dinner party in* Possessed *(1931). Only the slightest preparation is needed to affect the genteel image Crawford now desires: when she prepares to greet Henry Travers and his wife, she removes all but one of her bracelets and readjusts her dress so that her previously bare shoulders are now appropriately covered.*

Crawford lowers the shoulders of her gown as she squires Miss Laverne through the living area and back to the foyer, where Gable has already thrown Travers out.

Here Adrian draws the line between what is acceptable in dress and what is not. It is a harrowing moment in the film, as Crawford suddenly realizes the precariousness of a position unsanctified by matrimony. She can *look* the part, but that's all. "I wonder how many wives would be so understanding," Gable says as he seeks to smooth Crawford's ruffled feathers after Travers's departure. Her frank reply is withering: "These

MG-181
MGM

things don't happen to wives."

Crawford later offers to withdraw from the relationship, fearing she will hurt Gable's political chances. Toward the end of the film, she goes to a convention hall to hear Gable speak. They have not seen each other for months, and he does not know that she is in the audience. Adrian dresses Crawford in a solid-beige wool coat and matching hat with an enormous bow at the neck. No earrings. No bracelets. No rings. The costume signals to the audience that Crawford has arrived at a new place in her life. No longer poor, no longer kept, she is reunited with Gable at the end of the film, and marriage is in the offing. Crawford's outfit acts as a fashion forecast: This is what the respectable, upper-middle-class married or about-to-be-married woman will want to be seen in.

*Possessed* was an enormous hit, netting a $600,000 profit for MGM, and it set the wheels in motion for Crawford's new image as fashion arbiter for the 1930s, and for Adrian's emergence as the power behind that image. In an article for *Vogue* Cecil Beaton enthused over both of these developments:

Can it be that better taste has appeared in California, that good taste is coming into the movies? Can it be that sequin spangles, Kiki's moues, Ostrich feather trimming, swans down, and Pierette pompons have fallen out of popularity, together with the old, silent film? . . . Mr. Adrian, premier designer [at] Metro Goldwyn Mayer, is prized and guarded as one of its most important treasures, and rightly so, for he possesses astonishing talents in many directions; his paintings are extraordinary, and the costumes that he designs have the merits of being utterly photogenic, possessing the heightened smartness and exaggeration necessary for photoplays.

And look at the astonishing metamorphosis of Miss Joan Crawford! Two years ago her hair was fluffed up, and she insisted upon encasing her well-covered body in vulgar costumes with skin-tight waists and flaring, lamp-shade fringed skirts, but now she has transformed herself into one of the most brittle, exotic personalities in the colony, with her stark hair brushed to show off her archaic features.

In a fashion feature for *Modern Screen* timed to the release of *Possessed*, Crawford was more direct: "The right dress makes life an adventure, the wrong one makes it a dull bore!" Adrian's comments in the same article are more revealing, and they serve to validate the natural inclinations of thousands of young female film fans: "Joan is an example of the sophisticated, medium conservative 1931 girl. Hers has been a natural evolution. She first thought of herself in terms of a tight waist, a circular skirt and with bows on her shoes [as in *Our Dancing Daughters*]. Then, because she has an alert intelligence, she gradually acquired style sense. She dared new lines, saw that they became her and adopted them. In a way, motion pictures have been to her a belated finishing school. They have taught her to distinguish between a tawdry fad of the moment and a lasting style. She is eager to accept the most chic thing I can give her. The styles she wears are legion in number."

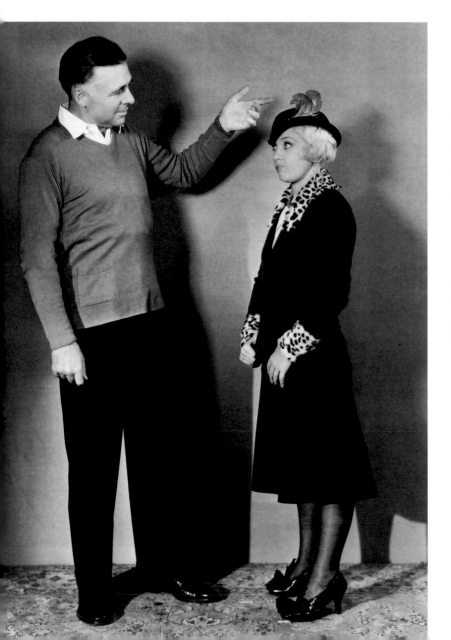

*In a publicity photo for* Possessed, *director Clarence Brown points out the incongruity of Vernice Laverne's "Empress Eugénie" hat when worn with a short black suit.*

OPPOSITE: *The final scene in* Possessed, *in which Crawford goes to hear Clark Gable speak at a political rally. By now she has shed the trappings of a kept woman and wisely chosen a stylish, solid beige coat signaling that she is ready for a proper middle-class marriage.*

# A Stenographer with Style: *Grand Hotel*

Not surprisingly, the lack of an opportunity to wear a "legion of styles" was the main reason Crawford initially resisted being cast in *Grand Hotel* (1932). As Flaemmchen (the "little whore-stenographer," as Crawford later described the character in her autobiography), she feared she would be relegated to a pair of simple frocks in her role as working girl, while Greta Garbo would no doubt have sumptuous costumes as the world-weary ballerina Grusinskaya. Despite Crawford's initial protests, however, Irving Thalberg was adamant, and she was cast in the film.

MGM, like many other studios in the early talkie era, had produced revue films using most of its lengthy talent roster. But in a feat of showmanship remarkable for its time, Thalberg decided to assemble the first all-star cast in a dramatic film. Crawford would join Garbo, John Barrymore, Wallace Beery, Lionel Barrymore, Lewis Stone, and Jean Hersholt in Vicki Baum's tale of life behind the walls of Berlin's luxurious Grand Hotel.

*Grand Hotel* today is almost more myth than film. In the late 1960s, when young baby boomers were rediscovering the films of the 1930s, it was one of the most frequently revived movies from Hollywood's "golden age." And in a spate of books that reexamined the studio system in the late 1980s, *Grand Hotel* was still regarded as the ultimate expression of early MGM "house style": "The archetypal MGM picture during Thalberg's regime," wrote Thomas Schatz in his book *The Genius of the System* (1988). "MGM's and perhaps all Hollywood's most typical film," wrote Ethan Mordden in *The Hollywood Studios* (1988). "Surely the most glamorous, possibly the most entertaining, and arguably the definitive Hollywood movie." Yet the evolution of Crawford's role in this production—as well as Adrian's unique contribution to the creation of Flaemmchen—has never been examined.

When the movie was first released, much was made of its cinematic opening; expert cross-cutting reveals Hersholt, the Barrymores, Beery, and Rafaela Ottiano (as Grusinskaya's maid, Suzette) inside individual phone booths in the hotel lobby. Tension is high, and each character is facing some kind of personal or professional crisis.

Finally we cut to Lewis Stone as the mysterious Dr. Otternschlag, sitting in the lobby, puffing on a cigarette, rather bored: "Grand Hotel," he sighs. "People coming . . . going . . . nothing

ever happens." The web has been cast, and the film's power has also been subtly defined: it will make voyeurs of us all.

*Grand Hotel*'s screenplay is credited to William Drake (he merely translated Baum's German into English), but director Edmund Goulding and Thalberg himself thrashed out many of the scenes before shooting began. And a fundamental change in the shooting script allowed Crawford to make a star entrance. Flaemmchen is not just another character occupying a phone booth as in the play. Instead, Crawford sweeps through the hotel's revolving doors, her face a mask of fierce resolve, her portable typewriter clutched tightly against her chest, wearing what will turn out to be one of her most famous costumes. She inquires after General Director Preysing (Wallace Beery) at the front desk, then gives away her social class by yelling after the elevator operator—*"Hey, wait a minute!"*—and brushing aside a baroness or two as she streaks across the lobby. Photographed almost entirely in long shot, this new entrance gives the audience a chance to take in the entire dress, something that would not have been possible in a phone booth.

And the dress is a masterpiece of design. Black with a tailored jacket bodice, it is cut low, cracked open with a "V" in front, and features white cuffs and an asymmetrical pleated white lace collar. Historically, at least, black dresses with white collars and cuffs recall the Puritan dress of seventeenth-century America. Almost ten years after *Grand Hotel* had its world premiere in the spring of 1932, the designer Renie designed a working-girl costume for Ginger Rogers to wear in *Kitty Foyle* that played another variation on this theme. It was made of navy wool with a boy's pointed collar in starched white linen. The collar and white cuffs were detachable (and practical!) so that Kitty could take them off every night and wash them. The dress became an instant classic with working girls in the early 1940s, and Renie later gave Adrian partial credit for the design, acknowledging her debt to Crawford's stenographer's outfit.

Adrian's dress for Flaemmchen had matching white gloves, and when Crawford wears them the entire ensemble resembles the uniform of a French maid. It suggests a domestic—a working girl—whereas the plunging neckline suggests something much more intimate. Crawford rarely wore her costumes with much sexual aplomb—the social aspirations lurking within each seam often negated this—but here she sizzles in silk crepe.

To accommodate Crawford's wish to appear in beautiful dresses, the action in the original play was rewritten for the screenplay. In the play Baron Von Gaigern (John Barrymore) meets Flaemmchen in the hotel bar. The scene is brief: He asks her to dance, but she has an engagement. There is a hurried promise to meet the next day, and the scene draws to its conclusion.

On film the encounter receives the MGM touch. The action has been transferred from the bar to a corridor of the hotel. Filmed almost entirely in close-up, Crawford and Barrymore dart and dance around each other like circling swans. Soon enough, the baron wears down all resistance, even discovering Flaemmchen's occupation. He then asks her to tea.

"Tea would spoil my dinner," she says. "I only have one meal a day, and I'd rather hate to spoil it."

"Why one meal a day?"

"Money. Ever heard of it?"

"Yes I have, vaguely. But I always thought little stenographers made little pennies."

"Very little. Did you ever see a stenographer with a decent frock on?"

The Baron looks her up and down. "I have indeed."

Flaemmchen moves in front of him, lips pursed, face set in plaster, her eyes narrowed and knowing. "One she'd bought *herself*?" she asks.

"Oh, I see what you mean. Poor kid. . . ."

Never mind how Crawford as Flaemmchen gets the dress, it appears thanks to Goulding, Thalberg, and MGM's cabal of screenwriters. At the same time, Flaemmchen's character is established immediately in this scene. She is much more than the character outlined in the play, that is, the "girl

Crawford as the stenographer Flaemmchen in Grand Hotel *(1932)*.

LEFT: *Crawford's Flaemmchen has the good fortune to wear a dress that really does go from day to night. As seen here with John Barrymore in* Grand Hotel, *Crawford is able to suggest that despite her lowly job, she has the wherewithal to attain higher pleasures.*

they pass around." This is a stenographer with ambition ("Oh, I'd love to be in the movies," she tells Preysing later, in his suite), one who is capable of attaining access to the high life ("A friend took me skiing in Switzerland last month . . .") and who is thoroughly aware of what men really want from her. Indeed, she is happy to provide it for a price. The audience is cued to assume she may take more than dictation from Mr. Preysing, but it lets her off the hook when she does: "I'll need clothes and shoes," she says when the industrial magnate asks her to travel with him to London. "And it's cold in England in March, and I'll need a suit. You'd want me to look nice, wouldn't you?" Even at the end of the film, with the baron dead and Preysing, her erstwhile benefactor, on his way to jail in handcuffs, plucky Flaemmchen hooks up with the ailing Kringelein (Lionel Barrymore) and heads off to Paris with 3,400 marks (Kringelein's gambling win) in her pocket.

Indeed, what critics and film scholars often overlook when discussing *Grand Hotel* is its celebratory middlebrow uplift. Of the five major principals, only Grusinskaya, Baron Von Gaigern, and Preysing have expensive rooms off the main corridor, with private bath. Von Gaigern's ability to pay for his quarters is based on illusion—a title and appropriate clothes, but no real capital to back it up. Kringelein, meanwhile, has initially been relegated to an inexpensive room for no other reason than the image broadcast by his shabby attire.

Yet at the end of the film, Von Gaigern and Preysing have met ignominious ends, and Grusinskaya faces an uncertain future, leaving the hotel without realizing that her lover, the baron, has been killed. Kringelein, however, parades through the lobby in new clothes: a top hat and morning coat. And, it seems, a new image along with them. "Is Your Excellency leaving?" asks a hotel employee. Yes, and with Flaemmchen on his arm, sporting the same costume she wears at the beginning of the film. This is no accident. For Flaemmchen, the adventure has just begun, and in Paris the dress shops are waiting.

> Any list of Hollywood-born clothes would be silly without mention of the "Letty Lynton" dress. Every little girl, all over the country, within two weeks of the release of Joan Crawford's picture, felt she would die if she couldn't have a dress like that. With the result that the country was flooded with little Joan Crawfords.
>
> —*Vogue*, February 1, 1938

When reviewing *Grand Hotel* in the April 1932 issue of

*Photoplay* James Quirk wrote, "Our interest is carried beyond the usual limits of a film. Perhaps one of the most interesting things about *Grand Hotel* is that when we have seen it, in our mind's eye it is never finished."

MGM would exploit the open-ended finale of *Grand Hotel* when promoting Crawford's next film, *Letty Lynton*. The two films were released within months of each other; in many cities across the United States, they opened at the same time, primarily because *Grand Hotel* was exhibited as a roadshow attraction, playing at one theater for months, while *Letty Lynton* received a general release on the Loew's circuit. The studio sent out a red alert to exhibitors who had booked the latter film; seen in retrospect it's a clever marketing ploy that demonstrates how a star's fashion image was both constructed and exploited, for the fact that Crawford has only three costume changes as Flaemmchen does not deter the publicity department: "A *Grand Hotel* roadshow engagement might have played your territory by the time you book this picture. If so, hook up both attractions in every possible way. You can also order the very smart collection of her latest style photos as shown in her *Letty Lynton* picture. Window photographs of *Grand Hotel* roadshow engagements reveal the willingness of stores and theaters to give them advantageous spots among the displays of summer fashions."

Studio photographer George Hurrell posed Crawford in her Lynton costumes against the sets of *Grand Hotel*. These stills, displayed in theater lobbies showing *Grand Hotel*, combined to create a third film in the mind's eye of the moviegoer exiting the theater, one that featured little Flaemmchen as she might have looked after spending Kringelein's marks in the Paris couture salons.

## *Letty Lynton* and *That* Dress

*Letty Lynton* is a difficult film to discuss because so few people have seen it. Several months after it was released, MGM was hit with a lawsuit accusing the studio of plagiarism. Although the screenplay for the film was based on a novel by Marie Belloc Lowndes, which in turn was inspired by the case of Madeleine Smith, the alleged "Edinburgh poisoner," the charges of plagiarism were brought by the author of a play entitled *Dishonored Lady*. The play told essentially the same story, but the studio had neglected to purchase it because the

*From left to right, Ilka Chase, Vivian Oakland, and Marion Davies in* The Floradora Girl *(1930), set at the end of the nineteenth century. The film caused a renewed interest in the fashions of the 1890s. The one person unsurprised was Adrian.*

Hays Office, Hollywood's watchdog, had objected to the title. Unfortunately for MGM, it was possible to prove that a portion of the play had been incorporated, however inadvertently, into the screenplay. The case accounts for the rarity of the film's public exhibition at revival houses or even on television. It has yet to be released on video. Nevertheless, Crawford's "Letty Lynton" dress, as it came to be called—a dress of white starched chiffon organdy with a rounded neck and gigantic puffed and ruffled peplum-edged sleeves—created a fashion furor across America and finally established Adrian's reputation as the most influential Hollywood costume designer.

More has been written about Crawford's shoulders and Adrian's emphasis of them than almost any other aspect of thirties fashion. Actually, Schiaparelli had hesitantly revived the padded shoulder and puffed sleeve look in 1930. A year later, *Women's Wear Daily* had reported that French designers were exaggerating the widths of shoulders with new cuts, sleeves, revers, and capelets.

The mutton sleeve, puffed at the shoulder and tight from the elbow down, was in itself a throwback to the 1890s. At the time *Letty Lynton* was released in 1932, the trend in fashion was toward an interest in such revival styles; a result, perhaps, of a search for solace during economic hard times by looking back at the accessories of a gilded past. The quixotic American designer Charles James, who worked out of London in the 1930s and was an inspired master of the intricate cut, would revive the raglan sleeve in 1933. Indeed, when Patou lowered hemlines in 1929, it seemed in retrospect almost perfectly in tune with what would become the dominant theme of the 1930s: retrospection. To many at the time it seemed as if he were trying to recall the days of *grand couture,* and the high-waisted gowns of Worth and Doucet. The puffed sleeve style, however, would remain virtually ignored until Joan Crawford wore it in *Letty Lynton.*

Adrian had precipitated this trend toward retrospection as early as 1930 with his costumes for Marion Davies in *The Floradora Girl,* which had an 1890s setting. Acting on a hunch, he worked with the MGM publicity department to sponsor a style contest in conjunction with the release of the film. It ran in Hearst newspapers across the country in the summer of 1930. Pictures of Davies in costumes from *The Floradora Girl* were featured with the following caption: "Do you like Marion's costume? Do you wish to see these styles return? Or do you prefer styles of today? Put your views in a letter. You may win $500.00. One man and one woman's letter will be selected."

MGM received literally thousands of letters, postcards, and telegrams, and the results were announced on August 11, 1930. While most respondents didn't want to return to the style *ordeals* of the 1890s—in 1930 there were many women who still remembered what it was like to struggle into a corset—they felt that many of the stylistic touches in Davies's costumes were lovely. One of the contest winners, Minna Marcus of New York City, said as much, stating that while her mother still recalled the difficulty of "getting dressed" in the 1890s, she herself felt that the "floradora style" had "great charm."

This response from the American moviegoing public provided Adrian with the impetus he needed to follow through on his intuition. In 1931 he designed a dress for Madge Evans in *Son of India* with fluted ruffles of organdy on a full, circular

skirt. Crawford wore a similar design in *This Modern Age,* which preceded *Possessed* onto the nation's screens by a few months. Around the same time, *Vogue* gave its blessing to the trend when it featured a sketch of a "startling" new design from Chanel—a formal evening dress in cotton with a full skirt. The dress, known simply as "578," was made of tucked apricot-rose organdy.

The *Letty Lynton* costume deviated from these efforts in one fundamental way, for Adrian reversed the drooping lines seen between 1930 and 1932. The lines in the dress moved upward instead of down. The fitted bodice above the circular skirt, and the hip emphasis created by the series of tucks appearing above the three-ruffled border, were all popular trends in the early 1930s. The shoulders were emphasized with huge, outsized ruffles that expanded and exaggerated a previously hesitant style. "Joan Crawford's organdie dress in *Letty Lynton* may have seemed to have several ideas," Adrian told *Ladies' Home Journal* in 1933. "The gathered ruffled sleeve; the Buster Brown collar; the hip treatment and the flared bottom of the skirt, both ruffled and tucked. But the ruffle was the repetitious note, and one was more conscious of it than anything else."

For Adrian, whose goal as a designer at MGM was to have a significant effect on American fashion, there was always the danger of time lag between creation and exhibition. "There is a definite evolution of styles which designers all follow," he said in 1936. "We may alter this or that, we may have our individual manners or twists or ways of doing things, but, after all, every change grows logically out of what has already developed, and in the end we all reach much the same conclusion." So the puffed mutton sleeve that Adrian had so confidently predicted would alter the prevailing silhouette of fashion came and stayed.

With *Letty Lynton,* Hollywood was finally ready to rival Paris as the leading exponent of style, at least among American moviegoers, and this was measured in dollars, cents, and the most sincere form of flattery, imitation.

When the film was released in May of 1932, Macy's department store chain had a Cinema Shop that specialized in gowns "worn by the stars." These star-fashion reproduction agreements had started in 1930 through a firm known as the Modern Merchandising Bureau, which acted as a sort of clearinghouse for the fashions marketed under their Cinema Fashions label. Through merchandise tie-in arrangements, the studios received free publicity on new releases in small-town

for it showed that film fashions could do more than just elicit interest in a picture and draw women to theaters. Ready-to-wear copies or reproductions of motion picture gowns could carry new fashion ideas into the emporiums of America on a mass scale.

A woman who bought a dress marketed by Cinema Fashions was not purchasing the exact dress she had seen on the screen, although some Hollywood designers' work was followed closely in these reproductions. Adrian, however, had a phobia about being imitated, and part of the reason his designs remain so distinctive even today is that it would be difficult to duplicate his lines exactly. Although the original "Letty Lynton" dress would remain unique, however, references to it abounded.

"I became conscious of the terrific power of the movies some months after *Letty Lynton* was released," Adrian said. "I came to New York and found out that everyone was talking about the "Letty Lynton" dress. In the studio we thought the dress was amusing but a trifle extreme. The copies of it made the

dry goods stores and city department stores as well as movie palaces. And the stores that carried these screen styles were listed by state in advertisements that appeared in the backs of movie magazines such as *Photoplay* and *Modern Screen*.

By late summer, Macy's claimed to have sold in excess of 15,000 copies of Crawford's *Letty Lynton* gown; eventually, some 500,000 copies were sold in stores nationwide. Yet MGM did not directly profit from the retail sales. The marketing arrangement that originally gave the studios a nominal one percent of the gross sales on copied designs was abandoned in 1931 when the studios realized the inherent publicity value of the transaction. *Letty Lynton* was a breakthrough film, however,

original 'Letty Lynton look' very modest and shy, which proves a fact I have long suspected, namely that the movies are giving the American woman much more courage in her dress and a much more dramatic approach to the whole subject of clothes."

And MGM began to reveal the intricacies of at least some costume construction in publicity that assumed the existence of resourceful female fans who could sew their own clothes. A photo feature in the July 1932 issue of *Photoplay* illustrated the steps taken by the MGM costume department to create the silver lamé cocktail dress Crawford wears in *Letty Lynton*.

But what of the film itself, so rich in design possibilities that it inspired an overnight flood of "little Joan Crawfords,"

*Joan Crawford with Nils Asther, looking cooler than the driest martini in the silver lamé cocktail suit Adrian designed for* Letty Lynton.

according to *Vogue*. Crawford plays a wealthy New York socialite who dallies with South American playboy Emile Renaul (Nils Asther) in Rio, then tires of him and heads back to New York. Aboard ship she is romanced by Jerry Darrow (Robert Montgomery), agreeing to marry him as soon as the ship docks. But Renaul turns up at the pier, his ardor and anger barely diminished in the weeks since Letty's brush-off. Threatened with exposure (she had written him several letters that were somewhat indiscreet), Letty goes to Renaul's apartment hotel and, in a mood of black despair, decides to kill herself, doctoring a glass of champagne with poison. When Emile proceeds to drink it by mistake, she doesn't try to stop him. Letty's case looks hopeless in court, until she is saved with an alibi concocted by Jerry.

The picture is noteworthy for 1932 in that its heroine is a murderess who goes unpunished, a radical departure from leading ladies who must pay the price if they have become even the least bit worldly. In fact, working titles for *Letty Lynton* when it was still in production included both *Redeemed* and *Promiscuous!* But there is about *Letty Lynton* an air of unreality

that makes its peccadillos easier to take. The critic for *Screenland* caught the essence of the film, and Crawford's appeal, in his review: "Besides her other assets, Miss Crawford has the great advantage of looking and acting like an actress and not a commonplace person encountered in real life. Her ability in this direction is skillfully enhanced by striking gowns that set her apart from everyday women."

The gowns served to set her apart, but they also illustrated her already implicit emotions, and one remembers Adrian's statement that a clever designer can substitute a single costume for whole scenes through the mere expedient of making clothes talk. Here he cues the audience to almost all of Letty's emotions by virtue of scissors, needle, and thread. "Adrian always played down the designs for the big scene," Crawford remembered. "For the lighter scene he'd create a 'big' dress. His theory, of course, was that an absolutely stunning outfit would distract the viewer from the highly emotional thing that was going on. There should be just the actress, her face registering her emotions, the body moving to express her reactions—the dress is only the background. But in the next scene, where she goes to the races and cheers for her horse, the costume would be just absolutely smashing."

For the dramatic turning points in the film, Adrian's ingenious designs allow Letty's clothes to speak for her. Encountering Renaul for the first time in New York, she wears a huge fur-collared black coat, and her head, with her hair slicked back under a black skullcap, rises from the collar like a cobra ready to strike its tormentor. Later, when she coolly watches Renaul drink the deadly cocktail, she is all lethal right angles in an icy silver lamé cocktail suit. The dress collar threatens Letty's jugular like a sharpened scythe, adding to the frosty encounter. Finally, the "Letty Lynton" dress brilliantly sums up the restless drive in Crawford's character in this film and her other 1930s vehicles. The oversized ruffled sleeves caught the air when Crawford wore the dress on the ship's deck, appearing to propel her forward like twin engines. At the same time, the billowing ruffles captured her at her most feminine. And the dazzling white cotton organdy helped lighten the gray Depression in America.

*Letty Lynton* neatly sums up a chapter in Crawford's MGM career. Beginning in 1930 with *Our Blushing Brides* she has promoted access to the high life through an assiduous application of knowledge, inherent good taste, and unrelenting ambition. In *Letty Lynton,* however, she has already reaped the rewards for all that hard work. She is a young socialite when the film opens, heiress to a family fortune. As important as Adrian's design for the "Letty Lynton" dress, then, was his decision to emphasize the exaggerated mutton sleeve in a costume for *Joan Crawford*—and not for Garbo, Shearer, Harlow, or any of the other MGM stars who were also wearing his designs in 1932. Letty Lynton is a well-bred American girl who would not have the slightest doubt about what was in or out of style. So is it any wonder that the clothes in this film—and this dress in particular—should have struck a special nerve with fashion-conscious Crawford fans all over the country? It was the sensational grand finale of a two-year fashion fireworks display.

Nor did the display go unnoticed by other designers in Hollywood. The following year, Walter Plunkett created a gown for Dolores Del Rio with "Letty Lynton" sleeves. She wears the dress in *Flying Down to Rio* (1933), and uses it to catch the eye of bandleader Gene Raymond while sitting at a table with five other women. Howard Greer adapted the style for Katharine Hepburn in *Christopher Strong* that same year, and Kalloch designed a gown with huge peplum sleeves for Glenda Farrell in *Lady for a Day* (also 1933).

Thanks in part to Adrian, Crawford reached the peak of her star power at MGM following the release of *Letty Lynton*. Joseph Schenck, the president of United Artists, soon asked his brother, Nicholas, the president of Loew's Inc., if he would loan Crawford to UA for a film they were planning: a talkie version of Somerset Maugham's *Rain*.

# Rain, Rain: Go Away

*Rain* would turn out to be a personal disaster for Crawford, and even as late as 1972 she wished that she could "burn every print of this turkey that's in existence." Yet many critics feel the film was severely shortchanged in its time, and that Crawford's performance as Sadie Thompson is little short of amazing, perhaps for being so unexpected. "Unpredictable in her playing and almost unrecognizable in her looks," wrote Alexander Walker in his biography of the star, her performance is "the least characteristic of all the performances Crawford was to give." Yet this was only one reason for the violent antipathy Crawford experienced when she opened her fan mail late in 1932.

Crawford's first appearance in *Rain* is executed in startling close-ups of Sadie Thompson's gaudy accessories—a bangled arm fills the frame, followed by a multi-ringed hand, legs encased in fishnet hose, a slave anklet, and finally, white patent leather shoes. Each of these shots is accompanied by the wail of a saxophone. Crawford then slithers into the frame done up in a tight gingham-check dress with a wide, scruffy white belt. A white fox stole is slung over her shoulder like a backpack.

*Rain* does not carry a credit for costume designer, although Crawford wanted Adrian to design her wardrobe. MGM refused to loan him to UA, and Adrian suggested an acquaintance, Milo Anderson, who was working as an assistant designer at Warner Brothers. Anderson bought the gingham check dress and other accessories Crawford wears in the film off-the-rack in downtown Los Angeles.

Alexander Walker has suggested that Crawford was unable to connect with her 1932 audience in *Rain* because the director, Lewis Milestone, revealed the male will that inhabited Sadie's assertively female body. "She is a woman here with power over men—and part of that power is the disconcerting

*Posing on the set of* Grand Hotel, *Crawford wears Adrian's fur-collared coat and matching black skirt from* Letty Lynton. *The black skull cap, neatly covering up Crawford's slicked back hair, further conveys the ruthlessness of Crawford's character at this point in the film.*

*Crawford as Sadie Thompson in* Rain *(1932). With little effort, she seems to have morphed into Vernice Laverne's wicked stepsister in* Possessed.

discovery a male makes that the power is the same gender as himself. It proved too unexpected a change, too raw a demonstration, for Crawford's fans to accept in 1932."

But a year earlier, Crawford had asserted power over her small-town boyfriend in *Possessed* during a tirade ("Why should men be so different? All they've got are the brains, and they're not afraid to use them. Well, neither am I!!"). The unexpected change that Crawford's fans could not accept was the fact that they found Sadie herself cheap and vulgar, with no real interest in changing her circumstances. These feelings were repeated again and again in the letters Crawford received.

At the end of *Rain,* after the Reverend Davidson has slit his throat in anguish over his attraction to Miss Thompson, as he calls her throughout the film, Sadie startles the friendly Marines by discarding the black robe she had worn during her brief religious conversion and appearing once again in what has become her native costume: tight gingham-check dress, white belt, dozens of jingling bracelets. "Surprised to see me all dolled up, huh?" she asks, registering the blank looks of two officers who have come to inform her of Davidson's suicide. "Well, why not? I had to put on my best for this gay and

glorious morning, didn't I? I'd race you down to the beach if it weren't for these pesky heels."

The message is clear. In reclaiming her identity, the costume is so much a part of who she is that she cannot remove even the smallest item, not even for a moment. And this is too much of a change for Miss Crawford's fans to accept in 1932.

Remarkably enough, Crawford's problems with what her fans expected resembled those that Gloria Swanson faced when she played Maugham's heroine in 1928. Swanson had been known throughout the 1920s as a clotheshorse; a meaty role like *Sadie Thompson* was thought beyond her range. But Swanson also had a long-term contract with UA, and the publicity material for *Sadie Thompson* alerted her fans what to expect: "In *Sadie Thompson,* Miss Swanson's latest screen offering, her wardrobe is a splendid example of what the well-dressed woman should *not* wear."

Crawford wasn't as fortunate as Swanson. A producer at United Artists might borrow an MGM star for one of his productions, but he was certainly not interested in giving that star any lasting publicity that might result in an upturn of her fortunes at a rival studio. The pressbook for *Rain* did not contain even one article about her wardrobe.

Returning to MGM in the late summer of 1932, Crawford was already working on her next film, *Today We Live,* when *Rain* was released in October, but it proved not to be the remedy she needed.

# Today We Live

Prior to the beginning of production, Crawford had visited Paris with her then-husband Douglas Fairbanks, Jr. While shopping she had discovered Schiaparelli's clothes. Returning stateside in August 1932, Eileen Creelman reported in an article for the *New York Sun* that Crawford had disembarked in New York with a number of Paris fashions, and would soon return to Culver City to begin fittings with Adrian.

And so she did. Full of enthusiasm for Schiaparelli's masculine style, Crawford persuaded Adrian to stress the width of her back rather than try to hide it, and to adapt some of Schiaparelli's lines for her. Adrian complied—he may even have been grateful, as he had once teasingly named Crawford MGM's "champion seam ripper": "She rips more sleeves than anyone else I know because she is always shrugging her shoulders." He made up a trio of dresses that were designed purely for publicity purposes. Each of the designs had squared

Following a trip to Paris in 1932, Crawford persuaded Adrian to adapt some of Schiaparelli's lines for her, and the result was a trio of suits originally designed purely for publicity purposes. Given Crawford's diva wiles, the clothes later found their way into Today We Live (1933). This suit is of gray tweed. Three silver buttons are arranged on each side of the set-in yoke, close to the rounded neckline, while an oversize silver buckle complements the four-inch-wide belt. The dress is complete with a mannish topcoat of wide lapel and patch-pocket trim.

LEFT: Another design that found its way into Today We Live. Director Howard Hawks hated this particular costume, complaining that the collar "stuck in everyone's eye." The dress is made of stiffly starched linen and has a close-to-the-throat neckline, with plainly tailored blouse and a kick-pleat skirt. A four-inch-wide belt outlines the waistline. This design marks Adrian's first experimentation with what would later become, in the 1940s, his trademark "coat hanger" silhouette.

shoulder lines, and later found their way, somewhat incongruously, into *Today We Live.*

Crawford was a last-minute addition to the film when the studio realized it stood to lose money if it did not put her to work immediately. Her later insistence on including Adrian's recent designs in the wardrobe for the film, which was set in 1916, was a star's prerogative at its most willful. What Adrian felt about the inclusion of these designs in the wardrobe for *Today We Live* remains unknown.

*Today We Live* was a Howard Hawks production, with a script by William Faulkner. But the original story (called *Turnabout*) was an Air Force melodrama set in an all-male milieu during World War I. Crawford was added to the cast as Diana Boyce-Smith, an English debutante in love with a British naval officer (Robert Young) who is seduced by an American flier (Gary Cooper).

*Letty Lynton* had played out its run by the time *Today We Live* went into production, and Crawford's ruffled sleeves in *Lynton* were creating an aftershock in the fall of 1932 ("Hollywood Ideas that Spread Over the World" read a piece in the October 1932 issue of *Screenland* that focused on Adrian's *Lynton* designs). The executives at MGM now realized that Crawford could do more than simply herald new styles. She and Adrian could *create* them. Although there was a nod to the "Lynton" gown when Crawford appears in *Today We Live* in a frock of white chiffon crepe with fluted ruffles, the Schiaparelli-influenced design that Adrian initially created for publicity was a preview of the tailored, padded-shoulder look that was to become Crawford's sartorial trademark throughout the middle and late 1930s. Adrian would later refine these designs in subsequent films throughout the decade to create the broad-shouldered and tapered waistline silhouette that became his signature in the 1940s.

MGM did its best to publicize the new Crawford look in the early months of 1933. "Hollywood is One Year Ahead!" trumpeted *Silver Screen* in a March 1933 pictorial spread on Adrian that featured three costumes from *Today We Live.* "Joan Wears Her Newest!" exclaimed *Photoplay* that same month. And the June 1933 issue of *New Movie* proclaimed that "The New Films Show the Smart New Fashions." Even *Vogue* got into the act, and the February 1, 1933 issue offered three costumes from *Today We Live* as fashions to watch for in the coming months—a tweed cap, a ribbon-laced dress, and a suit with a stand-up reverse collar.

Hearst's influential press machine, which had done so

much to create advance excitement for *Our Dancing Daughters* five years earlier, also went to work, sending reporter Jean Stevens from the *Chicago Herald and Examiner* to Hollywood in February of 1933. Stevens was a Chicago socialite, a member of the Junior League, and along with Irene Castle, a member of the *Chicago Herald and Examiner's* fashion advisory board. Her assignment was to write a series of articles about the latest fashion developments in Hollywood.

Stevens was an important tool in selling Hollywood fashion to Chicago's elite, and through them to high-end consumers throughout the Midwest. In one of the many articles she sent back to the paper, she herself was photographed in two costumes from *Today We Live.* "There is no doubt about it," Stevens wrote in her first dispatch to the *Examiner,* "the best looking clothes are being made in America—made right here in Hollywood. In my opinion Adrian is the greatest genius of them all. I believe the secret of Adrian's success is his great ability to dramatize fashion. Everything he creates has great dramatic feeling, and at the same time is perfectly wearable."

Stevens's trip had another purpose, too: Chicago was hosting a World's Fair in the summer of 1933. Forty years earlier, designers such as Worth, Paquin, Doucet, and other leading exponents of the French couture had sent elaborate exhibits to the Chicago Exposition of 1893. It was their first invasion of America, and it was accompanied by an advertising campaign that created an American demand for French clothes at the turn of the century. A Hollywood pavilion was planned for the 1933 Fair, where visitors would be able to see "actual pictures" being made on "soundstages" within the pavilion. They would also be able to view a traveling show of movie costumes from MGM, Paramount, Warner Brothers, Fox, and RKO studios. "We expect to show residents of Chicago and its visitors that Hollywood styles and fashions actually are far superior to those of Paris and other European capitals," wrote Miss Stevens. "We are going to prove to them that the clothes worn by Hollywood motion picture stars are months in advance of anything Paris can supply them."

*Today We Live,* however, was not the ideal vehicle either for promoting Hollywood fashion or for heralding Crawford's "new look." To begin with, she spends half the film's running time in a nurse's Army uniform after joining the English war effort and is constantly sniffling or on the brink of tears, saying good-bye to various lovers, her brother, even her maid. "Just when I think I can't cry anymore—that I haven't any tears left—I surprise myself," she tells her local vicar early in the film. He comforts her: "There are times in the lives of women when they must have a sublime, unreasoning faith."

"But I haven't any faith," she replies. "I don't even hope."

This is not a message any audience wanted to hear in 1933, at the height of the Depression. *Today We Live* failed to generate much excitement, and its message was too downbeat to inspire any real confidence in its fashion forecast. And while the costumes might have been interesting on a runway, they failed to embellish the narrative thrust of the film, as the costumes in *Grand Hotel* and *Letty Lynton* had done so successfully.

The film's failure made Crawford jittery. She now had two flops in a row, and her next film had to be a success or her career might be in serious jeopardy. She went directly to Louis B. Mayer with her concern, and he gave the matter of selecting her next picture more than his usual amount of interest.

## Dancing Lady: Crawford's New Deal

Mayer felt that Crawford would be helped by a change of producers, and he assigned the job of finding a project for the actress to a rising new executive on the lot, John Considine, Jr. He chose *Dancing Lady,* a novel by James Warner Bellah that had been serialized in the *Saturday Evening Post* and purchased by the studio in April of 1932. It was a twenty-year saga in the life of a young performer, from poverty to riches and fame, and its heroine's single-minded pursuit of a theatrical career offered a striking parallel to Crawford's own ambitions at MGM. Mayer approved his choice and tapped his new son-in-law, David O. Selznick, to take the picture into production.

The first thing Selznick did was to compress the scope of the story from twenty years to a period of several months. Then, figuring the title *Dancing Lady* implied music, he decided to add several musical numbers to the story. This was no whim, however. Warner Brothers had just reinvented the musical with

*Janie, with her roommate (Winnie Lightner), reads Tod Newton's note after returning home in* Dancing Lady *(1933).*

*42nd Street,* and the visual and sound dynamics of Busby Berkeley's numbers, all compressed at the end of the film, had impressed Selznick. The enormous box office success of *42nd Street* also suggested that a new musical cycle was beginning. (The first had begun with the introduction of sound in 1928 and had petered out around 1930 owing, in part, to the stage-bound limitations of the early sound cameras.) Thus, turning *Dancing Lady* into a musical would help assure Crawford of a hit. So would the eventual casting of Clark Gable as Crawford's co-star.

*Dancing Lady* is really a film within a film. It tells the story of Janie Barlow (Crawford), a young burlesque hoofer who tries for the big time on Broadway and makes it. It also reinvents Crawford's stardom, like a public relations campaign on celluloid. Gable, teamed with Crawford for the first time since their mega-hit *Possessed,* is an important part of the battle plan. So is the appropriation of Warner Brothers vitality. *Dancing Lady* is an amalgam of Metro gloss and Warner's New Deal can-do spirit. But it's also Crawford's New Deal. And the most important part of the deal is the costume strategy mapped out for the film by Adrian. *Dancing Lady* is a film that believes ardently in the magic of lucky clothes, and the near-magical transforming power of the right garment: clothing as talisman.

The film opens at the Empire Burlesque where wealthy

Tod Newton (Franchot Tone) and his society chums have gone "slumming" for the evening. "Hey Janie," whispers one of the dancers, spotting Tone and his tuxedoed friends front and center, "get a load of Park Avenue!"

"Yeah," Janie sneers. "Doin' the slums in ermine."

Janie barely has time to get her hat off before the theater is raided, and Tod follows Janie to night court to watch the fun. He then decides to bail her out after she is sentenced to jail for doing an "indecent dance." A wipe clears the screen, and the camera focuses on Janie's shoes. Shoes with ribbons on them.

Newton is treating Janie to dinner at a diner. She wears a plain black dress without puffed sleeves but she sports short-sleeved cuffs that end in plaid ribbons, which pick up on the pattern of the plaid tablecloth. Adrian has subtly connected Crawford with her working-class environment. When Janie gets home, she unfolds a note Newton has given her, and a $50 bill dribbles to the floor, replete with a list of instructions. She proceeds to read them aloud to the audience:

"Don't say 'them things.' Don't say 'can it.' Don't say 'guy.' Don't buy shoes with ribbons on 'em. Don't forget that striptease on Second Avenue is art on Broadway. The $50 is to buy yourself a dress without a zipper."

Janie mulls this over for a minute, then explodes: "Why that Park Avenue know-it-all! Don't buy shoes with ribbons on 'em! . . ." Then, brooding, she takes off her shoes and pokes at the ribbon. "Say, what's wrong with them

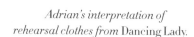

*Adrian's interpretation of rehearsal clothes from* Dancing Lady.

shoes?" she asks, pausing before she corrects herself. "*These* shoes," she says quietly. The seed has been planted, and when Crawford retires for the evening, she has already made a crucial decision: "I'm through dreamin'. I'm gonna start doin.' I'm goin' up where it's art. Uptown."

Janie's destination is a theater where Patch Gallagher's (Clark Gable) new show is in rehearsal. The following day, she is wearing the same outfit she had on at dinner the previous evening, with one crucial difference— she's removed the ribbons from her shoes. Still, it is not enough. She gets the brush-off. And even though Janie shadows Patch all over New York (or at least her ribbonless shoes do; the sequence is a breathlessly edited homage to Busby Berkeley's staccato style, in which Crawford's gams follow Gable's cordovans up and down the sidewalks of the theater district at breakneck speed), she fails to impress him.

So now Adrian's costume strategy takes center stage, and the script adds a touch of magic. Tod Newton tracks down Janie at her boardinghouse and offers her a letter of introduction to Gallagher's boss, Jasper Bradley. It's clear that Janie hasn't used the money she has received from Newton for clothes ("Don't pull that $50 gag again," she admonishes when he asks if she's low on coin), but she does have the good sense to show up at Bradley's office in a dress without a zipper. It is made of black silk crepe with starched white ruffles at the shoulders and sleeves. White gloves complete the ensemble. The scene opens after Janie's arrival, but even though she

An afternoon traveling suit from
Dancing Lady. Once Crawford
secures her position in Patch
Gallagher's (Clark Gable)
show, she is dressed like a star
on stage and off.

RIGHT: An ambitious, determined
Crawford arrives for her
audition in Dancing Lady.

doesn't get the advantage of an entrance, the camera circles
around her like John Barrymore in *Grand Hotel*. And indeed
the dress recalls her stenographer's frock; in a sense it is a
hybrid of that costume and the ruffled "Letty Lynton" dress.

Dressed for success, Crawford is at last ready to make her
mark. Although she gets her audition thanks to Newton's
entree, she secures the job *herself*. From now on, Crawford's
Janie Barlow will be dressed like a star in clothes designed to
make the audience swoon. She will turn up in evening gowns
of black silk crepe and silver sequins; she will stride into
rehearsal in an elegant black wool suit, gardenias fastened to
the lapel; she will travel to Tod Newton's country house attired
in a beige dress with an enormous gingham plaid collar
anchored by a tiny black bow. A black pillbox hat with matching black satin gloves will complete the outfit.

And the magic, as it turns out, is all in the zippers—or
the lack of them. For if Janie Barlow isn't using any of Newton's
money, how is she able to afford new clothes? Adrian was too
sensitive to the needs of both character and narrative to create
outlandish costumes that had no firm footing in reality. In many
of the films Crawford made after *Dancing Lady*, she played
women of means such as heiresses and socialites who could
easily afford lavish wardrobes. *Dancing Lady*, however, is the

Joan Crawford and Fred Astaire in a production number from Janie
Barlow's Broadway triumph. Adrian has taken the "Letty Lynton"
dress and reconfigured it for the stage in this scene.

exception. It is the only film Crawford made at MGM in which
her wardrobe cannot be explained away, as it was, for example,
in _Grand Hotel_. At the time, the critics didn't even notice.

The genius of Adrian's work for the film arrives at the
end. Janie has walked out on Newton and bullied Gallagher
into saving his theater. Finally, the show goes on.

The first number is called "Heigh, Ho, the Gang's All
Here," and all the chorus kids have pretzels and beer. (A
topical touch, for prohibition had been repealed only months
before.) They are clustered around a makeshift bar that slowly
breaks apart as Crawford waltzes in on the arm of Fred Astaire.
She is wearing a stylized, highly theatrical version of the white
organdy dress from _Letty Lynton_. Gold sequins sparkle on the
fluted skirt, and bands of gold braid that encircle her waist and
crisscross her chest end in simulated puffed sleeves of ostrich
feathers. In one brief production number Adrian has recon-
firmed Crawford's stardom through their shared fashion
influence. And even though she almost loses her balance as
she twirls for a few short minutes with Astaire, nearly falling
over at one point, it hardly seems to matter. _This_ is a star; she
saves the show, and she looks the part.

_Dancing Lady_ was a huge hit. On December 2, 1933, the
day after its New York premiere, the _New York American_
reported that police reserves were called to the Capitol Theater
before noon to handle the crowds. The largest single day's
business in fourteen months was recorded on opening day at
the theater, with paid attendance topping 18,256 people.

The film reaffirmed Crawford's popularity, but it also
hemmed her in. She and Adrian were now bound to each
other. The studio may have been slow on the uptake where
_Letty Lynton_ was concerned, but Mayer and Thalberg weren't
blind. Starting in 1934, the emphasis on fashion promotion in
Crawford's films would become overwhelming, to the point
where almost everything in the films, including the direction,
would take a backseat to the fashions. To facilitate that end,
Crawford found herself, for the moment, leaving the shopgirl,
the struggling chorine, and the stenographer on the make
behind; in the mid-thirties she was increasingly cast as a society girl with ready access to the high life, which included a luxurious wardrobe.

# Adrian Delivers American Fashion, Hollywood Style

_One main criticism is made by those who do criticize cinema
clothes. They say that the fashions are exaggerated. Hollywood replies to this, very adequately, that the technical side
of photography demands extremes. A sleeve that would look
very chic and new in a drawing room would miss its whole
force after a movie camera had finished with it. Besides, one
of the best ways to make the world conscious of a fashion is
to present it in an extreme form...._
— _Vogue,_ February 1, 1933

Adrian, via Joan Crawford's mid-thirties starring vehicles, was
about to give the American woman his own dramatic approach
to the whole subject of fashion, one he forecast in _Harper's
Bazaar:_ "What is coming? I feel that we are tired of being
clever at $14.50. I think that clothes are growing more impor-
tant in every way, even a little bit grand ... With a receptive,
even clamoring public ready to pounce on any new American
talent, with the power of the movies here to promote dramatic
ideas, the air of the American fashion world is teeming with
excitement. But we are still pathetically poor in truly original
and skilled designers. We are not so scholarly nor so light-
hearted nor so courageous as the French. We have not learned
how to be gaga in the grand manner."

We soon would. Several converging events in 1934 would
place both Adrian and Crawford in unique positions at MGM.
At the beginning of the year, Greta Garbo and Norma Shearer
would make their last modern-dress films for what would turn
out to be a period of five years. Garbo had fallen under the
influence of writer Salka Viertel, and in 1935 would resist
David O. Selznick's entreaty to star in _Dark Victory;_ Viertel's
taste leaned more toward the historical, the European, the costume epic. She encouraged Garbo's ambition to remake _Anna
Karenina_ in 1935. It would be followed in 1937 by _Camille_ and
then _Conquest,_ in which she played Napoleon's mistress, the
Polish countess Marie Walewska.

In the fall of 1934 Shearer would play poetess Elizabeth
Barrett Browning in _The Barretts of Wimpole Street,_ followed by
_Romeo and Juliet_ in 1936, and finally _Marie Antoinette_ (1938).
Adrian continued to dress both actresses, but opportunities to
promote dramatic ideas for modern American women in the

Bennett (1935) and *Biography of a Bachelor Girl* (1935) with Ann Harding come to mind—most of the films Crawford made between 1934 and 1938 became virtually the only major MGM showcases for Adrian's modern designs.

In almost all of these films Crawford plays a woman with a position in society, and in each of them Adrian created new and often startling fashion innovations that were assiduously marketed by the publicity department at MGM. Most of these innovations took the form of accessories rather than wholesale creations that attempted to change or challenge the prevailing silhouette, and for good reason. Whatever the budgetary limitations of women in the 1930s, their dresses had to go a long way. The designs they selected couldn't look dated after several seasons, which explains the simplicity of many of the clothes that were generated by Seventh Avenue. It also helps to explain the rise in the importance of accessories. Previously a hat, a pair of shoes, gloves, and a purse complemented an ensemble. In the 1930s, accessories became more dashing because they had to; besides, they could easily change the look of a relatively simple suit or dress from one wearing to the next.

Adrian would tap into this trend with the clothes he designed for Crawford's mid-1930s vehicles, and he had reached a position of power at MGM such that few directors or producers would interfere with his wardrobe decisions. "He was a loner, not a friendly sort of person, but a genius," says John Scura, who worked in the wardrobe manufacturing department and later became a supervisor in the 1940s. "He would sit in a meeting with a producer with his sketch pad and create. Most of the costume designers simply open a book of the period and copy. Adrian never even used sketch artists. Very few of our designers today do their own sketching. I don't think they have the talent. But when Adrian made a sketch, no producer or director dared to change it."

Adrian's importance to MGM's corporate profit was revealed in the prominence his name was given in the newspaper ads for *Chained* (1934), in which Crawford plays the wife of

*This elegant, bias-cut silk crepe evening gown, with accents in gold braid around the collar and arms, was first seen in Crawford's 1934 film* Sadie McKee. *The star was so fond of the dress that it found its way into the wardrobe for* Chained *the same year.*

costumes of fourteenth-century Verona or even nineteenth-century France were few and far between.

Jean Harlow, Myrna Loy, and Jeanette MacDonald were also major stars at MGM in the mid-thirties, but by 1935 designer Dolly Tree, who had been hired away from Fox by Howard Strickling and Adrian in 1932, was designing for Harlow and Loy on a regular basis. And MacDonald's forte was operetta, not an ideal vehicle to flaunt up-to-the-minute fashion. Aside from a handful of films Adrian designed with actresses on loan to MGM—*After Office Hours* with Constance

a shipping tycoon (Otto Kruger) being wooed by a wealthy South American rancher played by Clark Gable. Few films have ever introduced a heroine who led such an enviable life. Dazzling fashions, great wealth, travel, a position in society, a self-sacrificing husband, and a romantic lover—all these and more are Crawford's for the asking in *Chained*.

Over sixty years after its initial release, the plot and action of *Chained* may look moribund, but then the story hardly matters. It is simply a hanger on which some delectable costumes may be artfully draped, and director Clarence Brown puts every gown on prominent display, creating runway-model entrance shots for his star. Adrian vivifies Crawford in a series of creations that encompass every possible social situation: bathing attire, ensembles for a night at the opera, a day at the races, an afternoon on horseback, luncheon with the girls. His innovation for the film is his own version of a modernized hoop skirt. The dress was enhanced by yards of crisp tulle, flaring out suddenly from a point slightly above the knee. And the hoop, smaller in circumference than the old-fashioned kind, almost touches the floor.

As a concept that recalled another stylistic innovation of the nineteenth century, the hoop skirt was a fashion idea that was a natural progression from the mutton sleeve revival. For Adrian, the inspiration came from changing lifestyles for women. In 1933 he told reporter Jean Stevens that with the abolishment of Prohibition and the demise of the speakeasy, women were destined to concentrate on more elaborate food, drink, and gracious living in the home, which in turn would call for an expression in more graceful clothes. Noting that the French houses were exporting some dresses with a crinoline feeling late in 1933, this trend reaffirmed Adrian's sense that the re-introduction of the hoop skirt was an innovation whose time was ripe, and he jumped the gun

*Crawford wearing a bias-cut evening gown in* Forsaking All Others *(1934). Photograph, George Hurrell*

on Paris. Hoops returned as revived crinolines when Molyneux showed wide skirts in the fall of 1934, months after the release of *Chained*.

In *Forsaking All Others,* which opened on Christmas Day in 1934, Adrian took this idea one step further, introducing the hoop-skirt bridal gown. Crawford played a young society bride jilted by one suitor (Robert Montgomery), consoled by another (Clark Gable), taken for a weekend getaway by the first suitor, and then finally settling for matrimony with the second.

Fashioned of eggshell soufflé and rose-point lace, the wedding gown in *Forsaking All Others* utilized some forty yards of material. The bridal veil was also impressive. The veil

appears from beneath a small beret-like hat created in tulle and lace. It covers the face, is short in front and extremely long in back, edged in its entirety by appliquéd lace. The veil is starched to make it stand away from the head and body.

This trend toward embellishment was continued in 1935 with two sophisticated comedies, *No More Ladies* and *I Live My Life*. Crawford played society girls in both films, and each was rife with style innovations. A dinner dress in *No More Ladies* was one example of an adaptable style, although not in the fabric that was used onscreen. It was made of a gold lamé cloth called "moonbeam," and while the lines were simple and easy

ABOVE: *From left to right, Billie Burke, Joan Crawford, and Rosalind Russell in* Forsaking All Others. *Crawford is wearing Adrian's hoop-skirt bridal gown, which recalls the mutton sleeves and other period looks Adrian employed in* The Floradora Girl, *four years earlier.*

OPPOSITE: *A close-up of the hoop-skirt bridal gown. The hoops begin at the knees, and yards of the soft eggshell fabric, gathered at the hip line, fall in fluffy cascades over the rounds. Hand-appliquéd rose-point lace finishes the hemline. The waist of the dress is long and shirred to fit the figure. The sleeves are caught in puffs down the entire length of the arm ending in rose-point ruffles that cover the hands. The high Elizabethan collar is lace, but has been reinforced with wire so that it will stand erect at the back.*

RIGHT: *Crawford as Marsha Warren in* No More Ladies *(1935) wearing a gold lamé dinner dress. The accordion-pleated skirt was too delicate even for rehearsals, so the original muslin version was used instead.*

to copy, the accordion-pleated skirt was so delicate that during rehearsals for the film it was detached and the original muslin copy of the design was used instead.

For *I Live My Life* Adrian designed a large neckpiece of vari-colored flowers to be worn as an accessory with an afternoon dress. "It's just a new idea for a summer wrap," he said. "Instead of fur, I duplicated a fur design in flowers. I must admit I was a bit dubious about it at first—but it worked out most effectively, and Miss Crawford was more than pleased with the ensemble. I am sure that the flower wrap will prove a popular spring and summer wardrobe item. It solves the problem beautifully for both afternoon and evening wear."

Adrian also designed an evening gown with short-sleeved, tailored cuffs for Crawford to wear in the film, his own interpretation of the short-sleeved dinner gown that Lucien Lelong had introduced in 1932. In true Depression spirit, Lelong's idea allowed the dress to be worn more often than a very formal design, although Lelong either left his sleeves unfinished or completed them with bow-trimming. The finished cuffs Adrian designed resembled those found on a man's formal shirt, and served to complement his most startling innovation from this period: wide, tailored "kite lapels" on both suits and coats.

*Throughout the mid-1930s, Adrian continually emphasized the width of Crawford's shoulders, as in this gold lamé evening gown. Adrian called this dress "The Bounty," because he felt it looked like a ship under full sail.*

LEFT: *Joan Crawford with Brian Aherne in* I Live My Life *(1935) wearing Adrian's floral wrap, his warm-weather version of a fur stole.*

*Aherne and Crawford, again from* I Live My Life. *Everything about this dress seemed to get comments from critics, especially the so-called kite lapels and the short-sleeved tailored cuffs, which were inspired by French designer Lucien Lelong.*

These lapels stretched across the width of the chest from shoulder to shoulder, and had made their first, brief appearance on a polo coat in *Chained* the previous year. In *No More Ladies* the style was adapted as an accessory and dubbed the "Crawford Collar"; made of starched piqué, it was detachable and could be worn with formal or semiformal gowns.

While the "collar" shielded Crawford's chest like armor, the gown in *No More Ladies* that featured this accessory com-

*The kite lapel reappeared in* No More Ladies *(1935), only now it's been dubbed the "Crawford Collar" with some slight variations by Adrian.*

pletely bared her back. This was a reaction to the Hays Code's censorship dictates. Filmmakers worked around the restrictions and devised new situations for their characters, while the designers cut away at their dresses, but this time to reveal a "safe" area of women's bodies—their backs. It seemed the new rules of censorship which banned dresses cut low in the front contained no provisions regarding a lady's backside. Adrian, along with Travis Banton at Paramount, started this fashion flurry for backless dresses and Paris was quick to pick it up. In order to attract even more attention to the back, there was a brief vogue for wearing strings of beads hanging from the back of the neck. Elsa Schiaparelli even designed a backless dress with a bustle that jutted out like a shelf.

The "Crawford collar," however, inspired derisive comments from reviewers. Unforgiving, the collar made it almost impossible for Crawford to eat, smoke a cigarette, or do anything except maybe play bridge while she wears it. But perhaps people were looking at it the wrong way even then. Adrian always had a wicked sense of humor, which came out more often in his couture collections, after he had opened his own salon in 1942, than in his film work. For example, in 1946 he designed a white silk dress completely free of appliqué or other designs, except for a single bee on milady's derriere. And few people who have seen *Camille* will forget the bird's nest he planted amid the feathers on Lenore Ulric's ball gown—complete with eggs. Seen another way, then, the "Crawford collar" was Adrian's little inside joke. Here was the perfect fashion innovation for society women who never need to use their hands, as they always have someone on retainer to light their cigarettes or pour their drinks. Moreover, Adrian had a ready answer for his critics: "In motion pictures . . . there are scores of smart gowns that are adaptable and the problem of the intelligent dresser is to select the proper dresses displayed in a picture and to forget the impractical ones which have been designed to fit a certain character and to help create the story illusion."

Then, too, perhaps Adrian was simply ahead of his time. In 1995 a reporter for the *New York Times* visited the workrooms of Christian Lacroix and watched as Lacroix's business partner, Jean-Jacques Picart, constructed hats out of magazine clippings. When the reporter asked how much the hats would sell for, Picart smiled: they were only for the catwalk. "That's not a hat," he explained. "It's an *idea* of a hat."

Innovations and fads aside, one fashion trend that took firm root in Crawford's society-girl vehicles was Adrian's use of sequins and bugle beads as a dead giveaway for a woman with a questionable moral outlook or, more often, unscrupulous motives. By the mid-1930s he had completely forsaken bugle beads and sequined glitter in Crawford's costumes, relying instead on lamé, silk crepe, cotton, and wool. This trend began in *Forsaking All Others* when Frances Drake, Crawford's rival for the attentions of Robert Montgomery, is dressed for their first encounter in a crepe sheath with glittering gold braid, multiple bracelets on each arm, and large imitation jewels over each breast. In *No More Ladies* Crawford's erstwhile rival Gail Patrick attends a dinner party in an evening gown layered with glittering black sequins. Adrian kept glitter away from Crawford until she played the role of Anni Vivaldi in *The Bride Wore Red* in 1937.

*No More Ladies* and *I Live My Life* (both 1935) represent the pinnacle of Crawford's clotheshorse period at MGM, and also the beginning of its decline. There are several reasons for this, not the least of which was a hostile independent press that was beginning to turn on what it considered a calculated formula. Sneered the *New York Times* in early June 1935: "*No More Ladies,* despite its stage ancestry, is out of the same glamour factory as Miss Crawford's *Forsaking All Others.* Out of the labors of the brigade of writers who tinkered with the screenplay, there remains a sprinkling of nifties which make for moments of hilarity in an expanse of tedium and fake sophistication." And many of the films, however inadvertently, sent mixed messages to female moviegoers anxious to see what Miss Crawford was wearing.

*No More Ladies* opens with the face of a clock superimposed over a montage of New York high life: people in fast cars and at nightclubs, whooping it up all over town (for collectors of movie trivia: Hal LeSueur, Crawford's ne'er-do-well brother, can be glimpsed for a few seconds as one of the celebrants). Cut to Marcia's (Crawford's) boudoir, where the camera zeroes in on an alarm clock. It is 9:05 p.m. Four perfectly manicured fingers tap impatiently on an objet d'art. All dressed up with no place to go, Crawford wears a stunning white crepe de chine evening gown with wide black belt and matching black-velvet wrap collar. The collar is held in place with a diamond pin. She checks her engagement book, sharing it with the audience in a close-up: 11:30—manicure. 1:30—tea with Kate.

*Joan Crawford with Adrian on the set of* No More Ladies.

Top: *From left to right, Joan Crawford, Robert Montgomery, and Frances Drake in* Forsaking All Others. *By the mid-1930s, Adrian had begun using sequins and bugle beads as a visual key for a woman with unscrupulous motives.*

7:00—dinner with Sherry (Robert Montgomery). It seems Marcia has been stood up.

She has. First the engagement book goes flying. Then Crawford tears off the velvet collar and hurls it out of the movie frame, flings the belt to the floor with a resounding thud, and proceeds to grapple with the hooks and buttons on her dress like someone fighting a giant squid. And so to bed.

It is not only Crawford's apparent disregard for the sublime creation she is wearing that will impress itself on moviegoers; the underlying message is that clothing may not, after all, hold all the answers to life's difficulties. Crawford is dressed like that, and still she has been stood up.

If *No More Ladies* opens with a scene of furious undressing, *I Live My Life* closes out 1935 with a scene of furious destruction. Cornered by her obstinate bridegroom on the eve of their wedding, Crawford learns that Brian Aherne has

resigned his post as vice-president at Bentley and Gage, her father's company, and plans to return to archaeology. Any attempts to humor him ("If it's digging you want, we may be able to fix it so you can dig in Central Park") fall on deaf ears, and when Crawford refuses to give up the life to which she has become accustomed, her bridegroom walks out. She proceeds to vent her anger in typical spoiled movie heiress fashion, smashing lamps and ashtrays until she spots a better target,

*Gail Patrick vamps Arthur Treacher while Robert Montgomery, Edna May Oliver, and others look on in* No More Ladies.

Opposite: *Crawford in a stunning wool crepe suit and matching wide-brimmed hat from* No More Ladies. *The suit, with its side lapels and cinched waist, demonstrates a natural evolution from Adrian's Schiaparelli-inspired costumes for* Today We Live. *This photo adorned one of the windows in New York's Saks Fifth Avenue store to help publicize Giorgio Armani's fall collection in 1996.*

her wedding gown: "Well, look what we have here! Aren't you the beautiful thing! All full of sweetness and life, aren't you? Just a big, brave symbol. Two hearts that beat as one. Well, do you know what I think you are? I think you're just about twenty yards of satin, with a lot of lace and doohickeys spread all over you like the coating of a pill!" With this, Crawford stomps all over the dress, ruining it and her dreams. Not even a wedding dress has magic any more.

## The Bride Wore Red

Over the next several years Crawford would attempt to broaden both her range and appeal by appearing in a screwball comedy and a historical romance, genres she had never attempted before. The failure of these films to provide any real momentum to her career led her to begin taking risks that, just a few years before, she would have considered unnecessarily foolhardy.

In the opening months of 1937, Luise Rainer dropped out of MGM's planned film version of *The Girl from Trieste,* based on an unpublished play by Ferenc Molnar. Crawford snapped up the film, although it was much sterner stuff than she had played in the years following *Rain.* Molnar's story concerns a prostitute trying to go straight and then discovering that the high society she yearns to mix with is in reality more vicious and petty than her own class.

Unfortunately for Crawford, Irving Thalberg had died several months before the film went into production, and Louis B. Mayer's own preferences in story treatments—family sanctity, respect for one's parents, and a general wholesomeness—were beginning to exert a stranglehold on the MGM product. And so a hard-bitten tale about a reformed prostitute was rewritten as a Cinderella story for Crawford, and *The Girl from Trieste* became *The Bride Wore Red.*

In the opening scene, Count Armalia (George Zucco) and Rudi Pal (Robert Young) are whiling away an evening at the elegant Cosmos Club in Trieste on the evening of Rudi's departure for a holiday in the Swiss Alps. Armalia's plan is to prove to Pal once and for all that anyone who is appropriately attired can "pass" in high society, a popular Depression theme. Once Pal departs, it doesn't take long for the Count to pitch an offer to Crawford, who plays a cabaret entertainer named Anni Pavlovich: "How would you like a little holiday, Signorina Anni? Stop at a fine hotel, say, have servants wait on you.

Plenty of food, sunshine, beautiful clothes . . ."

She cuts him off: "I won't go unless I can have a red evening dress."

Rechristened Anni Vivaldi, she receives sufficient funds for a fantastic wardrobe and a two-week stay at a deluxe resort in the Swiss Alps. At the hotel in Terrano, Anni meets Rudi, just as Armalia intended. He is vacationing with his fiancée Maddelena (Lynne Carver) as well as two chaperones, the Contessa de Meina (Billie Burke) and Admiral Monti (Reginald Owen). By the end of her two-week stay, Anni must succeed in getting Rudi to break his engagement if she wants to keep living in society, but she is in a race against time; a telegram to the Contessa will arrive from Armalia at the conclusion of Anni's holiday, exposing her as a fake.

If it reads like an unremarkable Crawford programmer on paper, onscreen it speaks in forked sartorial tongues. When Anni arrives at the resort, she is delighted to discover an old friend, Maria, who is working at the hotel as a maid. She tells her excitedly about her red evening dress. Then, snatching the tissue paper from the top of the box, Anni waits for Maria's reaction. But Maria lifts the hanger and gives a disapproving look: "Not this red dress. Not here. You might as well wear a sign."

Suddenly Anni looks like a lost child. "Well, when will I wear it?"

"Perhaps two weeks from now."

And two weeks later she slips it on. Trying to talk herself into a happy marriage as she waits for evening, dinner, and her elopement with Rudi on her last day in Terrano, Anni suddenly begins singing. "Here comes the bride, all dressed in . . . red! The bride wore *red!*" She reaches for Adrian's bugle bead creation. "Oh, my wonderful red dress! You wouldn't let me wear it before, Maria. You were afraid and so was I. But now I'm not."

The waters part as Crawford sweeps down the stairs into the lobby, and people stop to stare. As Jane Gaines points out in her perceptive analysis of Arzner's work, "The dress becomes the character's means of revenge as she sits at the dinner table, glittering and seething, egging the admiral on to tell stories about how he remembers bouncing her on his knee as a child (but probably as a prostitute)." The dress also gives Anni away before the telegram arrives, but Crawford's fans probably weren't too surprised. They had already learned what is and is not acceptable in high society from watching *Chained, Forsaking All Others, No More Ladies,* and *I Live My Life.*

*Adrian's sensational red bugle-beaded evening gown, designed for* The Bride Wore Red *(1937). Crawford basks in the adoration of her co-stars, Robert Young (left) and Franchot Tone, completely contradicting the message in the film itself: that the dress is "too loud and too red and too cheap." Cut on the bias, the dress is form-fitting, with a cape that is attached to the shoulders with a jeweled clasp. The gown, which weighed 30 pounds, was made with more than two million beads. (Bugle beads are made from glass and weigh significantly more than sequins, which are gelatin-based.) Ten seamstresses worked for 2 weeks merely to bead the material, which was then hand-crocheted on crepe romaine. To conserve Crawford's strength while wearing the dress, director Dorothy Arzner rehearsed the sequence for a day in the muslin copy of the gown so that each scene could be done in one take.*

BELOW: *Crawford with Adrian's sketch for the infamous red bugle-beaded gown.*

And therein lies the problem. Earlier in the film, Count Armalia notices how Anni Pavlovich holds in her pinkie as she sips her tea, and can't help but comment, "Where did you learn such charming manners?" "I go to the movies," replies Anni. "I watch the ladies of your world." If Anni goes to the movies and picks up helpful hints on manners, why isn't she picking up the same hints for her wardrobe, as MGM expected millions of women to do when attending Crawford films?

It is the film's fatal flaw, although Anni does realize—albeit a bit too late—that the "harlot's dress" she is wearing condemns her. Adrian's red dress symbolizes the whore Anni would become if she married Rudi Pal, for she is interested in him only for his money. The publicity photos that decorated theaters nationwide, however, sent a different message to moviegoers. The photographs of Crawford all lit up in bugle beads and attended by her fawning male co-stars implied that the dress was a sartorial inspiration, just the ticket if you wanted men to fall at your feet.

The commercial failure of *The Bride Wore Red* had startling consequences for Crawford. Early in 1938 Harry Brandt, president of the Independent Theater Owners of America, placed a notorious advertisement in *Motion Picture Herald* and several other industry publications, labeling her "box-office poison." She was in select company: Greta Garbo, Fred Astaire,

Marlene Dietrich, and Katharine Hepburn also incurred Brandt's wrath. But a new contract in 1938 indicated that Mayer felt Crawford's reverses were only temporary. It ran for five years, offering her compensation at $330,000 per year, with a cap of three films per year. The agreement offered her less money than she had previously received, but this was more a reflection of a declining all-around box-office than Mayer's feeling that Crawford was washed up.

Her next film, however, revealed MGM's hesitancy to create a new image for her. *Mannequin*, released in January 1938, paired her with a new co-star, Spencer Tracy, yet the story seemed overly familiar: Jessie Cassidy (Crawford), a working girl who toils in a garment factory, marries Eddie Miller (Alan Curtis), a man of shady moral character, to get out of the tenement she shares with her parents. The newly married couple make the acquaintance of self-made millionaire John Hennessey (Tracy), whereupon her new bridegroom hatches a scheme: Jessie divorces him, pursues and marries Hennessey, and then walks away from the marriage, returning to Miller with a settlement. Disgusted, Jessie does leave Eddie, but not to chase after any millionaires. She gets a job as a mannequin in a department store and is courted by Hennessey, whom she eventually does marry, but for love, not money.

Despite the fact that the film showed Crawford as Cassidy wearing her one good dress (black with contrasting white collar) again and again to make the point of her poverty, much of the film seems to have been cobbled together in the editing room with clips from old Crawford successes. *Mannequin* seemed like a professional setback even before the first camera turned, and in Alexander Walker's words, induced in Crawford "a sense of recklessness in her search for a part, any part, that would get her career moving again and reassure her about the distance she had traveled from her origins."

## The Crawford Formula Turns Stale

By 1940 the problem facing Crawford and Adrian was twofold: Hedy Lamarr, Lana Turner, and Greer Garson, a Mayer import from England, were all challenging the positions of long-established MGM queens, and Crawford was heading into roles that ultimately strained the relationship between actress and designer. As she entered her late thirties, and romantic roles opposite Robert Taylor and Clark Gable began to go to the studio

*Crawford had a lot of uphill work to dispel the commonly held view that only finery was good enough for the actress in her films. Here's where Adrian's genius naturally shines, for not only does he make a point of showing how Crawford's character Jessie Cassidy in* Mannequin *must make do with wearing her one good dress again and again, but on a more subliminal level it proves to the public that Crawford is just as egalitarian.*

newcomers, Crawford began to actively seek an anti-star image for herself. In 1939 she begged producer Hunt Stromberg and Mayer to cast her as Crystal Allen, arch-bitch villainess in *The Women*. Mayer warned her it was a small role, but the studio was applying the "safety in numbers" principle that had shielded it from the Depression with *Grand Hotel* and *Dinner at Eight* by crowding the film with every top star it could muster.

Despite Mayer's reservations, Crawford knew that with a Broadway pedigree and an all-star cast *The Women* was hardly a risk; it was a guaranteed hit. "If I can't have a hit picture of my own," Crawford told the studio chief before production began, "at least let me sneak into someone else's." So she was able to broaden her range with an uncharacteristic (for the 1930s) hard-as-nails portrayal that did not rely on a fashion parade. The film marked a turning point both for herself and for Adrian. Emboldened, Crawford was ready for more risks.

Mayer had bought Rachel Crothers' hit play *Susan and God* for Norma Shearer, who turned the down part rather than play the mother of an adolescent. Crawford, increasingly anxious to keep a momentum going in her career, had no such qualms. She would dare comparison with Gertrude Lawrence, who had created the role on Broadway, and would again be put through her paces by George Cukor, Metro's most prestigious contract director. The nature of the part, however, did not demand a star turn. Susan Trexel is a silly New York socialite who catches a dose of moral rearmament on a trip to England. Returning stateside with a dowager guru, she proceeds to make a nuisance of herself by urging her family and friends to reform and repent. At the same time, however, she turns a blind eye to her own husband's alcohol problem and neglects the emotional needs of her daughter. Surprisingly confident at self-parody, Crawford created a bold, satiric character rather than trading on the image MGM had been meticulously burnishing throughout the 1930s. The advertising tag line for the film, though, indicated how successful Crawford's stab at devising a new image had been, and also served to vindicate Louis B. Mayer's worst fears: "Joan's a gorgeous meanie again!"

This was not the ideal image to sell fashion. The dark side that began to emerge in Crawford's characters after *The Women* necessarily affected any fashion influence they could have had. Audiences could be entertained by Joan Crawford as vain, silly Susan Trexel, but that didn't necessarily mean they wanted to *be* Susan. So why would they want to dress like her?

The situation implodes before the question can be fully answered. *A Woman's Face* follows *Susan and God* onto the nation's screens in less than a year. Based on a French play, *Il Etait Une Fois,* by Francis de Croisset, it had starred Ingrid Bergman in a Swedish film version in the late 1930s. When Crawford saw Bergman's portrayal of a woman whose horribly scarred face embitters her to a life of crime, she badgered Mayer to buy U.S. rights to the property. Mayer's reaction was emphatic: "Are you crazy? Do you want the public to see you looking ugly?" But Crawford persisted, and Mayer finally relented, but not without a word of warning: "If you want to destroy your career, go ahead!"

The role of Anna Holm hardly destroyed Crawford's career; to quote her biographer Bob Thomas, "Critics proclaimed that Joan Crawford had established herself as an actress." But the beginning of a new road was the end of

another, and Crawford in *A Woman's Face* takes few half measures in creating a new image. The studio would not release any publicity stills that featured their defaced star, but early in the picture, Crawford would defuse the power from her own temple. *A Woman's Face* would prove to be the antithesis of *Dancing Lady.* Here Crawford's character finally accepts that clothes no longer have any redemptive power. Even though she has purchased some new clothes, an unforeseen glance in the mirror provokes her rage. She smashes the mirror against the wall, opens a desk drawer, and reaches for a gun.

In one stroke, in a short sequence lasting only a few minutes, fashion, for Crawford, loses its fetishistic, magical powers once and for all. Its power has been neutered. Six months after the release of *A Woman's Face,* Adrian left MGM. And seen in retrospect, *A Woman's Face* seems like a warm-up for the *film noirs* Crawford would later make at Warner Brothers after she herself left MGM in 1943.

So after twelve years and thirty-one films, the partnership had played itself out, but it left a legacy that continues to this day. Contemporary critics might deride Crawford's 1930s clotheshorse vehicles, but the themes they serve up echo across the decades, for they are inherently American and, in essence, timeless. More than 50 years later, in 1988, Julia Roberts would go shopping with wealthy Richard Gere in *Pretty Woman* and emerge not as a prostitute but as Gere's companion for the opera, suitably gowned. The film grossed over $100 million and won an Oscar nomination for its female star. If it had been made in 1934 at MGM, one could well imagine Joan Crawford and Robert Montgomery in the leading roles.

After the release of *Mildred Pierce* in 1945, her first starring role after leaving MGM for Warner Brothers, Crawford expressed nothing but satisfaction with the role that would eventually lead to her own Oscar. "The role of Mildred was a delight to me," she told a magazine interviewer, "because it rescued me from what was known at MGM as the Joan Crawford formula. I had become so hidden in clothes and sets that nobody could tell whether I had talent or not." Thirty-odd years later, however, she had toned down her praise. Discussing *Mildred* Pierce with British journalist Roy Newquist, Crawford praised her director and costars but turned wistful as she summed it all up: "The only other thing I can say about the picture is the fact that it was not one of the dozens of films that made the critics rave about the way I dressed. No Adrian. I looked crummy through the whole thing."

*"The more that one tries to isolate the qualities that made Norma Shearer unique, the more one heads into an area of a kind of gracious dignity—a serene quality of bearing and attitude that eludes sensible definition. For certainly she played a good share of audacious, sometimes even wicked, and often déclassé women—but never without that special Shearer aura of special probity, along with most of the other positive attributes that have vanished wholly from a morally dismal world. The ghost flowers are gone; the bluebirds are rare; the likes of Norma Shearer are nowhere to be seen in contemporary film."*

—"Homage to Norma Shearer," from a program published in conjunction with a festival of her films at George Eastman House, Rochester NY, June 5–21, 1970

# Shearer Chic

"Clothes are a woman's first duty to herself," Norma Shearer told a reporter for the *London Daily Mail* in 1931, on a publicity trip to England. "It is when she is conscious of being well-dressed that she can do her best work and get that superiority complex that makes for success."

By 1931, after more than ten years as an actress in motion pictures, Norma Shearer was flush with success. A succession of roles that had begun with her Oscar-winning turn in *The Divorcee* the previous year, and which included *Let Us Be Gay* (1930), *Strangers May Kiss* (1931), *A Free Soul* (1931), and the film version of Noel Coward's *Private Lives,* had established her as one of the biggest stars in Hollywood: "Queen of the Lot" at Metro-Goldwyn-Mayer by virtue of her box-office clout and 1927 marriage to Irving Thalberg, the studio's production chief. More so than Greta Garbo or even Joan Crawford, however, Shearer's statement to the British press revealed how wedded she was to the Metro mystique, for no star under contract at MGM in the 1930s worked harder to achieve and sustain an image of enduring glamour.

Norma Shearer entered silent films as a bit player in 1920. After making low-budget programmers in and around New York for three years, she caught the eye of Louis B. Mayer as well as Irving Thalberg, Mayer's vice-president, who signed her to a short-term contract with the Mayer Company. She starred as a flapper in Mayer's

*For her role as the phony yet ultra-urbane, worldly-wise countess in* Idiot's Delight *(1939), Adrian adopted this off-the-shoulder style for Shearer, with a touch of Greek classicism in drape and trim to emphasize the effect.*

*Pleasure Mad* (1923) and was then loaned to a succession of studios, including Warner Bros., Fox, and First National. In the spring of 1924, when Mayer merged with the Metro and Gold-wyn Studios, Shearer suddenly found herself competing for roles at her home studio with an impressive new contract list of female stars, including Mae Murray, Aileen Pringle, Eleanor Boardman, and Nazimova.

But Thalberg had been watching Norma's progress in the nine films she had made while on loan to other studios, and he decided to reward her with the female lead in the new studio's first release, *He Who Gets Slapped* (1924). The assignment would prove to be a mixed blessing for Shearer. The story was adapted from a Russian play by Leonid Andreyev, and it told the story of a scientist, Paul Beaumont (Lon Chaney), who is humiliated when his work is usurped by his benefactor. Beaumont winds up as a notorious circus clown, and Shearer plays a bareback rider, Consuelo, who is also a member of the circus troupe. A succession of failed romances and misunder-standings ensues among the various characters, including Beaumont and Consuelo.

The wardrobe for the film was designed by Sophie Wachner, who had created costumes for Mae Murray and Aileen Pringle at Goldwyn. Shearer was not pleased with the fact that her circus costume revealed her somewhat heavy thighs, but her appeals to Wachner fell on deaf ears. The role of Consuelo was a supporting role almost any featured female player on the lot could have played, and Shearer did not have any input in the wardrobe she was to wear. And although *He Who Gets Slapped* was an enormous hit both critically and financially, Shearer personally benefited little from its success. After seeing the film—and keenly aware of the new competi-tion she would be facing at the new studio—she began work-ing out regularly with a fitness expert, a woman who called herself Madame Sylvia, in an attempt to improve her figure. She also consulted the film's cameraman, Milton Moore, for tips on how to look more glamorous onscreen. Experimenting with her makeup, Shearer began to use a bright green eye shadow, which she felt had a flattering effect on her eyes when she was photographed in close-up.

But while Garbo made an instantaneous impression on American audiences as a worldly vamp in her 1926 MGM debut, and Crawford was launched as the epitome of flaming youth in 1928, Shearer, throughout the decade, lacked an iden-tifying image that would in turn secure a fashion identity for her onscreen. Throughout the twenties her roles included an

ingenue aerialist in a circus (*The Devil's Circus*, 1926), chorus girl (*Pretty Ladies*, 1925), school teacher (*The Snob*, 1925), attorney (*The Waning Sex*, 1926), vaudeville performer (*Upstage*, 1927), and even a dual role, as debutante and gangster's moll (*Lady of the Night*, 1925). In a minor comedy called *His Secretary*, also released in 1925, Shearer was cast as Ruth Lawrence, a plain stenographer who turns the tables on her inattentive boss (Lew Cody) by transforming herself into a glamorous fashion plate. It would have been an unthinkable role for almost any of Shearer's rivals at MGM (although Aileen Pringle would play a similar role, also with Cody, in *A Single Man* three years later), yet the part seemed to cue one way the MGM publicity depart-ment could promote Shearer and the subject of fashion, always a major theme of exploitation for the studio: "Wise selection of clothes will deftly conceal any defect of the figure. Screen stars and players who make a scientific study of clothes and how to wear them know this only too well. 'The prevailing mode may always be adapted to one's own figure,' Miss Shearer says. 'The new draped skirts are suitable for both plump and slender—it all depends on how you drape the skirt.'"

Andre-Ani, who dressed Shearer frequently in the late 1920s, named Shearer a "perfectly gowned woman" in the publicity releases for *After Midnight* (1927), in which she played a party girl on the make. His most important stipulation for granting a woman that title: "She must have a good figure, or be wise enough to conceal her defects." But as Gavin Lambert has noted, in the wrong costume Shearer's figure looked awkward, and her movements ungraceful. She spent many an afternoon rehearsing in front of a mirror, but a camera was harder to fool than a looking glass.

And if Shearer was to serve as an exemplar for the woman who must make more with less, many of her roles in 1927 and 1928—a beer hall waitress in *The Student Prince* and a traveling saleslady in *The Latest from Paris* among them—did little to enhance this burgeoning image. The latter title merely confused the issue, with Shearer frequently dressed by Gilbert Clark in suits and vests tailored along masculine lines, and sporting stiff collars, starched shirtwaists, and heavy shoes. It completely abrogated the attendant publicity when the film opened: "It never pays for a woman to discard her femininity," as Shearer was quoted by MGM publicity prior to the movie's release. "The modern business woman is now distinctly femi-nine, except in such isolated instances where the same woman would adopt mannish attire even if she were not working in what was once supposed to be man's own particular sphere."

*Norma Shearer as a traveling saleslady with her wares in* The Latest from Paris *(1927). This photograph inadvertently symbolizes Shearer's own attempts to find an on-screen persona.*

Shearer's rescue came at the end of 1928, when Adrian was assigned to design the wardrobe for what would turn out to be her last silent film, *A Lady of Chance.* After playing a Victorian stage performer in *The Actress,* an adaptation of Pinero's *Trelawny of the Wells, A Lady of Chance* was a 180-degree turn in the opposite direction: Shearer played Angel Face, an expert in the badger game, who worked and traveled with a confidence man and his girlfriend. Despite the dull machinations of the plot, Shearer's MGM publicity as a fashion arbiter took a sudden turn under Adrian's guidance:

> The question that puzzles all feminine shoppers is whether to match the hat to the frock or the frock to the hat. This matching and blending of colors has been carefully followed by Norma Shearer in *A Lady of Chance.* In one sequence Miss Shearer appears in gray and green. The absinthe green frock matches the green suede purse and close-fitting hat, while the gray pumps, hose and gloves are of matching shade. A hammered silver hat pin is matched with the belt buckle, the trimming on the purse and the silver buckles on the pumps.

In February 1929, Adrian used his *Screenland* forum to introduce a new Shearer to audiences: "The Flapper is Passé," read the article's headline. "Norma Shearer is an Ideal Example of the Smart Young Woman who has Taken her Place: the Physically Fit and Mentally Alert Maid of the Moment!" Adrian's style credo for Shearer and the "Shearer type" lay in carving out a fashion domain for her that lay somewhere between the realms dominated by Crawford (Shearer types should "choose clothes that have grace rather than pep," he counseled) and Garbo ("charm rather than an exotic quality"). "She [Shearer] represents the American girl at her most charming best."

Adrian's prescience, it would turn out, was startling once again, for as the 1920s came to a close the characters Shearer began to play at MGM would become noted for their "direct frankness of manner." The wardrobe Adrian created for Shearer in these parts determined the boundaries of social conventions in the early 1930s, and they were at least partially responsible for making Shearer one of the top ten box-office stars among a "host of sisters" watching her in the audience.

## A New Look for Shearer

Jerry: *"You sound as if you were proposing to my grandmother. What am I going to be doing while you're saving the first million?"*
Ted: *"Waiting for me."*
Jerry: *"Waiting isn't my idea of the king of indoor sports. I have no intention of sitting around for three or four years, while you harvest an additional crop of wild oats. You're no St. Anthony. You're just human — so am I. That's why I don't want to wait."*

—Norma Shearer and Chester Morris in *The Divorcee*

Ursula Parrott's *Ex-Wife,* published in 1928, explored a topic that was becoming much discussed in the late 1920s: the fact that women were beginning to free themselves from social conventions that relied on the double standard. Jerry, the heroine of Parrott's novel, wants a perfect marriage, but she leaves her husband when she realizes he is unfaithful, and yet cannot accept the fact that she may have sowed a few wild oats of her own.

MGM purchased the rights to Parrott's best seller in 1929, retitling the property *The Divorcee,* and the story of how Shearer won the role of Jerry has passed into Hollywood legend. Thalberg did not think his wife was glamorous enough to play a wayward divorcee, so Shearer enlisted the help of photographer George Hurrell to convince him otherwise.

*Norma Shearer as Jerry in* The Divorcee *(1930) wearing Adrian's revealing cotton lounging pajamas.*

Hurrell's photographs revealed a newly sleek, seductive Norma: "a woman of the world, waiting for an invitation" in an assortment of Adrian-designed lamé negligees. Thalberg was astonished when he saw the photographs, and Shearer got the part of the "strong, almost ruthless" Jerry.

*The Divorcee* opens with a group of "smart young things" on holiday in the Adirondacks. The girls are all in smart summer dresses, but Jerry, fishing at a nearby creek with Ted, a journalist, wears a khaki blouse with matching skirt: the simplest of sports clothes to complement her fierce, masculine,

independent spirit. She doesn't want to wait for Ted to save enough money before they wed. He's no St. Anthony, she tells him, but then neither is she.

"Jerry, you certainly say it straight," says her intended. "And you know, you've got a man's point of view."

"That's why we're going to make a go of it," Jerry replies, "everything equal!"

Three years later, when Ted is about to leave on a business trip, Jerry discovers that her husband has been having an affair. When she confronts him with the evidence, Ted is hardly contrite: "Darling, you've got to get a broader look at things, that's all. Why, you're out in the world doing a man's work. Was that just a lot of talk about a man's point of view?"

And Jerry has been working, with a thriving career at a fashion house to supplement the family income; her husband is, by his own admission, "just a poor newspaperman." Toiling overtime at a desk in her apartment, Adrian dresses Shearer in a smart one-piece pajama suit of bright red cotton with patterns of white forming a yoke and blouse trimming. A tie sash outlines the waist of the widely flared trousers. Not overtly stylish, but a wearable costume fashioned along lines that allow for freedom of movement.

The costume gives Jerry just enough freedom, it will turn out, to allow her the opportunity of seeing the world from "a man's point of view." She spends the night with Ted's friend Don (Robert Montgomery), and when her husband returns from his trip, she tells him, without drama or a hint of rancor, that "I've balanced our accounts."

Ted is disbelieving: "I always thought you were the most decent thing in the world. It can't be true!" But Jerry's simple reply reverses the tables on the traditional roles of husband and wife. "Well, it is," she tells him quietly. "I'm going to work, Ted. I'm late. See you tonight."

When Jerry returns to find Ted packing a suitcase, she reverts to the traditional role of suffering wife. Dressed in a virginal white gown, she pleads, "I'll forgive you anything, dear. Can't you please forgive me?" But Ted's pride won't let him. He tells Jerry that he'll always be wondering which of his friends is laughing at him. This triggers an outburst from Jerry that becomes the film's manifesto: "I thought your heart was breaking like mine. But instead you tell me your man's pride can't stand the game. . . . So look for me in the future where the primroses grow. And pack your man's pride with the rest! From now on, you're the only man in the world my door is closed to!"

Ted and Jerry eventually reconcile at the end of the film for another go at married life, but only after a series of affairs that established Shearer as a star "on the crest of a new and powerful sexual wave." For her performance in *The Divorcee* Shearer received an Oscar for Best Actress in 1930. And in order to establish a beachhead, Shearer needed a follow-up film as soon as possible.

*Let Us Be Gay,* by Rachel Crothers, filled the bill. A popular success on Broadway, the play made romantic comedy out of the same dramatic material in *The Divorcee,* suggesting that women, like men, can also play the field in order to allure the opposite sex and find fulfillment. In the opening scenes, Shearer eschews makeup as bedraggled, put-upon housewife Kitty Brown, appearing in hair curlers and a pince-nez. When she discovers her husband, Bob (Rod LaRocque), is having an affair she tells him to leave, even though he begs her forgiveness. Three years later, having been completely made over in Paris, Kitty comes between her husband and a second marriage when both find themselves weekend guests at the Long Island estate of a mutual acquaintance, Mrs. Bouccicault (Marie Dressler).

In *Let Us Be Gay,* Adrian begins to toy with Shearer's new image, creating a frisson of sexual tension between the image her clothes project, and what the audience suspects is really going on in her character's mind. Making an entrance at Mrs. Bouccicault's after her Paris transformation, Shearer appears in a yellow flannel double-breasted suit exemplifying, in Adrian's words, "the typical conservative young woman. Shearer looks her truest self in simple, tailored things, but she is able to wear the sensationally daring dresses of *The Divorcee* and similar films because, in her heart, like so many conservative women, she longs for a freedom that she would never really enjoy."

But Shearer's disciples, in theater auditoriums across the country, were able to live out their fantasies vicariously watching her onscreen. And the power of Adrian's designs for this film span the decades; at a showing of *Let Us Be Gay* at the Museum of Modern Art in New York in 1997, the audience burst into applause when Shearer made her entrance in this suit.

The very titles of Shearer's next three films—*Strangers May Kiss, A Free Soul,* and *Private Lives*—continued to flaunt the production code. *Strangers May Kiss* was based on yet another Ursula Parrott novel, about a woman who foregoes marriage, falls in love with a traveling journalist, and then becomes promiscuous when he leaves her. Shearer would turn the pajamas she wore in *The Divorcee*—a big fashion craze in the early 1930s for at-home entertaining—into a seductive tool in this film, suggesting indolent lounging and the boudoir all at once.

*A Free Soul* was based on an autobiographical novel by Adela Rogers St. John that dealt with episodes in the life of her famous lawyer father, Earl Rogers. Adapted for the screen by Becky Gardiner and John Meehan, the film tells the story of an

*Above: She may be wearing a blazer like any nice, educated young woman of her day in* Let Us Be Gay *(1930), but Shearer, with Adrian's help, was beginning to suggest a more sensual image on-screen.*

*Right: Also from* Let Us Be Gay, *a more womanly, sensual Shearer in a black crepe gown accented with silver disks.*

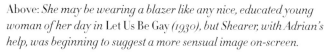

alcoholic lawyer, Stephen Ashe, and his relationship with his free-spirited daughter, Jan.

The film opens with an Adrian tease: The credits appear over the skyline of San Francisco, and the camera pulls back through an apartment window to reveal Ashe (Lionel Barrymore) reading the newspaper in his bathrobe over breakfast. The bathroom door then swings open to reveal the silhouette of a young woman, drying herself with a towel. "Come on," comes an insistent, girlish voice from the bath, "give me some-

thing to put on!"

Ashe looks perplexed. "For instance?" he asks.

"Undies!" comes the impatient voice from the bathroom. "In the bag! A complete outfit."

"A complete outfit? Stockings?" Ashe asks.

"Yes, my love, and other confections."

Ashe walks to the bathroom and hands the girl a pile of filmy lingerie. "See what you can make out of this," he says, but he hesitates by the doorway, as if trying to steal a glimpse of the girl within.

"Why, that's three complete outfits, you goose!" the girl giggles.

"For what?" he replies. "A sparrow?"

"Poor busy man, doesn't know what the modern girl should wear! Be with you in a minute, darling."

"I can hardly wait, my angel. Now, don't interrupt me again."

"Why not? Tired of me after one night?"

And then Shearer makes her entrance as Jan Ashe, returning home after an extended stay with her grandmother, dressed in a medium-length black skirt, a white short-sleeved sweater, and a contrasting scarf. "Morning, dad," she says brightly, as the two settle down to breakfast. This opening vignette plays on pre-code expectations—middle-aged roué entertaining a tootsie—but Adrian dresses Shearer in the height of respectability, a distinct and sophisticated simplicity at odds with the spicy dialogue the audience has just heard. As she prepares to leave the apartment, she dons white gloves and a white suit jacket with lapels that match the scarf. Once again, Adrian creates an underlying current of tension between what is heard and what is seen.

We soon meet gangster Ace Wilfong (Clark Gable), who has just gotten off a murder charge thanks to Ashe. Not surprisingly, Ace and Jan begin an affair that not only upsets her engagement with fiancé Dwight Winthrop (Leslie Howard), but which eventually leads to a dramatic confrontation.

Retiring upstairs to his living quarters, Ace finds Jan waiting for him. "Say, it's great to come up and find you here like this," he says surprised, but with a cursory yet knowing glance downstairs. Entrapment is on his mind as director Clarence Brown's camera pans across the room and settles on Shearer, standing in the doorway of the bedroom with her hands on her hips, in a tangerine velvet negligee showing sleeves and bodice in one. It is cut to fit tightly over the hips with a train-like finish. A gold cord holds the waistline in snug closeness. It looks as if one pull on the cord would send the costume tumbling to the floor, which prompted a critic from *Photoplay* to comment, "Shearer's clothes are breathtaking in their daring, but you couldn't get away with them in your drawing room!" Melodrama aside, Adrian manages to capture Jan's moods and changes of temperament (dutiful daughter, cunning mistress) in a series of wardrobe changes.

*Private Lives* (1931) plays on the same tricky heights, this time with sophisticated comedy substituting for ripe melodrama. The film's opening shot focuses on a set of stained glass windows in a church where Elyot Chase (Robert Montgomery) and Sybil (Una Merkel) are about to be married. As the two exchange vows, the scene abruptly shifts to a close up of Amanda Prynne (Norma Shearer), Elyot's ex-wife, in a white cloche hat, replete with a feather, and a crisply tailored

*Shearer as Jan Ashe certainly was a free soul. She may have been her daddy's baby, but she sure knew how to turn on the charm for Ace Wilfong (Clark Gable) in this slinky negligee.*

white suit worn with a ruffled, checked blouse. She is about to be married to Victor (Reginald Denny), but the setting here is as non-traditional as Amanda's wedding apparel—the office of a French justice of the peace.

Both couples honeymoon at a hotel in the south of France, where they receive adjoining rooms. Elyot and Amanda bump into one another and set about rekindling their romance. But love turns feisty, and soon enough Amanda and Elyot engage in another petty quarrel. The two end up slapping each other and destroying their hotel room just as Sybil and Victor arrive, looking for their respective spouses. Director Sydney Franklin films the sequence in a series of long, sustained takes, allowing Shearer to give the scene its combustible edge. She is aided by Adrian, who dresses her in a sleek lounging ensemble. The wide, flared pants allow for a wide variety of well-aimed kicks to Montgomery's posterior.

ABOVE: *A white wool blazer and plaid blouse from* Private Lives *(1931).*

LEFT: *Una Merkel as Sybil Chase in* Private Lives, *wearing an exquisite black silk gown.*

# The Riptide Effect

*There is no other personality on the screen today quite like Norma Shearer. When you check the stars and the leading women of all studios — this fact becomes all the more apparent. Norma Shearer gave to the screen a distinct type of entertainment . . . sparkling, gay (never use the words "sophisticated" or "smart" because they are not understood by the mob) . . . always clever, always a trifle naughty . . . stopping just at the right second . . . advocating the "right thing to do" for every woman . . . to live and laugh and love — as her heart dictates . . . the sort of woman who makes her own conventions . . . the type of woman who can do the very thing that, in other women would be cheap and common — that is the Norma Shearer screen character.*

—Suggested MGM advertising copy to promote *Riptide*, 1934

Lord Rexford: *"In New York, you were the kind of girl who didn't stop at a kiss."*
Mary: *"I always knew that one day you'd say that!"*

—Norma Shearer and Herbert Marshall in *Riptide*

*Private Lives,* in 1931, capped the definitive Shearer screen persona in the early 1930s: the rich, spoiled, independent woman who parties it up, fools around, and repents—in chic style—before the closing credits. She followed it, against her own instincts, with *Smilin' Through,* based on Jane Cowl's sentimental 1920 play. Discarding sophistication for old-fashioned innocent romance, she bowed to Thalberg's wishes, and scored an enormous hit in a lush, escapist film that appealed to audiences at the height of the Depression.

There followed an eighteen-month absence from the screen when Thalberg suffered a heart attack in December 1932 and Shearer traveled with him to Europe where he recovered at a spa in Bad Nauheim, Germany. While he was away, Thalberg was relieved from his post as head of production for all of MGM and given his own production unit. Upon his return to the studio in the summer of 1933, he began to plan a big comeback for his wife. He talked to Charles MacArthur about a remake of *The Green Hat,* which Garbo had made as a silent film, *A Woman of Affairs,* in 1928. But MacArthur's reaction to this idea was negative: *The Green Hat,* he felt, was old hat, and "nobody cared any more about a beautiful misunderstood woman whose search for true love ended when her Hispano-Suiza crashed into a tree." Thalberg then approached

director Edmund Goulding, who outlined an idea for a variation on the story. Thalberg liked it and assigned Goulding to write and direct the movie, which was tentatively titled *Riptide.* It was scheduled to start shooting at the end of October 1933.

Upon its release in the spring of 1934, MGM planned a publicity build-up for *Riptide* at least as noteworthy as the one that had heralded Garbo's return six months previously in *Queen Christina.* The campaign centered around Adrian, and the timing was ideal. Early in 1933 a number of Seventh Avenue manufacturers had tried, unsuccessfully, to market wholesale suits and dresses with the impression that they had been designed by Adrian. The threat of lawsuits on his behalf by MGM's legal department put a halt to these manufacturing schemes, but by the end of the year, Adrian was learning how to disarm his "competition."

"Style design is such a fragile thing," Adrian told the *Los Angeles Times* in December 1933. "If there were a copyright law, someone could hop in and copyright every conceivable style of sleeve, for instance. Yet fashions are actually a bigger industry than the film industry itself . . . we are the unpaid designers for the wholesale houses of the country—since their scouts manage to pirate our styles before the picture in which they will appear starts shooting."

The many monthly magazines that reported on the film industry, among them *Photoplay, Modern Screen,* and *Screenland,* were indirectly responsible for this situation, as they needed material far ahead of the actual publication date. Once the photographs and costume sketches had left the MGM publicity department, they were an easy target for style pirates. With *Riptide,* however, MGM planned to change all this, and reap some good publicity in the bargain. "Adrian's designs for Norma Shearer in *Riptide,*" said Howard Strickling, head of the MGM publicity department, "are so original and provocative that we have decided not to send out a single still, and Adrian's own drawings will only be seen by those immediately interested in connection with the picture. Every one of this group is being sworn to secrecy."

Other studios such as Paramount and Warner Bros., with high-profile designers, were talking about following MGM's lead, to the point where the major studios even discussed forming a guild with codes. There was also talk about drawing up an agreement with some of the smarter shops throughout the country to boycott all copyists. "If we can get retailers to back us on this," Strickling maintained, "and then advertise our styles as coming out of the USA instead of Paris, we

*A velvet and silver lamé evening gown from* Riptide *(1934). Adrian called this costume "Retake," as Norma Shearer made several changes to the final design. The costume is designed with tails like those in a man's full dress suit.*

eccentric—which is also why directors sometimes find them too startling and tone us down."

In its April 1934 issue, *Movie Mirror* scooped the other fan magazines with its article on *Riptide*:

Adrian of Metro is more mysterious than the Parisian salons about his interpretations of the new silhouette. Over there in Europe they require a special stamp on your passport before admitting you to the showrooms where their fashions are displayed. In Hollywood, where Adrian reigns supreme, not even that would get you a glimpse of the costumes Norma Shearer is wearing in *Riptide*. She says, "Adrian has outdone himself!" Hollywood, says, "How much longer must we stand this suspense?" Adrian himself says, "I believe in this pre-war revival and as soon as *Riptide* is ready for release you'll see what I mean."

But in spite of all this secrecy and suspense, *Movie Mirror* has a little bit of advance, exclusive information about one of Norma's most important gowns in the picture. . . . She wears a cocktail dress which is a significant phase of repeal's influence on style. It is a shirtwaist and skirt arrangement with a black skirt of ankle length, quite tight and split so nearly to the knee that every time she steps that knee is visible. The skirt is not draped but follows the directoire line.

"Repeal's influence on style" and "prewar revival" were clues to the designs Adrian had created for Shearer in *Riptide*. Shearer's role as Lady Mary Rexford in Goulding's original screenplay gave her ample opportunity to appear in more graceful clothes. She played an American woman who marries British Lord Philip Rexford (Herbert Marshall), and then has a fling with an old flame from New York, Tommie Trent (Robert Montgomery). Tommie has an accident in his physical pursuit of Mary, and when she visits him in the hospital, a photo of them kissing, subsequently published, causes a scandal. Mary tries to explain the situation to her husband, but he denies he is upset, forgiving but not believing her. "In New York," he tells her, "you were the kind of girl who didn't stop at a kiss!"

should soon become the style center of the world."

"In Paris," Adrian said, "they start styles by having fifty or sixty very prominent women wear the gowns, hats, etc. Some 'take' and some don't. Patou's effort to lower the waist line two seasons ago was a flop, for instance. The time was not ripe. There is a curious psychology about styles. We are handicapped because ours must necessarily be 'premature' to some extent, and they must photograph well—in grays, blacks and whites. For this reason, our styles must seem a little

BELOW: *A white crepe gown from* Riptide, *topped by a chartreuse and black-striped scarf bodice, held high about the throat on a shirred halter neckline falling in soft draped folds under the arm. Adrian called this costume "Close-Up," because of the busy detail around the neck.*

*Norma Shearer in* Riptide. *Classic simplicity is seen in this negligee of white velvet with huge draped sleeves of crimson velvet. The braided cotton cord accent at the neck is repeated in the Grecian girdle that falls to the hemline.*

*Riptide* aroused morality concerns about pre-marital sex and adultery among the nation's moral guardians. The production code that had been initiated in 1934 made the moral speculations of Ursula Parrott unfit for screen material, and *Riptide,* for all its lords, ladies, and English country-house settings, was essentially a Parrott morality tale. In the end, Lady Mary learns that for intimacy to develop the truth must be uncovered. And Lord Philip's inability to recognize and express his real feelings almost cost him his wife. A life of risk is followed by a return to safety.

For Shearer and Adrian, *Riptide* represented the last word in Parrott-like permissiveness, its peccadillos cushioned with osprey feathers, black velvet, and silver lamé. The film would also turn out to be Shearer's last film in modern dress for a period of five years.

# A Return to Romance and History

Romeo: *"Oh, she doth teach the torches to burn bright! It seems she hangs upon the cheek of night like a rich jewel in an Ethiop's ear."*

—Leslie Howard in *Romeo and Juliet*

While en route to Europe early in 1933, Irving Thalberg had discovered Stefan Zweig's newly-published biography of Marie Antoinette in the ship's library. When he asked his wife to read it, she pronounced it "the part of a lifetime," and Thalberg immediately began to talk of buying the rights to the property when he returned to MGM. A suitable screenplay eluded Thalberg for years, however, and at the end of 1934, when Shearer became pregnant with her second child, he decided to postpone the project. Then, as an act of happenstance, Katharine Cornell revived *Romeo and Juliet* on Broadway. Thalberg, who had thought before about filming Shakespeare's tragic romance, was convinced by the success of Cornell's revival that its time had come. In Juliet, too, he felt he had found a perfect role for his wife, despite the fact that Shearer would turn thirty-three in 1935, and Juliet, as described by Shakespeare, was a girl of fourteen.

George Cukor, whom Thalberg chose to direct the film, wanted to bring a young designer from England to MGM to supervise the creation of the sets and costumes. Oliver Messel had designed two films in England, *The Private Life of Don Juan*

(1934) and *The Scarlet Pimpernel* (1935), each produced by Alexander Korda. Thalberg had admired Messel's stage sets for Max Reinhardt's production of *The Miracle* in New York, and he instructed Cukor to contact the designer on a trip he made to Europe in 1935.

"Cukor wanted a fresh outlook on Hollywood," Messel told the London papers. "That was why I was invited. Another reason was, perhaps, the fact that I had been brought up on Italian art, and traveled to Italy over several years."

Messel's reputation impressed neither Adrian nor Cedric Gibbons, nor did this decision sit well with either of them. According to Robert Riley, Adrian marched into Louis B. Mayer's office and announced, "Don't think that I'm just the MGM workhorse, because I'm not. I'm the MGM designer, and since *Romeo and Juliet* will be an MGM picture, I'll design it." For Shearer, however, there was no decision to be made. Intensely loyal to the practitioners of illusion that helped her to sustain an image of glamour at MGM, she insisted that Adrian design her costumes. Thalberg bowed to her wishes, assigning Adrian to the film at the same time Cukor was making an offer to Oliver Messel in London. In the end, Gibbons and Adrian shared the task of designing *Romeo and Juliet* with Messel. "We all worked in peace and harmony," Messel said when filming had concluded. "I saw no signs of jealousy and no temperament." The press, however, reported that while there were no hard feelings between Adrian and Messel, "they were both slightly embarrassed for the other."

On July 29, 1935, the day of Messel's departure for California, the *London Daily Express* reported that MGM was paying him £250 a week (approximately $600) for at least five weeks of work. After meeting with Cukor and Thalberg upon his arrival, Messel was dispatched to Verona with two cameramen to take pictures that would form the basis of the research for the costumes and settings. Messel and his men spent four months scouring Italy, taking more that 2,769 photographs of buildings, balconies, old paintings, frescoes, drawings, and engravings.

When Messel returned to Hollywood early in 1936, he and Adrian began the task of studying the paintings of Bellini, Carpaccio, Botticelli, Ghirlandaio, and Pietro Della Francesca. They chose one celebrated painting, Gozzoli's *Procession of the Magi,* and used it as inspiration to fashion all of the costumes for the entrance of the Prince of Verona and his followers at the beginning of the film. Adrian's headdress for Shearer in the balcony scene was inspired by Fra Angelico's painting *The*

*Norma Shearer as Juliet. Her costume was*
*inspired by a gown in a portrait by Botticelli.*

*Annunciation,* and her ball gown was adapted
from Michel de Verona's *The Betrothal.*

"Even the smallest, most insignificant
item had to be absolutely correct," Adrian
declared when he finished work on the film.
"Such minor details as slippers, the hang of a
sleeve, the drape of a veil, had to be exactly as
it was during the Italian Renaissance."
Messel discovered Dozian's, a shop in Los
Angeles that sold, in his words, "every kind
of material ever made." He bought yards of
unpatterned fabric, which was then painted
and stitched by hand in the MGM
workrooms.

*Romeo and Juliet* was one of the most
intricate costuming operations in MGM's
history. More than 1,200 costumes were
created, and 500 people worked on the production for two months. Several looms were
set up in Los Angeles, and two mills were
engaged in New York to weave tights, all in
one piece. A total of 18,000 yards of cotton,
silk, satin, velvet, and wool went into the
glamorous gowns of the court ladies of
Verona and the crowds of townspeople,
soldiers, and nobles in the film. The
costumes for the actors, which were executed
by Messel, were almost as elaborate as those
designed for the actresses. Leslie Howard wore one cloak that
required nine yards of Fortuny cloth imported from Italy.
Shearer's costumes required 100 yards of assorted silks, satins,
and other materials, all specially hand-embroidered or beaded
to reproduce, as much as was possible, the embroidering of
the time.

"The period is most interesting from a costume standpoint," Adrian explained. "It was during the early portion of
this period that women as well as men began to become interested in personal adornments. With this new found freedom
in dress, however, came the tendency to overdress. As time
passed, plain surfaced fabrics, regardless of how lovely, began
to pall in their plainness. Then began the elaborate jewel
embroideries, the slit sleeves through which it was possible to

pull even more costly fabrics. Men as well as women indulged
in these fancies."

Thalberg's determination to produce a "classic of a classic," however—from the Folger Library imprint that appears at
the bottom of the screen during the credits, to the sepia tone
images of Verona that open and close the film—frustrated any
real inventiveness in costume creation. Paintings were duti-
fully reproduced, and Adrian's and Messel's insistence on
the finest tailoring and the best fabrics gave the film a sheen
of authenticity that could not be found in the sets, which
vacillated between Gibbons's penchant for geometrics, and
Messel's dark, dreamlike interiors.

Despite some preliminary tensions, however, Adrian's
designs played off Messel's creations to great effect. Messel

studded his costumes for Lady Montague (Virginia Hammond) and Lady Capulet (Violet Kemble Cooper) with jewels and other fussy, elaborate embroidery. Most of Adrian's designs for Juliet, by contrast, were simplicity itself, and through the use of costume Adrian was able to widen the gulf that separated the young lovers from the authority figures that sought to control their lives. For the balcony scene, the softest blue chiffon peeks out from a pale pink cape lightly embossed with the most delicate of spiral designs. And when Shearer enters the ball at the beginning of the film, lifting high Adrian's dress of pure silver satin, the material seizes all the light in the room, highlighting her face and at once outlining and distinguishing Juliet from the dancing graces that surround her. As an infatuated Romeo proclaims, she truly does teach the torches to burn bright.

In the first week of its New York run, attendance figures for *Romeo and Juliet* were somewhat short of record-breaking. Ticket sales picked up, however, when a number of fashion columnists drew attention to Norma Shearer's "Juliet cap" in the balcony scene. Soon thereafter copies began to appear in department stores.

# Marie Antoinette: Nearly Pure Confection

*"What could be more perfect than the costumes Adrian designed for* Marie Antoinette *starring Norma Shearer? They have the most beautiful lamé and lace and tulle, with scrolls and festoons, designed of total wonderment."*

—Diana Vreeland in *Hollywood Costume: Glamour! Glitter! Romance!*

While researching the costumes for *Marie Antoinette* in the Royal Archives in Vienna during the summer of 1937, Adrian came across a letter the Empress Maria Theresa had written to her daughter in 1775, when she was still Dauphine of France. The Empress had become greatly disturbed when Count Mercy, the Austrian ambassador to Versailles, had sent her a picture of her daughter wearing the latest fashions of the

French court. Marie's head could hardly be turned either to the right or the left, so elaborate was the headdress that towered above her masses of waved hair. And her gown was exceptionally wide, flaunting yards and yards of embroidery, ruffles, and lace. "Dear Toinette," the Empress wrote in response to the portrait, "you know that I have always held that it is well to be in the fashion to a reasonable extent, but that one should never be *outré* in one's dress. A good-looking queen, endowed with charm, has no need of such follies. On the contrary, simplicity of attire enhances these advantages."

"Maria Theresa," Adrian commented after he returned to MGM, "preached the same theory then that Hollywood designers do today!" Yet it was in this letter that Adrian would find the inspiration for many of his *Marie Antoinette* designs: "At no time in history," he said as he began work on the film, "has woman's dress been as elaborate as during Marie Antoinette's time."

And never before, and most likely never again, would such an enormous effort in costuming be undertaken by a major Hollywood studio. During his 1937 trip to Austria and France, Adrian had purchased bushels of silks, embroidered velvets, and gold and silver lace for the film. And to supervise the manufacture of the hats and headdresses, he engaged a milliner formerly employed by the Russian Imperial Opera. The clothes that came out of the MGM wardrobe department for *Marie Antoinette* were the most lavish and sumptuous of Adrian's career, extravagant with intricate embroideries, ruffles, precious gems, and arabesques of the most exquisite precision.

The opulence and scope that Adrian was able to give his *Antoinette* designs were due to forces that went beyond his control, yet ironically worked in his favor. Irving Thalberg had begun planning the film as early as 1933. His untimely death in 1936 nearly derailed the project, as Shearer put pressure on the studio for a new contract, and threatened to retire from the screen. By March of 1937, MGM had spent nearly $400,000 in preproduction costs, a hefty amount for the 1930s. When Shearer signed a new six-picture contract with the studio on July 14, the wardrobe department had been working on *Marie*

*Some of Adrian's hand-colored sketches from* Marie Antoinette.

OPPOSITE: *A ball gown with magnificent fur trim.*

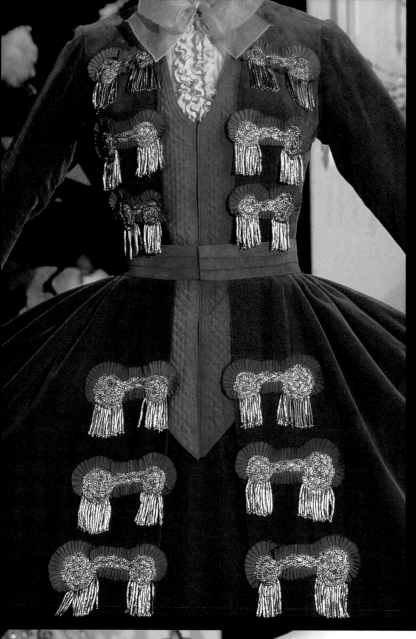

*Details of gowns from* Marie Antoinette.

*Antoinette,* off and on, for a little over three years.

Beginning on February 14, 1934, and continuing through the summer of 1937, Metro-Goldwyn-Mayer's research department logged 59,277 specific reports on historical personages, settings, costumes, language, and furnishings that detailed the last years of the Bourbon monarchy in France. In the course of research, 1,538 books, 10,615 photographs, paintings, and sketches, and 5,000 pages of unbound manuscripts were perused.

As with *Romeo and Juliet,* Adrian carefully scrutinized paintings from the period, in particular the eight surviving portraits of Marie Antoinette by her favorite court painter, Madame Vigée-Lebrun. Many of his costumes for the Queen were based on these paintings. "We have followed the gowns in Mme. Lebrun's paintings to the letter," he explained. "Microscopes were placed over indications of embroidery that the work on Miss Shearer's gowns might be identical. Fabric patterns to match those in the paintings were especially woven in many cases."

Factories in France were engaged to weave specially needed fabrics, and Adrian once again hired scores of beaders —many of them the same people who had worked on *The Great Ziegfeld* the year before—to trace his intricate designs with delicate needles threaded with strands of metal. Some of the embroidery was too fine for the naked eye and was done under a magnifying glass.

Throughout the entire procedure, M. E. Greenwood, the gaunt studio manager at MGM, kept an eye on Adrian's expenses. Greenwood, who was once a faro dealer in Arizona, had been with MGM almost from its inception. He was chiefly responsible for informing MGM's New York office how much the company had spent every week, and how much to place on deposit for the studio's account at the Culver City branch of the Bank of America.

Greenwood's memos to Adrian, raging at the money that was being spent on both costume materials and labor for *Marie Antoinette,* began to arrive in the wardrobe department as early as September 1937. For the most part, Adrian ignored them, although he must have been aware of the political situation that motivated Greenwood. Thalberg was dead, and Louis B. Mayer was revenging himself on his widow, who claimed that Thalberg's share of the studio profits should now be paid to her, in a number of small and petty ways. At the last minute, he switched directors on the film, replacing Shearer favorite Sidney Franklin with W. S. Van Dyke, known for his

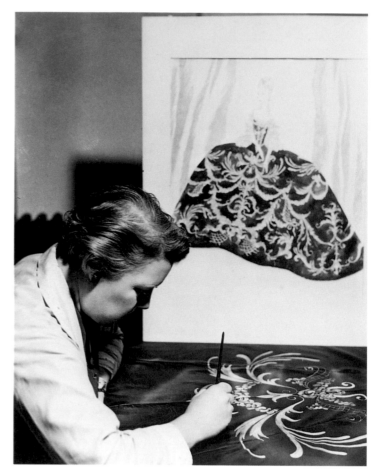

*A woman in the wardrobe department painstakingly re-creates Adrian's design for* Marie Antoinette *(1938).*

speedy reputation in completing films. Actually, he had given Franklin a choice: guarantee he could finish the film in sixty days or resign.

Adrian did not receive any such direct ultimatums from Mayer himself during production on *Marie Antoinette,* and it may have been the lack of any official authority behind Greenwood's memos, as well as the fact that Adrian was somewhat bitter about not getting a raise in salary when his contract option was picked up in July, that contributed to his defiance. In the end, as far as the costumes were concerned, it was a move that paid off handsomely.

Norma Shearer, who stood 5'3", wore 34 costumes in the film, with an aggregate weight of 1,768 pounds, approximately seventeen times her own weight of 110. The heaviest of these, Marie Antoinette's wedding gown, which weighed 108 pounds, included more than 500 yards of sheer white satin, every inch covered with hand-embroidered, silver fleur de lis edged in minute seed pearls. Steel-wired frameworks for this and the other billowing gowns of the period were not available in commercial quantities, so a factory was commissioned to fill

*Norma Shearer in the title role of* Marie Antoinette. *The exquisite embroidery on this costume prompted Diana Vreeland to comment, "Hollywood had the most expensive couture in the world. The details, the workmanship, are second to none."*

the specifications: more than 90 feet of shaped wire for each of 1,000 separate costumes. Each dress was draped over a steel hoop which in turn was fastened to a foundation that was adjusted so the weight of the costume hung from the shoulders. The hoop had a petticoat under it, a second frilled petticoat fastened to it, and a third frilled petticoat over it. It took a lady of the French court several hours to climb into this formal apparel. Thanks to talon fasteners and zippers, it took the actors at MGM about 12 minutes.

For Shearer's costumes, the prop department created 34 of the largest hangers ever manufactured. The hoops of steel holding each skirt in position proved too heavy for ordinary hangers, in some instances even breaking holders placed in the plaster walls of the wardrobe department. A handyman at the studio created hangers eight feet across, and equipped with clips of wire to keep the drapes of elaborate skirts, with their various festoons, from trailing on the floor.

Adrian's costumes are at the center of *Marie Antoinette*, even more so than Cedric Gibbons's extravagant sets, and his designs in the first part of the film visualize the spectacle of hundreds of people living purely for pleasure. His costumes for Shearer support a long dramatic curve, cueing the audience's responses to both the young princess and her denizens at court. For Marie's arrival at Versailles: a silk gown handpainted with spring blooms and garnished with ribbons; white ruffled sleeves and a large straw hat embellished with an enormous white ostrich plume evoke the innocence and freshness of a young milkmaid. For the young Dauphine's entrance into Parisian society, and the sequences that detail Marie's rise to become "the brightest, highest figure in this court": dresses that become ever more elaborate, adorned with sequins, pearls, and gar-

lands of silk flowers, and headdresses composed of feathers and plumes from every variety of bird. One headdress flaunted a mechanical canary in a gilded cage. Adrian deployed the most outrageous motifs to visualize what Maria Theresa referred to in her letter as the *outré* in fashionable dress, culminating in a headdress of symbolic, sparkling stars as the Dauphine reaches her ascendancy. For Marie's confrontation with her rival at court, Madame du Barry (Gladys George): excessive extravagance transmuted into a white ball gown adorned with ostrich feathers—purity of spirit in contrast with

*Adrian called this costume the "Rocket Gown." The star burst effect on the sheer chiffon was inspired by the French love of fireworks.*

OPPOSITE: *Ruth Hussey as Madame de Polignac in* Marie Antoinette.

*A wardrobe mistress makes a last-minute repair to a costume on the set of* Marie Antoinette.

Left: *Gladys George as the scheming Madame du Barry.*

Opposite: *Anita Louise as the Princesse de Lamballe in* Marie Antoinette.

du Barry's heavily embroidered black gown, decorated with garish gold thread that glitters like a pinwheel. After Marie's dismissal by Louis XV (John Barrymore), and her second meeting with Count Axel von Fersen (Tyrone Power), with whom she would fall in love: a voluminous satin cloak, the burden of royalty lying heavily on the Queen's shoulders in a hood heavily bedecked with fur. On her way to the guillotine: a rough, wool dress topped by a small white cap, made with absolute historical accuracy.

According to her biographer Stefan Zweig, Marie Antoinette was neither "the great saint of royalism nor yet the great whore of the Revolution." She was, rather, a simple woman "jolted out of her untroubled play-world" and forced into a heroic role. It may be more than fortuitous, then, that before she stepped before the cameras as the Queen of France, Norma Shearer told Louis B. Mayer that she wanted to follow *Marie Antoinette* with the role of Irene Fellara in the film version of *Idiot's Delight,* Robert Sherwood's Pulitzer prize–winning play. For Irene, a vaudeville acrobat performer who passes herself off as a Russian countess, lives in another kind of untroubled play world of her own invention while the rest of the civilized world prepares for World War II. Sherwood was commissioned by MGM to adapt his play for the screen, and the changes he would make to the story to satisfy Metro-Goldwyn-Mayer's overseas marketing department would result in the ultimate Norma Shearer movie, and the apotheosis of Shearer's professional relationship with Adrian.

# Shearer Triumphs:
## *Idiot's Delight*

Harry: *"The world you live in isn't a world of facts and figures. It's a world of dreams. Maybe that's what I like about you, Irene. You're so beautifully phony."*
Irene: *"And maybe you're wrong, my darling. Maybe we two cheap people with our cheap lives— maybe we're the only ones in this crazy world who are real."*

—Clark Gable and Norma Shearer in
*Idiot's Delight.*

Robert Sherwood's *Idiot's Delight* opened on Broadway in March 1936, a production of the Theater Guild. It offered a vigorous arraignment of the war madness then threatening both Europe and the world, in particular those countries that had already succumbed to Fascism. Set entirely at the Hotel Monte Gabriele, which was a former sanatorium in the Austrian Alps, *Idiot's Delight* was essentially a comedy with an overlay of philosophic antiwar conviction, just as Sherwood's earlier *Petrified Forest* was a hostage melodrama tied in with modern social problems.

No one, however, could accuse Sherwood's original play of glossing over a delicate situation. But Louis B. Mayer expressly wanted Sherwood to remove any incendiary political references. For the film, a group of people are now stranded at a hotel somewhere in Europe as there is some "serious trouble on the frontier." The visitors are unable to get to the "border," because "we're on the verge of a war." But who's fighting? Mayer even insisted that Sherwood eliminate any mention of Nazi Germany as the major threat to world peace.

Mayer, like many of the other largely Jewish studio heads, was still anxious to continue deriving profits from the German market in 1938 when *Idiot's Delight* went into production, and was reluctant to make a film that was blatantly anti-Nazi. In addition, Vittorio Mussolini, the head of the Italian Censor Board, refused to approve a first draft of the script. As a result, Sherwood's antiwar message was neutered, and Esperanto (an artificial international language) was employed whenever a foreign dialect was needed. *Idiot's Delight* was turned into a Shearer-Gable vehicle with a new opening set in the United States.

Harry Van (Clark Gable), a small-time entertainer, returns from the First World War to find his career on the skids. While working in vaudeville as an assistant to an alcoholic mindreader in Omaha, Nebraska, Harry meets Irene (Norma Shearer), an acrobat with an overactive imagination on the same bill. He invites her to eat with him at a local diner, but makes the mistake of continually calling her "Babe."

"My name isn't Babe," she tells him, "It's Irene."

"Don't worry about that," Van replies, "I call everybody Babe."

"Perhaps that's why I don't like it. I'm not everybody. . ."

"Oh, I beg your pardon," Van says, bemused. "I should have realized. You're pretty exclusive."

"I am," Irene quietly insists. "I was really born to live in a palace. So it isn't always easy for me to adjust myself to Daka's Place—Eats."

When Harry and Irene part, he tells her that she lives in a world of dreams, but it's a dream that's about to come true. Several years later, when Van is touring Europe and is stranded at the Hotel Monte Gabriele with his troupe, Irene—now Countess Irina—appears in the lobby as a traveling companion to a munitions magnate. She sweeps into the hotel with a blond wig and a Slavic drawl. Finally, clothes and character have become one. Shearer is wearing a stunning karakul ensemble with a large cape and muff made of gray Persian lamb, sporting gray suede boots, the whole outfit topped off with an enormous shako.

Throughout the early part of the film set in Omaha, Irene is diminutive, almost childlike in comparison with

Harry Van. Adrian dresses Shearer in frilly white blouses with puffed sleeves, and hats that fit snugly, allowing her curls to billow softly around her face. As the phony countess, Adrian's boots, cape, and shako allow Shearer to tower over everybody else in the hotel lobby. Irene's ambition—"I was born for excitement, adventure, danger"—has been fully realized, and Adrian's costume allows her to finally grow even larger than her dream. Harry thinks he dimly recognizes Irene, but she repels all his efforts to refresh her memory of the Royal Grand Hotel in Omaha.

Later that evening, entertaining the other guests in the hotel cocktail lounge, Adrian dresses Shearer in a variation of a black pleated silk tea gown, with a collar and waistband of jet beads. Her long batlike sleeves punctuate every one of Shearer's exaggerated gestures as she holds court with her preposterous stories about escaping from the Bolsheviks during the revolution. This costume replaced a black pants suit designed by Adrian that Shearer decided, at the last moment, made her look too wide across the hips. Although it was rare for a costume at MGM to be discarded once it had been created, Shearer was famous for changing her mind about a design at the last minute. Costume fittings became an important ritual for her total realization of a role.

"Norma Shearer has a perfect passion for details," Adrian told Hedda Hopper in 1939. "She will stand for hours admiring every angle. Never puts on a dress without its wig, sometimes makeup, and will come in two or three times a day for the same gown. If there are seven or eight ways to put in a sleeve, she wants to see all of them." Shearer

*In Adrian's nimble hands, costume is always character. This pleated black silk crepe gown, with a collar and waistband of jet beads, featured long batlike sleeves that served to accent Shearer's exaggerated gestures as she held court at the hotel with her stories about escaping from the Bolsheviks during the Russian Revolution.*

*For the final scenes in* Idiot's Delight, *when Irene confesses her real identity to Harry Van (Clark Gable), Adrian dresses Shearer in the essence of simplicity and honesty.*

was also the only star at MGM whose costumes were not fitted on a dress dummy. "[She] has the patience of Job in this," Adrian once remarked, "and while she often changes her mind about details, she is practically always right. She never grows tired. My technicians and I can be wilting and she will look as fresh as the proverbial daisy."

Shearer's passion, more often than not, paid off in performance. The large, chunky bracelets Shearer wore with the black gown were the only accessory she retained from the discarded pantsuit. When Shearer told Adrian she planned to use a cigarette holder in the film, he knew that the bracelets, with each gesture, would lend dramatic authority to her every move. And the collar of jet beads on the new costume sparkled under the lights, providing a visual accompaniment to Irina's rippling, theatrical laugh.

As the film builds to its climax, the bombing escalates, and Harry makes a dramatic effort to rescue Irene. For these final scenes, Adrian outfits Shearer in a simple black dress with a strand of pearls. The sleeves are shirred, and the outfit includes a hood that gives Shearer's character a nunlike appearance appropriate for her redemption at the end of the film. "The age of chivalry still lives!" Irene crows when Harry comes back for her. "Romance is not dead!"

In the play, Harry and Irene, who were played by Alfred Lunt and Lynn Fontanne on Broadway, do a softshoe shuffle offstage as the stage directions read "the din is now terrific! Demolition—bombs, gas-bombs, airplanes, shrapnel, machine guns!" Sherwood's scathing critique of American isolationism, however, is turned into a happy ending for Gable and Shearer. They embrace long enough to dream about a new world that may not be brave, but will stay intact long enough

for them to create yet another illusion.

*Idiot's Delight* was recalled by Adrian as one of his favorite films long after he had left MGM, and no wonder. As a costume designer, he may have found a kindred spirit in the character of Irene Fellara. For Norma Shearer, the role of Irene summed up her personal feelings about costume in general: "the right dress can triumph over any situation," she said in 1932, "build any mood, create any illusion, and make any woman into the sort of person which she most desires to be."

In Adrian, Shearer had found her own real-life Harry Van, a man who could facilitate almost any illusion.

With 135 Women to Gown, Adrian Had Field Day

*When a woman feels blue she goes out and buys herself a new hat or dress . . . . But a man can only find solace in a picture of himself mirrored in the eyes of another woman. Upon this bit of philosophy from* The Women, *Adrian has whipped together an astounding collection of gowns and hats to make any woman forget her troubles. The fact that every woman in the cast, and there are 135 of them, are "blue" at some period during the film has given Adrian ample excuse to buoy their sagging spirits with frocks destined to set fashion agog for the next 12 months.*

—Exhibitor pressbook for *The Women,* 1939

# Putting It All Together

*Adrian and* The Women

For Adrian, eleven years of designing at Metro-Goldwyn-Mayer reached a kind of theatrical climax with his costumes for the film version of Clare Boothe Luce's *The Women* in 1939. The play, mercilessly flip, was an instant comic hit when it opened on Broadway in 1936. The property was purchased by MGM in 1938 as a showcase for its star actresses and it would prove to be a showcase for its star designer as well. In much the same way that *The Great Ziegfeld* summed up Adrian's Broadway revue background, and *Marie Antoinette* was his last word on the costume spectacle, so *The Women* offered his definitive take on the subject of costume vs. fashion. More than any other film he worked on at MGM, *The Women* was a dazzling example of what Adrian felt was his most important task as a costume designer: the ability to interpret character and mirror the mood of the scene.

By the time *The Women* went into production in the late spring of 1939, each of the leading actresses cast in the film was at a crossroads in her career, and each saw the film as a kind of testing ground for the development of a new image. Rosalind Russell

*Always the scene stealer, Crawford doesn't hold back in the final scene of* The Women. *As Crystal Allen, she upstages Norma Shearer, left, and Rosalind Russell, right, with a bare midriff. This is Adrian's first design with a bare midriff since* Mata Hari, *made 8 years earlier in 1931. In creating this costume for Crawford, Adrian was inspired by the basic Hollywood "vamp suit" first worn by Theda Bara in* Cleopatra *(1917).*

had been under contract to MGM since 1934, usually playing brittle "other woman" roles, and losing Gable or Robert Montgomery to Jean Harlow or Joan Crawford in the final reel. She saw the part of vicious, gossip-mongering Sylvia Fowler in *The Women* as a comic opportunity that would give her career a whole new dimension. Norma Shearer had initially resisted being cast as the virtuous Mary Haines, but after playing Marie Antoinette and a phony Russian countess in *Idiot's Delight,* Mayer felt it was time for Shearer to come down to earth and attempt a role that would put her back in touch with Middle America.

The star who had the most to lose, or, as it turned out, to gain from the film, was Joan Crawford. Having been labeled "box-office poison" in *Motion Picture Herald* a year earlier, she lobbied relentlessly for the role of Crystal Allen, seeing the part as a reversion to a successful type, but with a twist: this shopgirl marries well, but only after stealing another woman's husband.

From the very beginning, Mayer was against adding Crawford to the cast, but not for the reasons that have been popularly assumed. "The role is that of an outright bitch, a homewrecker," Mayer told Crawford. "It could hurt your career." What Mayer really had on his mind, however, was concern over Crawford's ability to sell fashion in a role that would receive little audience sympathy. His misgivings, in fact, would result in a showdown with Adrian that very nearly resulted in Adrian's resignation.

Crawford felt instinctively that the role of Crystal Allen was a vital presence in *The Women.* As the perfume salesgirl from Blacks Fifth Avenue who entraps, and eventually marries, the husband of socialite Mary Haines, she was a middle-class standout in a stable of society ladies, the spark that lit and fueled the entire plot. Mayer finally gave in, but he remained nervous all through filming. He attempted to have one of Crawford's costumes changed midway through production, and even tried to have the ending of the film rewritten so that her character would receive at least a modicum of sympathy. He was eventually talked out of both attempts.

Still, much of the film *was* rewritten from the original play, with some of the dirt "cleaned up." (In the play Mary's husband, Stephen Haines, for example, is depicted as a constant, rather than a first-time, philanderer). As a way around the censors, screenwriters Anita Loos and Jane Murfin also concocted new words in response to the question, "When is a lady not a lady?" So that all of the women in the cast would remain strictly ladylike, any demeaning references to "less

fortunate" members of their sex were couched in gibberish. Topping the list was the noun "beazel," followed in rapid succession by "micklish," "sleeper," "chotsie," "trech," and "kronker."

Many of the rewrites also put an increasing emphasis on fashion. The front office insisted on the inclusion of a fashion show, which was easy enough, since in the play Mary first encounters Crystal at a couturier shop. Shot in the new technicolor process (the rest of the film was in black-and-white) the show was a clever bit of salesmanship that met with almost universal scorn when the picture was released:

> "The fashion show, bursting forth in vivid colors from the alleged continuity, is simply downright bad from any standpoint except that of the clothes." (*New York Herald Tribune*)
>
> "There is really no reason for the inserted fashion show which slows up a story that has been stretched a little far for durability." (*New York Daily News*)
>
> "Some of the new sequences are so good Miss Boothe might have thought of them herself. Among these, however, we do not include a style show in Technicolor, which may be lovely — at least that's what most of the women around us seemed to think — but has no place in the picture. Why not a diving exhibition or a number by the Rockettes?" (*New York Times*)

The use of technicolor *was* intrusive, but the fashion show itself was hardly a mistake from a dramatic viewpoint. It provided a turning point in the plot that could not have been accomplished as successfully any other way, and its ramifications would be felt up to the film's final scenes.

Thirty-five professional models, transported to Hollywood from the New York World's Fair, were used in the show, which featured beachwear, sportswear, afternoon frocks, and evening dresses worn against appropriate backgrounds: at the pool and country club, at the theater, and at a zoo (where three monkeys, named Dizzy, Featherbrain, and Stupid, eat peanuts, dressed in costumes that duplicate those of the models. In keeping with the selling point of the picture, the producers made sure they were *female* monkeys).

As Mary Haines and her friends Sylvia, Edith (Phyllis Povah), and Peggy (Joan Fontaine) congregate in one of the salons at the conclusion of the show, they encourage Mary to purchase a nightgown. But just as Mary decides to buy it, she is interrupted by Crystal Allen.

"I'll take that," she says. "I could use a few more gowns on the same order—you know, imports with hand embroidery." Crystal and Mary are wearing similar black suits, making them social equals at first glance. Then the audience realizes that Crystal was also present at the fashion show, and that by laying claim to a garment that Mary Haines intended to purchase, she is also staking her claim to the lifestyle she has just seen on display—Mary Haines's lifestyle, where fashion takes center stage. After all, the plot of *The Women* kicks into high gear when Sylvia Fowler is thumbing through an issue of *Vogue* at a salon and a manicurist sees a picture of Mary in the magazine wearing a Beaux-Arts costume. She then proceeds to tell Mrs. Fowler all the gossip about "that poor Mrs. Haines. . . ."

A remake of *The Women* was bandied about the major studios in the late 1970s and again in the early 1990s (it was remade by MGM in the mid-1950s as *The Opposite Sex*), but it is difficult to imagine how this scene would be handled today, when couturier salons no longer serve as outposts in the class war, and when anyone with a credit card is welcomed with open arms. In 1939, clothes were still a uniform and sign of status; society matrons never wore pants, let alone designer jeans. So Crystal's three little words—"I'll take that"—momentarily, and quite literally, freeze the action.

Mary then proceeds to her fitting. Crystal has the dressing room next door, and Sylvia encourages Mary to have it out with her rival. Gathering her resolve, Mary bursts in on Crystal.

Adrian dresses Shearer in a voluminous black ball gown with a huge, billowing skirt for this dramatic confrontation—conventionally sober, isolating, and distinctive. Crawford whirls around to face her in a tight gold lamé dress with puffed sleeves and a matching turban. Adrian had dressed Crawford in lamé before, for her roles as a woman of society in *No More Ladies, I Live My Life,* and, most especially, *Letty Lynton.* But here he adds a slight tweak: Crawford's costume is short in front, revealing shapely legs behind the gathered lamé folds.

This prompts a withering exit line after Mary and Crystal have introduced themselves and exchanged verbal blows. "May I suggest if you're dressing to please Stephen," says Mary, "not that one, he doesn't like such *obvious* effects." Crystal thrusts her torso forward in reply, coming face-to-face with Mary: "Thanks for the tip! But when anything I wear doesn't please Stephen I *take it off!*"

This scene marks a turning point in Crawford's career at MGM: The woman who has made a career out of dressing for success not only admitting to an occasional lapse of taste, but brazenly suggesting that fashion is not at the heart of her appeal.

In the final scene of the film, when the entire cast is present in the ladies' lounge of the Casino Roof nightclub, Adrian validates the fashion show again by dressing Peggy and Miriam Aarons (Paulette Goddard) in variations of the gowns presented onstage, thus reinforcing their taste and rightful inclusion in high society. But Crystal makes her entrance in Adrian's first design with a bare midriff since *Mata Hari* in 1931, the brassiere and full circular skirt done entirely in gold sequins. A wide belt embroidered in gold completes the outfit.

On Broadway, costume designer John Hambleton dressed the actress playing Crystal Allen for this scene in a veil of black tulle sprinkled with gold coins, a sleekly-fitted black satin dress, and black kid gloves, cut out to reveal brilliantly polished nails. In creating a costume for Crawford, Adrian was inspired by an enduring design from Hollywood's earliest days: the basic vamp suit first worn by Theda Bara in *Cleopatra* (1917). This outfit, as costume historian Anne Hollander has pointed out, has hardly changed in 80 years, and consists of a jeweled brassiere, more or less revealing, and a jeweled, beltlike arrangement with a centrally placed flap, patch or medallion on the stomach, with tight gathers around the hips. "This vaguely belly-dancerish costume," Hollander has written, "although it resembles nothing specific in history, is an all-purpose Hollywood device, used over and over, decade after

decade, to signal unscrupulous sex in a barbaric setting. It will do for ancient Egypt, Babylon, Greece or Rome, for all Eastern nations old or new, for other planets, and for the future."

And it will do for the Casino Roof nightclub in New York City. Adrian adapted the design to indicate how out of place Crystal was in this setting: a pushy, overdressed hussy whose blatant intentions are announced in screaming sequins. When Louis B. Mayer saw Crawford wearing the dress in the rushes, however, he became apoplectic. Summoning both Adrian and the film's producer, Hunt Stromberg, to his office, he exclaimed that the dress was in "very poor taste" and insisted that it be changed. According to Stromberg, Adrian tried to explain his conception of the character to Mayer, but his explanation fell on deaf ears.

Following the death of Irving Thalberg in 1936, Louis B. Mayer began to take a more active role in the day-to-day operation of MGM, not only in the larger matter of assignment and casting but also in concept and execution. The studio's films of the twenties and thirties were notable for the sophisticated adult themes that producers such as Thalberg and David O. Selznick had chosen for Metro's powerful female stars. By the middle of the latter decade, with Thalberg's passing and Selznick's resignation, there was a noticeable change in emphasis. Male leads, family themes, and child stars were growing in favor. Even in Metro's musicals, the slightly naughty capriciousness of *The Merry Widow* (1934) had given way to the pastel sweetness of *Maytime* (1937).

Adrian was beginning to chafe under Mayer's moral vigilance, and at first he refused to change the dress. It was producer Hunt Stromberg who reminded Adrian of Mayer's far-reaching wrath and influence in the Hollywood community. Cooler heads soon prevailed, but Crawford remained anxious. She knew that the sequined dress would make her a standout in a climactic scene that included almost all the speaking parts in the cast, and if it were going to be replaced, she wanted final approval. Crawford and producer Hunt Stromberg were supposed to meet with Adrian on March 20, 1939, to go over sketches for a replacement dress, but Stromberg couldn't make it, and he sent the following telegram to Crawford's home to allay her qualms over the impending decision: "Must stay home today on account of severe cold. Will see you and Adrian tomorrow 12:30. Have talked with Adrian regarding general treatment. He will try to have something to show us tomorrow."

Attempting to comply with Mayer's wishes, Adrian chose

Following a confrontation between Adrian and Louis B. Mayer over the respectability of Crawford's bare midriff outfit, the designer was instructed to create something more suitable. He did: a crepe gown nearly identical to one that Shearer wears in the same scene, with only minor modifications. The upshot: Crawford returned to her gold sequins and Shearer stayed in white crepe.

would wear the gold sequined dress.

Adrian's costumes for his two leading ladies in this scene underscore the dramatic tension and serve to tip off the audience in advance. "Stephen's fed up with you, Crystal, and in your heart you know it!" Mary says, but we could have already guessed after seeing Crawford in that dress.

*The Women* provided Adrian with one of his best opportunities not only to create fashion, but also to actually effect character through clothes. The fact that his costumes stand up after sixty years, and can still reveal the brazen instincts of one character while laying bare the childish maliciousness of another, is a credit to the power of his designs. And never do they lapse into unbridled camp.

Perhaps his most successful creations were not for the two principals but for Rosalind Russell as Sylvia Fowler. "I may not be a model, but nobody disputes how I wear clothes!" she sputters at one point. But

a dress for Crawford that closely resembled the one he had designed for Norma Shearer to wear in the same scene: an evening gown of white crepe, the only decoration a wide jewel-encrusted belt. It was originally created for the fashion show and then discarded at the last moment.

Designing virtually the same gown for two leading stars to wear in the same scene might seem like madness, but for Adrian there was a method to it. He knew that Crawford would never consent to wearing the dress (although she gamely donned the gown and posed in it for costume tests), and that Shearer would also object. He hoped to bring matters to a head, and he did. In a meeting in Mayer's office at the end of March, director George Cukor, Crawford, Adrian, and Hunt Stromberg prevailed on the studio head, and he finally gave in. Crawford

Adrian's cockeyed costumes for Russell give lie to her outburst. In little-girl dresses with puffed sleeves and button-down collars, and saddled with enormous purses, veils, and hats that make her look like a whirlybird about to take off (one was adapted by Balenciaga as late as 1963), her venom is given the comic coating it needs through her costumes. At the fashion show, Adrian dresses Russell in a navy blue and white taffeta dress that is vertically striped in the bodice and features diagonal stripes in the skirt. The design itself seems to be pulling Sylvia in opposite directions as she flits about the showroom and Mary's dressing room, attempting to stay one step ahead of the action. The fitted jacket on the costume is cut a bit too short in back to allow for a full bustle on the skirt, which jiggles amusingly as she walks.

*Rosalind Russell as Sylvia Fowler in* The Women. *Her navy blue-and-white taffeta dress is deliberately "all sixes and sevens," an indication that her character is more comedy than comely. Even the hat amuses, with its flattened felt cyclamen and pert grosgrain bows of cyclamen and fuchsia.*

BELOW: *Adrian escorts Rosalind Russell to the set.*

In the grand finale atop the Casino Roof, Mary has Sylvia locked in a broom closet to get her out of the way. And when she is finally released, a yellow mop that has become entangled in her lace cape literally becomes a part of the costume, for Sylvia is so intent on participating in the general hoop-de-do that she carries the mop with her, oblivious, until the film's denouement. Earlier, attending a luncheon at Mary's country home, Sylvia is a walking metaphor in a beige sweater studded with glass doll's eyes of fuchsia that look out at the world from under long metal eyelashes. "Great guns, what are you made up for," asks Nancy (Florence Nash) when she spots her, "the seeing eye?" Exactly. *All*-seeing, and Sylvia tells all that she sees.

One of Adrian's most outrageous creations for Russell ended up on the cutting room floor, but photographs of it survive. Designed for a scene set at the

*Another white crepe gown that never made it to the final cut of* The Women. *Just as the Munchkins in* The Wizard of Oz *had costumes with floral motifs to complement the lush flowerscape of Oz, so Adrian made Rosalind Russell's gown complement the Reno, Nevada, ranch setting. The full sleeves are caught tight at the wrists with wide hand-tooled leather gauntlets. Hand-tooled leather is also employed in the belt and saddle epaulets with flat silver stirrups.*

*The repetition of a rose on this white silk bathing suit and beach coat is both fanciful and fantastic. Even the fastening on the neck of the jacket is playful—a wooden hand holding a rose. The amusing beach hat is of fine white braided straw with a neck shield of white silk jersey.*

*OPPOSITE: Another great evening gown from the fashion show in* The Women, *bearing the influence of Surrealism: a single jewel-encrusted gold kid glove, which also matches the wide belt.*

divorce ranch in Reno, it was made of white wool jersey and featured shoulder pads constructed out of gold kid in the shape of miniature saddles.

The costume hinted at Surrealism, and several of Adrian's creations for the fashion show featured some of his first dabblings in this fantastic imagery. Adrian was fascinated by the trend, but the narrative demands of the films he designed for usually precluded any Surrealist touches. The fashion show in *The Women,* however, provided him with a unique opportunity to experiment, and he was able to create a number of designs for the runway that were divorced from character. One crepe evening gown featured a cape with eyes embroidered in sequins, accented by a single embroidered eye on the right shoulder. A beach jacket featured a clasp in the shape of a wooden hand clutching a rose, a decorative motif repeated in the lining and on the bathing suit.

One costume with a surreal feel to it, however, perfectly suited the character for whom it was designed. When Hedda Hopper joins the action on the Casino Roof as columnist Dolly ("Got any dirt for the column?") DePeyster, Adrian outfits her in a suit jacket with a giant butterfly design embroidered entirely of sequins. The matching hat features antennae, presumably ready to pick up gossip from the Casino Roof, and points west, all over Manhattan.

Many of the designs worn by the principal actresses in *The Women* were marketed to moviegoing consumers after the film was released. In the exhibitor's pressbook, MGM publicity offered this helpful suggestion to theater owners who might want to order fashion stills for their lobbies: "You will note that in some of the stills the footwear is white although the fashions are distinctly fall. This is due, in part, to the longer Hollywood summer season which permits women to wear white footwear past our time. Crop off the shoes simply by using the photos in ovals or vignetted effects!"

Macy's, in its Cinema Shops, featured adaptations of four evening gowns, one daytime ensemble, three hats, and a negligee from the film. A black tulle evening gown was inspired by one of Adrian's creations for Russell. The inspiration for the

*Adrian must have found it amusing to design this costume for Hedda Hopper, far left, with Rosalind Russell, Norma Shearer, and Joan Fontaine in the Casino Roof powder room. You can practically hear the "buzz" around her as she plays the gossipy columnist Dolly DePeyster.*

bulk of the Macy's collection, however, came from Norma Shearer's wardrobe, including a swingy wool day dress with a velveteen collar and lively red wool jacket, and a soft wool negligee with long, full sleeves ("blue or fuchsia—and quite dignified enough for dinner at home," read the Macy's ads).

Director George Cukor had warned Shearer before production began that the part of Mary Haines could easily become a worthy bore, and Shearer responded by never playing for sympathy. In contrast to her broad portrayal of the phony countess in *Idiot's Delight,* her technique here is admirably restrained, and so are Adrian's costumes. Mary Haines comes to life in his reedy tailored suits, simple blouse-

and-skirt combinations and sober dinner gowns that prefigured many of the ready-to-wear and custom-made clothes he would design for his own couture house in the years to come. "Mary suffers by contrast to the other more eccentric and amusing characters," Norma Shearer said, "but she gives strength and meaning to the story. She is like a Christmas tree, while the others are like the trimmings that provide the glitter."

The defining note for Shearer's costumes was verbalized early in the film when Mary Haines's daughter asks to help her mother dress for a luncheon she is hosting for a group of friends: "Mother, let me pick out your dress for you. They'll all be so fancy—why don't you be plain?"

Crawford's wardrobe for Crystal Allen was far from plain, but it was meager. She has only four costume changes in the picture, and plays one scene submerged in a bubble bath. This was hardly a mandate for "the cinema's leading wearer of clothes" (as Walter Winchell tagged Crawford in a review of *Mannequin*), and so, to a certain extent, Louis B. Mayer's prophecy was borne out. The success of *The Women*, however, gave Crawford the hit she needed, and emboldened her to begin taking more risks in her choice of roles.

Adrian designed 237 gowns for the cast of *The Women*. Five complete, identical changes of wardrobe were needed for the fight that erupts on the Reno divorce ranch due to the multiple takes that were required for each scene. And amid all the criticism for the inserted fashion show, a critic for the *Hollywood Reporter* was astute enough to recognize Adrian's contribution to the film: "Regarding the production as a whole, I would give major honors to Cedric Gibbons and Adrian, whose contributions made it possible for Oliver Marsh's and Joe Ruttenberg's cameras to make the film one of the season's outstanding visual treats. Against the background of the Gibbons sets, the women wearing the Adrian creations are grouped by Cukor in a manner which must have delighted the artistic souls of Marsh and Ruttenberg."

*The Women* was the last big Metro "all-star" film of the 1930s, and the production was as lavish behind the scenes as it was in front of the camera. There were so many personal maids, hair dressers, fitters, tailors, and makeup artists on the stage during the filming of the final scenes that the completion of a take marked a veritable subway rush as each "crew" hurried to its own "victim" to ready her for the next "take." At the end of one sequence, in which practically the entire cast was before the cameras, Cukor screamed, "Duck everybody! Here come the grasshoppers!"

Adrian did not allow any of the players in the picture to see the costumes designed for the other members of the cast until the actresses arrived on the set, ready to work, and stories that have circulated for years of Shearer changing Crawford's dress in this scene or that scene are completely untrue. Yet the fourteen-year rivalry between the two actresses did erupt into a feud on the set, and Crawford refused to attend the cast party Shearer threw at the conclusion of filming. Their feud made good publicity for the film ("when the two meet," *Look* reported in its March 28 issue, "farmers for miles around set out smudge pots to keep the frost from nipping their fruit."), but was ultimately rendered pointless, for the ground Shearer and Crawford were fighting over was already slipping from beneath their feet. As Mark Vieira has written, 1940 was just around the corner, and with it would come the Twilight of the Goddesses.

*After he left MGM, Adrian started his own couture business. Some of the garments he made for Norma Shearer as a well-heeled New York house-wife in* The Women *influenced his fashions for his retail customers.*

Lambert: *"The prologue ... sums up the way the marriage between Hepburn and Grant ended without a word. He walks out of the house carrying a bag of golf clubs. Hepburn appears in the doorway carrying a club he's forgotten. Instead of giving it to him, she breaks it in two. Grant looks furious, then does this marvelous thing of advancing on her as if he's going to hit her—then gives her this contemptuous push, sending her into a pratfall."*

Cukor: *"You know, we shot that as an afterthought! We realized we needed something to reconstruct their marriage, and we didn't want to do it with a lot of dialogue."*
—Gavin Lambert and George Cukor discussing *The Philadelphia Story* in *On Cukor*

# End of an Era

*1940–1941*

The *Philadelphia Story*, released in 1940, was Katharine Hepburn's first film at Metro-Goldwyn-Mayer, after almost a decade of stardom at RKO-Radio Pictures that had essentially ended when she was labeled "box-office poison" in 1938. Philip Barry had written the original play specifically for Hepburn as a comeback vehicle on Broadway; she owned the screen rights, in conjunction with Howard Hughes, and was part of the package when the property was ultimately sold to MGM.

Throughout the 1930s at RKO, Katharine Hepburn had played a number of arch, privileged characters, often stubborn, and always independent and temperamental. Hepburn's character in *The Philadelphia Story*, Tracy Lord, is no less arch, no less stubborn or temperamental, but Barry cleverly fashioned the play partially as a reprimand. The screenplay, by Donald Ogden Stewart, made some changes to the original play— it is C. K. Dexter Haven (Cary Grant), Tracy's ex-husband, and not her brother, who invites two tabloid reporters to Tracy's wedding, in exchange for a vow from the magazine's publisher to keep the extramarital affair of Tracy's father under wraps. Yet one important aspect of the play remained untouched: character after character reproaches

*Adrian's party gown for Katharine Hepburn in* The Philadelphia Story *(1940) epitomizes in many ways what classic Hollywood design was all about. It was both elegant and flamboyant, and perfectly visualized James Stewart's rapturous declaration of love: "You are the golden girl, Tracy ...." The dress became one of Hepburn's favorites.*

Tracy, a bright, attractive young member of Philadelphia's Main Line. She's "a prig, a spinster" according to her own father, and a woman "who will never be a first-class human being until (she) learns to have some regard for human frailty," according to her ex-husband. In the opening scene of the film, which was added "as an afterthought" according to director George Cukor, Tracy is shoved to the floor by her departing husband. It is a gesture, as Foster Hirsch has written, that "echoed the popular rejection of 'Katharine Hepburn.'"

This scene is also, however, the beginning of a miraculous comeback, for along with all this overt disapproval the film also celebrates Tracy's—and Hepburn's—rarefied presence: "There's a magnificence in you, Tracy," reporter Macaulay "Mike" Connor (James Stewart) tells her, "a magnificence that comes out of your eyes, and your voice, and the way you stand there and the way you walk." And at the end of the film, Mike will help Tracy discover her humanity, and become a "first-class human being."

On the stage, Hepburn's costumes were designed by the New York couturiere Valentina. For the evening garden party scene in which Connor professes his love for Tracy, Valentina dressed Hepburn in a long pleated dress of plain white silk crepe that bore a marked resemblance to one of Mariano Fortuny's Delphos tea gowns. The Delphos was a columnar dress of thin silk satin, finely pleated, that was named for the pleated linen chitons worn by maidens in Delphic Greek sculpture. It was back in vogue in the 1920s and 1930s among society women, and on stage the similarities were clear: "I'm going to build you an ivory tower with my own two hands," Tracy's fiancé, George Kittredge (John Howard) tells her. "There's a kind of beautiful purity about you, like a statue." Valentina's costume served to venerate the chaste, exalted goddess.

Adrian saw Tracy Lord differently. To start, he smoothed out the pleats in her gown. As an accent around Hepburn's collar, he added an embroidered pattern in gold braid and sequins to the stark white costume, repeating the motif in a band around her waist that encircled the bodice. The bodice itself was plain, with a deep V decolletage and a turned-back shirtmaker collar.

This dress ultimately became a contributing factor in the success of Hepburn's film comeback. Some might call it typical Hollywood excess, and it was somewhat flamboyant, but the gold braid perfectly visualized Mike Connor's enraptured declaration of love: "You're lit from within, Tracy! You've got

*Adrian's original sketch for Hepburn's gingham plaid skirt in* The Philadelphia Story. *Katharine Hepburn, opposite, wearing the finished costume in the film.*

fires banked down in you! Hearth-fires and . . . holocausts!" And on this special night, in this special dress, these fires glow very near the surface.

Throughout the film Adrian's costumes seem to celebrate Hepburn not only as a creature of rare "magnificence," but one who is uniquely American as well. When Tracy Lord meets the reporters from *Spy* magazine onstage, she wears a dress of clinging jersey, with alternating wide and narrow stripes—horizontal along the top, and vertical on the bottom.

*A costume sketch for Katharine Hepburn in* The Philadelphia Story. *Although Louis B. Mayer objected to Hepburn in slacks, the designer and star prevailed. The garment made from this sketch was a short lumber jacket in navy blue crepe and tailored trousers. Carved white ivory was used for the trio of buttons on the jacket.*

Adrian's costume for the same encounter on film turns Tracy into a billowing Dresden shepherdess, with an orchidaceous organza blouse and a skirt built from layer upon layer of gingham check. The gingham was a touch of Americana that Adrian had found on a trip through Appalachia in 1938. He used a blue shade of the material for Judy Garland's farm dress in *The Wizard of Oz,* and here he employs it to connect Tracy with a kind of driven, never-say-die American pioneer spirit.

For the opening scene, when Tracy walks out the front door carrying C. K. Dexter Haven's golf clubs, Adrian talked Hepburn out of the pants she wanted to wear. Instead, he dressed her in a diaphanous white nightgown. The scene was partially written as an act of defiance: Tracy throws the bag of clubs at Haven's feet, and then breaks one for good measure. It's our first glimpse of the "goddess," all in ethereal white, yet despite her defiant, brazen act she is rendered vulnerable somehow by dint of the breeze that ruffles the hem of the thin, cotton material.

Pants were, however, an important part of Adrian's costume strategy for Tracy Lord. Part of his vision for the character—if not necessarily in the opening scene—was as an assertive, commanding presence who would naturally be attracted to slacks, which had become less and less shocking on women as the 1930s gave way to a new decade. One costume sketch that survives reveals what Adrian was up against as late as 1940. The drawing, a smart pantsuit, had been approved by producer Joseph L. Mankiewicz, who queried Adrian on the sketch: "Are you sure these, too, should be pants? Fine by me if fine by you." But it wasn't fine, as it turned out. Louis B. Mayer objected, and Hepburn, along with Adrian, had to convince him. After his battle with Mayer over one of Joan Crawford's costumes in *The Women,* Adrian was growing tired of fighting with the front office over every last bit of "permissiveness."

While *The Philadelphia Story* was still in production, Herbert Marcus, the patriarch of the Neiman-Marcus retailing family, paid a visit to MGM in order to meet Adrian. Marcus's visit was not merely a social call. The occupation of France in 1940 had closed most of the great couture houses in Paris, and

from the moment the city was occupied there was speculation in New York as to whether American fashion could function cut off from the inspirations of the great French designers. This concern was not only reflected in Marcus's visit to MGM, but also in the marketing campaign the studio devised to help sell *The Philadelphia Story* when it opened in December 1940. The following notice was sent to exhibitors who had booked the film:

*Paris Style Headquarters Moves to America*
*America Now Sets the Style Pace!*
When France declared an armistice with Germany a few months ago, its economic and political consequences meant less to American fashion designers than the loss of Parisian style influence on the women of this country.

For, despite frequent publicity to the contrary, Paris still was the biggest and most influential source of fashion right up to the demise of the French republic.

There was plenty of newspaper conjecture at the time as to whether NY or Hollywood would become increasingly important in the fashion picture. Many big N.Y. City stores are now coming out with costly display ads in which they feature American fashions by American designers exclusively.

This change, along with the fashionable background of *The Philadelphia Story*, leads us to believe you can promote an exceptionally interesting style show with the assistance of a prominent store. Wave the promotion flag a little. Stage a 100% American style show in a store or on the stage of your theater.

In an article in the *New York Times Magazine* four months earlier, fashion editor Virginia Pope had speculated on the effects the eclipse of Paris would have on American design:

The functions of the two dynamic fashion capitals have up to now been totally different. That of Paris has been inspirational, that of New York practical—speaking from the American point of view. On the Rue de la Paix the art of dressing was aristocratic: in the New York garment center it has always been democratic. The Paris couture was the product of luxury. To Paris have flocked the opulent to indulge their tastes for the extravagantly beautiful.

New York began at the opposite end of the social scale, with complete democratization of style as its purpose. Not the few but the many must be well-dressed, and at price levels fitting the budget range of all. The wide swing of New York's pendulum today covers the cotton dress that retails for $1.99 and the elaborately trimmed gown that may bring as much as $500. Into every item goes "styling effort."

During the 1920s a fictitious name, the Famous Forty, was applied to the style leaders of Europe, a group that bought their clothes in Paris, found their fun in the well-heeled watering spots on the Continent, and were the proving ground for French style. No comparable style stars, however, lit up the American scene. The socially prominent of Fifth and Park Avenues had always taken their cues from Paris—until, of course, the ascendance of Hollywood design in the 1930s. The creations of designers such as Adrian, Travis Banton, Orry-Kelly, and Edith Head served not only to challenge the pervasive influence of Paris, but to inspire the design rooms that looked out on the turreted skyline of Manhattan.

An upscale retailer like Herbert Marcus believed the time had come to move Adrian onto the stage of American ready-to-wear and couture fashion. Some of the Hepburn dresses from *The Philadelphia Story* were displayed on mannequins in the MGM wardrobe workroom when Marcus called on Adrian at the studio, and during the course of his visit he began to examine them closely. Quite casually, Adrian held up the beaded party dress and asked, "I'm curious, how many of this dress do you think you could sell?" Marcus replied, "Oh, I could sell at least fifty of them at each store." Adrian just stared at his guest and was quite thoughtful for the rest of the afternoon.

Marcus's visit to Metro-Goldwyn-Mayer was one of the catalysts that prompted Adrian to begin thinking about striking out on his own. A year earlier, he had married actress Janet Gaynor, who had encouraged him to set up his own shop, even offering to help him bankroll his own business. From his past experience at the studio, however, Adrian also realized that he could not undertake this kind of business venture while still under contract to MGM.

Throughout most of the 1930s, the lucrative possibilities that might result from marketing Adrian's film designs had not been lost on MGM, nor was it lost on clothing manufacturers in New York and Los Angeles. In the aftermath of the enormous popularity of Joan Crawford's "Letty Lynton" dress in 1932, a number of companies that produced ready-to-wear clothing and accessories on both the east and west coasts began slyly trading on the Adrian name. In 1933, the Morris Nagel Company in New York began advertising "Adrienne" suits as "created by America's foremost designer of fashions for stars of stage and screen." The line of clothing featured a suit called "The Norma" and one called "The Greta," with pictures of Norma Shearer and Greta Garbo wearing each suit. "Garbo's likeness is almost real," read the studio file on the matter, but "Norma's doubtful."

MGM sued, but that didn't stop a firm by the name of Leo Joseph, with headquarters in the Jeweler's Building in downtown Los Angeles, from manufacturing hats under the style names "Adrian Deb" and "Adrian Sport"—"Styled in Hollywood." Adrian himself alerted MGM, and again they threatened a lawsuit. "The obvious purpose of this firm is to lead the public to believe that our Adrian is the designer of the hats," wrote MGM's legal counsel in a memo to Howard Strickling, Eddie Mannix, and Louis B. Mayer. "This is particularly true by reason of the language 'Styled in Hollywood.'"

Each of these incidents alerted executives at MGM that there was money to be made from Adrian's designs, and beginning in 1933 they began to listen to legitimate proposals for commercial tie-ins. By far the most aggressive of these overtures came from M. J. Kane Lloyd Weil, a wholesale dress manufacturer located at 498 Seventh Avenue in New York. In January 1933 Weil contacted MGM with the following business proposition: "To furnish Weil with the dresses and a pattern of each said dress designed by Adrian, which have been worn by starred actresses of Metro in their feature photoplays. Metro will furnish the pattern of said dresses in the size of the original dress as soon as they can be spared after the photography."

Also—and this was a first—Weil wanted original dress patterns designed by Adrian in addition to those worn by the Metro stars. He left it up to MGM, in its discretion, to decide whether Adrian had enough spare time to design for this purpose during the period of the agreement.

Weil agreed to pay MGM $20,000 for the first year of the contract. Additional compensation to the studio for Adrian's services would be as follows: First million in sales—5% to MGM; Second million in sales—7½% to MGM; Over two million in sales—10% to MGM. Once the offer was discussed with him, Adrian stipulated that he wanted a $1.00 royalty for each dress sold. The term "dress" included evening gowns, street dresses, sport dresses, negligee wraps, capes, and coats. Accessories were not part of the deal.

Strickling saw two major stumbling blocks to this arrangement. For one thing, the termination date of the contract superseded Adrian's with MGM, so Weil and Adrian would have been free to make their own arrangements if Adrian decided not to renew his contract with Metro. In a letter to Weil dated April 15, 1933, Strickling gave the New York clothing manufacturer a brief picture of Adrian and his association with the studio. "He is in a class by himself," Strickling wrote:

> While his use of the best materials is somewhat expensive, the fact remains that he (Adrian) is extremely economical in that during his period with us, approximately 4½ years, only two of his designs have been unaccept-

able. He is very loyal and happy with us which accounts for his remaining with us at compensation much lower than paid for similar services for other studios. We have wanted the entire matter to be workable as otherwise we might be the loser through a letdown in his creativeness.

In other words, if Adrian spent too much of his time on independent designs for Weil, MGM would ultimately be the loser in any business agreement they might reach with the dress manufacturer. Then, in early May, Weil chose to revise the terms of the contract. He stated that in order to make the venture profitable for his firm, his annual requirements would call for a total of 240 dresses and 80 coats. MGM felt that these terms would be impossible considering the methods Adrian used to design each costume: from sketch to watercolor design to muslin pattern. Strickling explained this and other obstacles to the agreement in a final telegram to Weil dated May 6, 1933:

> We have always been concerned as to the risk of impairing Adrian's reputation as a designer by manufacturing his designs for public consumption. That is why we stipulated that the manufactured product should not deviate from Adrian's design and that difference as to colors, fabric and quality of fabric should be only with our consent. I have reviewed this with Adrian several times and he and ourselves are in agreement that we should make all stipulations possible to keep the marketing of the mdse on the highest possible plane.
>
> In the majority of cases, there are material changes made between each phase of operation, so the finished product is not exactly reflected in either the sketch or the muslin pattern. Since Adrian personally supervises the progress of the design, you will readily see that each design takes considerable time from inception to completion and therefore, Adrian and Joe Rapf, our wardrobe manager, agree that it is not feasible for Kane to manufacture models from Adrian's original sketches or the muslin patterns.
>
> When all is said and done Adrian's importance to our pictures outweighs any revenue that we could realize from a manufactured by-product. I have always seen that the proposal had two sides which were extremely difficult to merge: 1) the manufacturer could not make a success if the designs were limited in quality, and 2) to provide

enough designs to make manufacturing profitable would mean interference with (Adrian's) duties for us. Even if it were possible to meet Kane's requirements, we still would not do it for two reasons: 1)For his guarantee of $20,000 per annum, Kane would have a great designer at a fine bargain. 2)Kane could, if so minded, build up a reserve of designs for use after the contract termination.

Joe Rapf figured that MGM's annual production schedule would produce approximately thirty designs that could be turned into ready-to-wear clothing. Further, Adrian's film designs did not conform to the seasons, which would further complicate matters if he were required to furnish quotas of seasonal designs.

Adrian was satisfied with MGM's decision to forego a contract with Weil—or any other clothing manufacturer for the present time—but the discussions had planted an idea in his head, and when negotiations were underway for his new contract with the studio two years later, in 1935, he proved more tenacious than he had been before. By this point, he was becoming increasingly reluctant to sign over his life to MGM. Adrian informed studio manager M. E. Greenwood that he was opposed to committing himself for more than one year, despite efforts by the studio to sign him for a longer period of time. He explained to Greenwood that he had been with MGM for seven consecutive years, and felt that he should either have a long rest, or an opportunity to travel and broaden himself.

Greenwood stated in a memo to Louis B. Mayer and Eddie Mannix that he had clarified for Adrian the fact that costs were mounting, and that the studio desired his present compensation, $750 per week, to apply through the four-year period of the contract—one year, followed by three yearly options. In response, Adrian pointed out that Travis Banton's compensation at Paramount ($800 a week) exceeded his and he felt that he should receive an increase, the amount of which he would leave to the studio's suggestion. He mentioned, and Greenwood verified the fact, that Paramount not only sent Banton to New York each year, but to Paris as well.

Adrian did not desire a trip to Paris, but he suggested the following arrangement to MGM: With Garbo away and Norma Shearer pregnant in the summer of 1935, and with Joan Crawford's two annual productions taken care of, he would leave in three weeks for a trip to Europe of approximately twelve weeks on salary. MGM would pay reasonable transportation and

expenses. There would be no more trips to Europe for the duration of the contract, and no trip to New York during the first year. Further, Adrian wanted the right to use his name in connection with commercial interests other than motion pictures, and where it did not conflict with the studio's present interests. (He had an interior design business and a flourishing antique shop on Olvera Street in Los Angeles). He also would not commit himself to a fourth year, saying that if his association with MGM had been agreeable at the expiration of the third year, then the studio would have no difficulty re-signing him.

MGM informed Adrian that if he did take a European trip the studio would not pay his expenses. Without MGM's support, he decided against the trip; beginning July 1 he took a vacation of approximately four to five weeks in Mexico City, then New York, and finally in Taos, New Mexico. And his salary was raised to $800 a week, which would increase to $900 and then finally $1,000 a week for the final year of the contract.

These negotiations revealed a designer who was aware of his power at MGM, and was certainly interested in using the reputation he had earned to cast a wider net. After re-signing with Metro in 1935 Adrian would go on to complete some of his most exacting and celebrated work—the costumes for *The Great Ziegfeld, Romeo and Juliet, Camille, Marie Antoinette, The Women,* and *The Wizard of Oz.*

As his fame grew, and his designs became an important factor in selling the MGM product to exhibitors, Adrian became increasingly exasperated with his lack of control over the way these designs were ultimately marketed and promoted to the moviegoing public. One attraction to opening his own business was the opportunity to control how his designs were publicized. Garbo's cone-shaped hat in *Ninotchka* was a case in point. At the time, Adrian discouraged any special endorsement of the hat. Yet Adrian's opinion on the matter did not stop MGM's publicity department from promoting the design in the following publicity release, which accompanied stills from the film that were sent to local exhibitors:

*The New Garbo Hat Will Be One of the Most Talked About Things in the Picture*
Fashion experts say that variations of it will sweep the country. As a fashion innovation that is radically different from what women are now wearing, we believe it will cause plenty of local feminine twittering. Even if local

stores have nothing like it in stock they can, nevertheless, feature these scenes in their windows as eye attractors [sic] and with copy which conjectures whether this new Garbo hat will change the current mode.

Who these "fashion experts" were remained a moot point, but few exhibitors pressed the issue with MGM.

In 1938, Adrian had complained privately to his friend Hedda Hopper that he was beginning to abhor the studio's lack of appreciation for created beauty. He wanted many of the costumes for *Marie Antoinette* to be preserved for posterity, but "the studio thinks nothing of cutting up those beautiful things, and eventually these bits and pieces will find themselves covering the backs of character women." A year later, Adrian was devastated when MGM decided to burn some of the costumes in the wardrobe department. By the end of the 1930s the main wardrobe building had become overstuffed with thousands of costumes, and the excess was stored in hastily constructed Quonset huts that were built on various locations around the lot. A number of costumes were inadvertently hung on wire hangers, and over time some of the heavily embroidered gowns had begun to rip and tear. And so one night in the summer of 1939 the studio had a big bonfire, and hundreds of costumes that could no longer be used or sold to resale shops went up in flames.

This event was precipitated by the economic problems that hit the major studios at the close of the 1930s. For the first time since the very early years of the Depression, the film business was in trouble. According to a Gallup Poll, weekly attendance between 1936 and 1940 had shrunk from eighty-five million a week to fifty-five million. Film industry analysts judged that radio entertainment was keeping moviegoers at home. Moreover, Edward R. Murrow's broadcasts on the Battle of Britain were drawing people to radio. As a result, Hollywood slowed down. Budgets were trimmed, and fiscal reality became the order of the day. Adrian, so accustomed to working with only the finest materials, was plunged into a depression that was further exacerbated by the imbroglio over Garbo's costumes in *Two-Faced Woman*. In the summer of 1941 Louis B. Mayer suggested to Adrian that he had been working too hard, and that perhaps a rest might change his point of view. But Adrian's point of view had already changed in ways Mayer couldn't have guessed. He was beginning to see that Hollywood would never be quite the same as it had been in the

1920s and 30s. An age he had played no small part in creating was coming to an end.

It makes for dramatic narrative to picture Adrian tearing up his *Two-Faced Woman* sketches in a fury, and stalking out of the studio, as has often been reported. Anyone who knew him even slightly would recognize that this kind of behavior would have been totally out of character. If anything, it may have been sheer boredom, as well as the tantalizing prospect of launching his own business, that was the major reason behind his decision not to renew his contract with MGM.

"My father once told me that after he had finished working on *The Wizard of Oz* he felt like he had done it all," Robin Adrian says. "By the early 1940s everything on his schedule seemed boring and repetitious to him." Indeed, the exhibitor pressbook for one of his last films at MGM, *Keeper of the Flame* (1942) with Katharine Hepburn and Spencer Tracy, featured the following fashion tie-in suggestion, timed to coincide with America's entrance into World War II: "Fall, winter and spring are the seasons for raincoats. Usage of this garment has received a new impetus because it is worn by all servicemen. Suggest a fashion promotion with this versatile garment with a local department or women's clothing store." For Adrian, there seemed to be no new worlds to conquer, let alone create, on the soundstages of MGM.

When the end came, it was without melodrama or theatrics. Adrian's contract with Metro was terminated on July 16, 1941. According to the studio's personnel department, during his last three-year term of employment, 1938–41, Adrian had been absent from the studio due to illness for an aggregate period of eighteen days, for which he was paid. "The contract provides we may extend term for period equivalent to any period of incapacity," M. E. Greenwood wrote in a memo to Mayer. "Will you please advise whether you wish to exercise any right of extension for all or part of this 18-day period?"

Mayer did not. On August 15, 1941, Adrian advised personnel, prior to his departure, that he had informed Mayer of his desire to open a shop of his own, but that he would stay until such time as everything was under control. Mayer wired Adrian that he appreciated the gesture, and three weeks later, on September 5, 1941, he was officially removed from the MGM payroll.

"My mother always told me," Robin Adrian says, "that when my father left Metro, the studio had to hire five different designers to replace him."

# Epilogue

On his numerous shopping forays into downtown Los Angeles in the early and mid-1930s, Adrian had made the acquaintance of a merchandise manager named Woody Feurt at the Bullock's-Wilshire store. He had once accompanied Feurt on a buying trip to the East Coast, and now, in the fall of 1941, Adrian approached him about launching his own business, Adrian Ltd.

Initially, Feurt balked: with impending American involvement in the war overseas, there were new government restrictions in the works on fabrics and other goods that would make a new business undertaking even more perilous than usual. But Adrian persevered, and though the birth of his own clothing line was dogged by a series of potential disasters—mounting bills, limited cash flow, missing fabrics—and his salon was not ready for his first showing, which had to be held at his home, both buyers and the press were impressed. *Vogue* celebrated the collection in three full pages of photographs, and Stanley Marcus, son of Herbert and heir to the Neiman-Marcus retailing fortune, was one of the first to place an order. He was followed by buyers from Bonwit Teller, Best's, and Garfinkel's.

By the mid-1940s, Adrian's California success was repeated in the showrooms and workrooms of Seventh Avenue, where his pioneering "silhouette"—the narrow dress with broad shoulders and narrow skirt, enlivened with pleating, embroidery, or other ornamentation—became a wartime staple. As the war escalated, and France remained occupied, Adrian arranged speaking engagements and granted interviews, urging American designers to grab the opportunity and work out their own solutions to American life and style.

Awards soon followed, from a Fashion Critics' Award to the prestigious Coty Award in 1944 for his ready-to-wear designs. The wartime press hung on his every word, up until the conflict ended and Christian Dior presented his "New Look" in the Paris collections of 1947. *Vogue* and *Harper's Bazaar,* in Robert Riley's words, proclaimed the New Look the only look, and soon most prestigious stores and manufacturers came around to their position.

Adrian took the change in fashion philosophically. After suffering a heart attack in 1952 he closed up shop, traveled to Africa and Brazil, painted, and built a house in the Amazon jungle. Then, in the late 1950s, he and his wife were both lured back to work. Janet Gaynor was offered the lead in a play on Broadway, and Adrian was engaged to design the costumes for two lush Broadway musicals, *At The Grand*—a musical version of *Grand Hotel*—and *Camelot.*

The strain proved to be too much, however. On September 13, 1959, Adrian suffered a second, fatal heart attack. Tony Duquette, a friend and fellow designer who had helped Adrian plan his salon in 1941, took over the task of completing the *Camelot* costumes. Both men received Tony awards for their work, with Adrian's being awarded posthumously.

It seems incredible, in retrospect, that Adrian never won an Oscar for his film work. As a category, the Academy Award for costume design was not inaugurated until 1948, twenty-one years after the inception of the Academy, and well after the bulk of Adrian's film work had been completed. Yet it still seems incongruous to see that among the list of nominees in 1940 for *The Wizard of Oz*—when Cedric Gibbons, Harold Arlen, and Victor Fleming were all nominated for their work on the film—Adrian's name is missing because there was no category for costumes. His peers, however, recognized their debt to him, both as a designer and as a pioneering influence in American fashion.

"No one can forget Adrian's romantic period clothes," said Orry-Kelly after Adrian's death. "His imaginative period costumes were unforgettable. He stood for something in fashion." "As a designer," said Edith Head, "he created a type of clothes so individual, they will always stand out in the history of design. He created a look, something achieved by few in the world of fashion." Howard Greer commented that Adrian "was the one who really started the couture here. He was responsible for what dignity this market achieved," while Walter Plunkett, who did the clothes for *Gone With the Wind,* maintained that Adrian was "one of the greatest influences in design. He had a flair for knowing what was the coming trend and utilizing it."

Adrian's costumes at MGM flagged moods and attitudes onscreen as surely as William Daniels's expressive lighting or Cedric Gibbons's masterful set design. More so than almost any other Hollywood designer, he understood how dramatic style enhanced the persona of an actress, and how clothing could be either decadently sensual or heartbreakingly sympathetic. His most successful creations took on a life of their own, nurturing and sustaining the character onscreen. They remain potent artifacts of the American dream—of that limited and romantic vision of life's possibilities that once dominated American film.

# Endnotes

All numbers in **bold** refer to page numbers
in the book

## Preface

**7.** "For the past five years. . .": *Fortune*, December, 1932, p. 51.
**7.** "MGM pictures are always superlatively well-packaged. . .": *Ibid.*, p. 122.
**7.** "All the studio dress designers have been thinking. . .": *Modern Screen*, April, 1930, page 36.
**8.** "For years motion picture clothes were conceived. . .": *Screenland*, February, 1929, p. 112.
**8.** "is particularly chic. . . .": *Vogue*, February 1, 1933, p. 56
**8.** "Screen presentation is vital and living. . .": *Cinema Arts*, September, 1936, p. 28.
**9.** "In 1934 Adrian's costumes inspired a young girl in Los Toldos, Argentina. . .": Gavin Lambert, *Norma Shearer: A Life*, p. 204.
**9.** "Few people in an audience. . .": Stephen Watts, ed., *Behind the Screen: How Films Are Made*, p. 57.

## A Predilection for Design

**12.** "Neither of us had any money. . .": Honor Seligman to author, July 27, 1991.
**13.** "The new revue is ablaze with color. . .": *New York Times*, September 22, 1921, n.p.
**14.** "Rambova 'hated the designer's crabbed little sketches'. . .": Robert Riley, *American Fashion*, p. 20.

## Going Hollywood

**21.** "My only scene was a futuristic dream sequence. . .": Myrna Loy, with James Kotsilibas-Davis, *Myrna Loy: Being and Becoming*, p. 42.
**21.** "No help came from anyone. . .": Michael Morris, *Madam Valentino*, p. 167.
**22.** "no hint of the nature of the spectacular prologue. . .": *Los Angeles Times*, June 21, 1925, Part III, p. 18.
**22.** "impressively artistic dances by fascinatingly pretty young women. . .": David Robinson, *Chaplin: His Life and Art*, p. 356.
**22.** "Paris fashion shows had been accessible only to the chosen few. . .": Sumiko Higashi, *Cecil B. DeMille and American Culture: The Silent Era*, p. 162.
**22.** "The dramatic situations in a picture must be costumed. . .": *Motion Picture*, May, 1926, p. 42.
**23.** "Less than a year after my break-up with Famous Players-Lasky. . .": Cecil B. DeMille, *The Autobiography of Cecil B. DeMille*, p. 290.

## A Studio Takes Shape

**25.** "More important, his insistence on highly crafted production values. . .": Beverly Heisner, *Hollywood Art: Art Direction in the Days of the Great Studios*, p. 58.
**26.** "Goldwyn refused to let one of his stars. . .": *Moving Picture World*, January 25, 1919, p. 48.
**26.** "Gibbons became one of the most autonomous. . .": Heisner, p. 61.
**26.** "he hated wallpaper, for example. . .": Ronald L. Davis, *The Glamour Factory: Inside Hollywood's Big Studio System*, p. 206.
**26.** "Shades of a golden past still hovered. . .": *Photoplay*, May, 1919, p. 100.
**27.** Caption: "Ivory walls and an ivory barrel ceiling. . . .": *Los Angeles Telegraph*, June 7, 1925, n.p.
**27.** "Mayer's expectations were borne out. . .": *New York Review*, March 1, 1925, n.p.
**27.** "Erté's advent into motion pictures. . .": *New York Morning Telegraph*, March 14, 1925, n.p.
**28.** "Somehow the final garments were never. . .": David Chierichetti, *Hollywood Costume Design*, p. 12.
**28.** "Adoree refused to wear. . .": *Photoplay*, February, 1926, p. 32.
**28.** "I thought he would know just how Mimi should look. . .": Lillian Gish and Ann Pinchet, *The Movies, Mr. Griffith, and Me*, p. 278.
**28.** "Erté's final declaration. . .": *Los Angeles Daily News*, November 4, 1925, n.p.
**29.** "Coulter had spent fifty years making. . .": Barrett C. Kiesling, *Talking Pictures*, p. 113.
**29.** "he even advised Constance Bennett to go on a milk diet. . .": *Seattle Daily News*, December 22, 1925, n.p.
**29.** "the real story behind the designer's sudden departure. . .": *Variety*, November 11, 1925, p. 93.
**29.** "Thalberg had been displeased enough. . .": *New York Times*, January 31, 1939, p. 21.
**30.** "Rapf's real coup, however, was signing Bennett Nathan. . .": *Los Angeles Telegraph*, July 26, 1925, n.p.
**30.** "Gilbert Clark walked off the lot. . .": *Modern Screen*, June, 1928, n.p.
**30.** "Andre-Ani had also had difficulty with Garbo. . .": *Motion Picture*, February, 1927, p. 110.
**30.** "You have to have the patience of Job. . .": *The Glamour Factory*, p. 207.
**31.** "David Cox, Andre-Ani, and Gilbert Clark were not really respected. . .": Robert Riley to author, October 25, 1996.
**31.** "MGM promised Adrian 'a certain amount of dignified publicity'. . . .": *MGM Employment File, Gilbert Adrian, Contract File 616 [42617–000]*.

## The Advent of Adrian at MGM

**33.** "looked like giant gaping mouths. . . .": Whitney Stine, *The Hurrell Style*, p. 11.
**34.** "Every costume should have one note. . .": *Ladies Home Journal*, February, 1933, p. 40.
**36.** "I knew, of course, what the old goat wanted. . . .": *Films in Review*, March, 1990, p. 155.
**38.** "'I remember he frowned,' she said. . . .": *Films in Review*, October, 1979, p. 475.
**38.** "Adrian saw the transformation in symbolic terms. . .": *Hollywood*, August 15, 1928, p. 17.
**38.** "The costume took nine seamstresses fifteen days to make. . .": *Photoplay*, October, 1928, p. 34.
**38.** "He presented me with a series of sketches. . .": Aileen Pringle to author, August 22, 1987.
**38.** "When we were working on a film together. . .": Anita Page to author, August 21, 1997.
**38.** "I have always liked wearing clothes up to my throat. . .": Sven Broman, *Conversations with Greta Garbo*, p. 25.
**40.** "There are not many Aileen Pringles. . . .": *Screenland*, May, 1929, p. 54.
**41.** "the studio chief had been fascinated with Erté. . . .": Charles Higham, *Merchant of Dreams*, p. 90.
**41.** "a look of 'austere simplicity'. . . .": Robert Riley, *American Fashion*, p. 41.
**41.** "Thalberg's 'gentle, dreamy' air. . . .": Peter Hay, *MGM: When the Lion Roars*, p. 42.
**41.** "he would sometimes assume a convincing Chinese accent. . . .": Leonard Gershe to author, May 16, 1996.
**41.** "One April Fool's Day. . . .": *American Fashion*, p. 42.

## A New Beginning

**43.** "Adrian finally decided on a neutral color scheme. . .": *Christian Science Monitor Magazine*, January 22, 1936, p. 14.
**44.** "Adrian's fitting room was 'nirvana'. . .": *Oral History Collection, Southern Methodist University, Dallas*.
**44.** "He was extremely well organized. . .": Robert Riley to author, October 25, 1996.
**44.** "Adrian once told me that the stars would get. . .": Leonard Gershe to author, August 1, 2000.
**44.** Caption: "It wasn't just floor after floor of clothes. . .": *Oral History Collection, Southern Methodist University, Dallas*.
**44.** "he hired good people who had training. . .": Robert Riley to author, October 26, 1996.
**44.** "A truck from Malone Studio Service. . .": Aljean Harmetz, *The Making of the Wizard of Oz*, p. 239.
**44.** "In the mid-1930s, the MGM cleaning bill came to. . .": *Good Housekeeping*, January, 1946, pp. 12–13.
**44.** "the racks in the studio's wardrobe department. . . .": *Good Housekeeping*, January, 1946, p. 13.
**44.** "Adrian was also instrumental in hiring. . .": Joseph Simms to author, September 13, 1996.
**44.** "They brought their lunch in brown bags. . .": Ronald Davis, *The Glamour Factory*, p. 216.
**45.** "At one table several middle-aged women. . . .": *Good Housekeeping*, January, 1946, p. 13.
**45.** "He lined about seven or eight of us up in a row. . .": Jane Gaines and Charlotte Herzog. eds., *Fabrications: Costume and the Female Body*, p. 166.
**46.** "Once Adrian received the costume script. . .": *Behind the Screen: How Films Are Made*, p. 55.
**47.** "Like Chanel, who worked directly on her mannequins. . .": Caroline Rennolds Milbank, *Couture*, p. 122.
**47.** "By the mid-1930s, there were eight cutters and fitters. . .": *Fabrications: Costume and the Female Body*, p. 166.
**47.** "Adrian instituted the practice of using dress dummies. . .": *Hedda Hopper Adrian Collection, Academy of Motion Picture Arts and Sciences*.
**47.** "I often felt pangs of inadequacy. . .": Paddy Calistro and Edith Head, *Edith Head's Hollywood*, p. 41.
**47.** "In 1931, actress Madge Evans was signed. . . .": *Talking Pictures*, p. 116.
**48.** "Designers in real life seldom worry about dramatic values. . . .": John Paddy Carstairs, *Movie Merry-Go-Round*, p. 83.
**48.** "I gave her moulded lines. . .": *Modern Screen*, July, 1934, p. 87.
**51.** "There is no question that Hollywood. . .": *Christian Science Monitor Magazine*, January 22, 1936, p. 9.
**51.** "Motion picture style designers cannot give the effect. . .": *Christian Science Monitor Magazine*, January 22, 1936, p. 9.
**54.** "The ostrich-feathered negligee. . .": *Los Angeles Herald Examiner*, March 8, 1934, n.p.
**54.** "I wore it in the scene in the library. . .": Katharine Hepburn to author, October 26, 1991.
**54.** "When Adrian showed me the sketch. . .": Katharine Hepburn to author, October 26, 1991.
**54.** "Adrian was my favorite designer. . . .": Program for the 1985 Council of Fashion Designers of America Awards/CFDA Lifetime Achievement Award to Katharine Hepburn. Interview conducted by Calvin Klein.

## The Spectacle Films

**57.** Caption: "Ten thousand yards of pleated chiffon. . . .": Souvenir Programme, *The Great Ziegfeld*, p. 3.
**57.** "He had no assistants—he designed for all players. . .": Margaret Bailey, *Those Glorious*

*Glamour Years*, p. 269.

**58.** "that left Ziegfeld himself 'green with envy'. . .": *New York Sun*, September 23, 1924, n.p.

**58.** "the classiest biopic ever to emerge from Hollywood. . .": Clive Hirschhorn, *Great Hollywood Musicals*, p. 118.

**58.** "This huge inflated gas-blown object. . .": Graham Greene, *The Graham Greene Film Reader*, p. 139.

**62.** "I remember the Munchkins all had long mustachios. . .": MGM Exhibitor Pressbook, *The Wizard of Oz*, p. 9.

**62.** "Adrian reported to Hedda Hopper. . .": *Ibid.*, p. 9.

**62.** "A full picture of Munchkinland. . .": *Ibid.*, p. 10.

**62.** "We came into the fitting room. . .": Margaret Pellegrini to author, November 19, 1999.

**63.** "Green shoes, green stockings, green dresses, green coats. . .": Aljean Harmetz, *The Making of The Wizard of Oz*, p. 236.

**64.** "He had modeled the wings after those of the South American condor. . .": MGM Exhibitor Pressbook, *The Wizard of Oz*, p. 9.

**64.** "None can be adopted in its entirety. . .": *Ibid.*, p. 10.

**64.** "I was anxious to see just how much material we could get. . .": *Los Angeles Herald-Examiner*, September 21, 1930, n.p.

**66.** "It is not a gown which will be generally copied. . .": *Ibid.*, n.p.

**67.** "Before motion pictures, the public never anticipated Paris. . .": MGM Exhibitor Pressbook, *Madam Satan*, p. 3.

## Greta Garbo

**71.** Caption: "Paris is still fashion dictator of the world on paper. . .": *New Movie*, March, 1933, p. 47.

**71.** Caption: "Garbo wears the unexpected. . .": *Ladies Home Journal*, June, 1932, p. 8.

**71.** Caption: "Gowns worn by Sembrich and Gadski. . .": *New York Evening Journal*, February 18, 1926, n.p.

**72.** "Miss Garbo, as it happens. . .": *New York Post*, February 23, 1926, n.p.

**72.** "great sensual tension. . .": Alexander Walker, *Garbo*, p. 42.

**73.** "'Dresses!' Garbo exclaimed in one of her rare. . .": *Detroit News*, October 26, 1931, n.p.

**73.** "She has foreign ideas about clothes. . .": *Ibid*, n.p.

**73.** "On *Flesh and the Devil* Garbo attempted. . .": Walker, p. 54.

**73.** "Everyone remembers Greta Garbo in *The Temptress*. . .": MGM Exhibitor Pressbook, *Flesh and the Devil*, p. 5.

**74.** "They could not use *The Green Hat*. . .": *New York Times*, January 27, 1929, p. 36.

**74.** "They feared she would lose all her allure if she came down to earth. . .": *Ladies Home Journal*, June, 1932, p. 8.

**74.** "her natural aloofness and the manner of her bearing. . .": *Screenland*, January, 1929, p. 27.

**75.** "She thus shielded her pure and private thoughts. . .": Alison Lurie, *The Language of Clothes*, p. 177.

**76.** "In fashion—as in everything else—.": MGM Exhibitor Pressbook, *Wild Orchids*, p. 5.

**76.** "The tall girl accentuates the great difference. . .": MGM Exhibitor Pressbook, *The Single Standard*, p. 5.

**77.** "Garbo can dress as she darn well pleases, and does. . .": *Photoplay*, January, 1930, n.p.

**77.** "Greta Garbo strolls around the lot [at MGM] in duck sailor trousers. . .": *New York Evening World*, July 24, 1930, n.p.

**78.** "Garbo is a mighty fortunate person. . .": *Variety*, February 11, 1931, n.p.

**78.** "As critic Andrew Sarris has observed. . .":

Andrew Sarris, *You Ain't Heard Nothin' Yet*, p. 378.

**79.** "How fitting that Garbo's first talkie. . .": *Ibid.*, p. 379.

**79.** "Until the arrival of talking pictures. . .": *Modern Screen*, July, 1931, n.p.

**79.** "The old gods go, and with them the young goddesses. . . .": *New York Times*, March 23, 1930. n.p.

**80.** "Imagine the alluring Miss Garbo. . .": *Ibid.*, n.p.

**80.** "Irving Thalberg was well aware that Garbo's sound debut. . .": Karen Swenson, *Greta Garbo: A Life Apart*, p. 232.

**80.** "A pert, audacious hat which Greta Garbo wore. . .": *Cinema Arts*, July, 1937, p. 66.

**81.** "The French designers can sell their models for huge prices. . .": *Los Angeles Times*, December 17, 1933, n.p.

**81.** "I want to create a style for Garbo. . .": *Ladies Home Journal*, June, 1932, p. 8.

**81.** "That hat was part of the plot. . .": Hedda Hopper, *From Under My Hat*, p. 212.

**83.** "The noted Adrian once more scores another style scoop. . .": MGM Exhibitor Pressbook, *The Painted Veil*, p. 5.

**83.** "Beware of overdoing the Chinese fashion influence. . .": *Ibid.*, p. 5.

**84.** "Adrian's costumes for the film were considered 'so—well—distinctive'. . .": *Omaha News*, December 23, 1934, n.p.

**84.** "(Garbo) must never create situations. . .": Bob Thomas, *Thalberg: Life and Legend*, p. 291.

**87.** "The costuming in *Queen Christina* presented numerous problems. . .": MGM Exhibitor Pressbook, *Queen Christina*, p. 5.

**87.** "By modification of Sweden's exorbitant styles. . .": *Ibid.*, p. 5.

**87.** "(Director Rouben) Mamoulian kept impressing on me. . .": *Modern Screen*, March, 1934, n.p.

**90.** "Kitty had been seeing Anna every day. . . .": Leo Tolstoy, *Anna Karenina*, p. 83.

**91.** "At first we had difficulty in finding data about the demi-mondaine of the period. . . .": *Vogue*, November 15, 1936, p. 70.

**91.** "Adrian's glamorous costumes for Garbo follow the period but are dramatized. . .": MGM Exhibitor Pressbook, *Camille*, p. 5.

**94.** "We're getting sick and tired of hearing, 'of course, Garbo can get away with it.'. . .": *New York World Telegram*, October 21, 1938, n.p.

**96.** "boyish yet exquisitely feminine, which follows the basque line. . .": MGM Exhibitor Pressbook, *Queen Christina*, p. 11.

**96.** "I have in mind presenting him on radio. . .": *MGM Employment File, Gilbert Adrian, Contract File 616 [42617-000]*.

**98.** "*Ninotchka* did the last thing left to do to the Garbo myth. . .": Walker, p. 155.

**98.** "It's a little bit of a hat—a crazy little hat. . .": MGM Exhibitor Pressbook, *Ninotchka*, p. 7.

**101.** "One gown, which she wanted to wear but the Hays office banned, is so beautiful. . .": Swenson, p. 411.

**101.** "It's like seeing Sarah Bernhardt swatted with a bladder. . .": *Time*, December 22, 1941, n.p.

**101.** "I'm very sorry that you're leaving. . ." Barry Paris, *Garbo*, p. 381.

## Joan Crawford

**103.** Caption: "From Boston to Budapest to Bali. . .": *Motion Picture*, May, 1937, p. 30.

**103.** "Who would have thought. . . .": *Time*, July 1, 1940, n.p.

**104.** "Something new has entered the world of clothes. . . .": *New York Evening Journal*, September 30, 1928, n.p.

**104.** "'The Crawford Romp,' a new dance craze.

. . .": *Dallas News*, September 21, 1928, n.p.

**105.** "None of us was starred in the picture. . . .": Joan Crawford, *A Portrait of Joan*, p. 63.

**105.** "the first [film] that gave the wardrobe department. . . .": Roy Newquist, *Conversations with Joan Crawford*, p. 70.

**108.** "The editors were also able to give readers. . . ." *Vogue*, January, 1930, p. 123.

**108.** "Beginning with this season, the swing toward originality. . . ." Metro-Goldwyn-Mayer pressbook, *Our Blushing Brides*, p. 5.

**108.** "One of the latest modes that continued to sweep Seventh Avenue. . . .": Caroline Rennolds Milbank, *New York Fashion: The Evolution of American Style*, p. 102.

**109.** "The idea of false economy is past. . . .": Metro-Goldwyn-Mayer pressbook, *Our Blushing Brides*, p. 5.

**109.** "Economic depression has historically encouraged mass-produced fashion. . . .": Michael Harrington, *The Other America*, p. 5.

**111.** "He urged women to be 'terribly careful'. . . .": *Ladies Home Journal*, January, 1932, p. 43.

**112.** "Can it be that better taste has appeared in California. . . .": *Vogue*, June 15, 1931, p. 35.

**112.** "The right dress makes life an adventure. . . .": Mark Bego, ed., *The Best of Modern Screen*, p. 86.

**112.** "Joan is an example of the sophisticated, medium conservative. . . .": *Ibid.*, pp. 86–87.

**114.** "The archetypal MGM picture during Thalberg's regime. . . .": Thomas Schatz, *The Genius of the System*, p. 119.

**114.** "MGM's and perhaps all Hollywood's. . . .": Ethan Mordden, *The Hollywood Studios*, p. 105.

**116.** "Our interest is carried beyond the usual limits. . . .": *Photoplay*, April, 1932, p. 12.

**116.** "A *Grand Hotel* roadshow engagement might have played. . . .": Metro-Goldwyn-Mayer pressbook, *Letty Lynton*, p. 6.

**117.** "The quixotic American designer Charles James. . . .": *The New Yorker*, September 21, 1998, p. 99.

**117.** "Do you like Marion's costume?. . . .": *New York American*, June 11, 1930, n.p.

**118.** "Around the same time, *Vogue* gave its blessing. . . .": *Vogue*, September 15, 1931, p. 140.

**118.** "Joan Crawford's organdie dress in *Letty Lynton*. . . .": *Ladies Home Journal*, February, 1933, p. 11.

**118.** "There is a definite evolution of styles. . . .": *Christian Science Monitor Magazine*, January 22, 1936, p. 9.

**119.** "I became conscious of the terrific power of the movies. . . .": *Harper's Bazaar*, February, 1934, pp. 135-136.

**120.** "Besides her other assets, Miss Crawford has. . . .": *Screenland*, July, 1932, p. 10.

**120.** "Adrian always played down the designs for the big scene. . .": Diana Vreeland with Dale McConathy, *Hollywood Costume: Glamour! Glitter! Romance!*, p. 103.

**121.** "Unpredictable in her playing. . . .": Alexander Walker, *Joan Crawford: The Ultimate Star*, p. 92.

**121.** "MGM refused to loan him to UA. . . .": David Chierichetti to author, June 1, 1997.

**121.** "She is a woman here with power over men. . . . :" *Joan Crawford: The Ultimate Star*, p. 92.

**122.** "Returning stateside in August of 1932. . . .": *New York Sun*, August 21, 1932, p. 23.

**122.** "She rips more sleeves than anyone else I know. . . .": *Los Angeles Herald Examiner*, July 25, 1935, n.p.

**124.** "There is no doubt about it. . . .": *Chicago Herald and Examiner*, February 27, 1933, p. 46.

**124.** "We expect to show residents of Chicago. . . .": *Los Angeles Herald Examiner*,

February 21, 1933, n.p.

129. "The largest single day's business in fourteen months. . . .:" *New York American*, December 2, 1933, n.p.

129. Caption: "One main criticism is made by those who do criticize cinema clothes. . . .:" *Vogue*, February 1, 1933.

129. "What is coming? I feel that we are tired. . .:" *Harper's Bazaar*, February, 1934, p. 135.

130. "He was a loner, not a friendly sort of person. . . .:" Aljean Harmetz, *The Making of the Wizard of Oz*, p. 238.

131. "In 1933 he told reporter Jean Stevens. . . .:" *Screenland*, February, 1935, p. 22.

134. "It's just a new idea for a summer wrap. . . .:" Metro-Goldwyn-Mayer pressbook, *I Live My Life*, p. 5.

136. "In motion pictures there are scores of smart gowns. . . .:" *Christian Science Monitor Magazine*, January 22, 1936, p. 15.

136. "That's not a hat,. . . .:" *New York Times Magazine*, January 15, 1995, p. 42.

137. "*No More Ladies*, despite its stage ancestry. . . .:" *New York Times*, June 22, 1935, p. 18.

140. "The dress becomes the character's means of revenge. . . .:" Costume Clipping File, New York Public Library for the Performing Arts, n.p.

142. "a sense of recklessness in her search for a part. . . .:" *Joan Crawford: The Ultimate Star*, p. 127.

143. "Are you crazy? Do you want the public to see you. . . .:" Bob Thomas, *Joan Crawford*, p. 134.

143. "Critics proclaimed that Joan Crawford. . . .:" *Ibid.*, p. 134.

143. "The role of Mildred was a delight to me. . . .:" *Conversations with Joan Crawford*, p. 95.

143. "The only other thing I can say about the picture. . . .:" *Ibid.*, p. 95.

## Shearer Chic

145. Caption: "The more that one tries to isolate the qualities. . .:" James Card, *Seductive Cinema: The Art of Silent Film*, pp. 174–175.

145. "Clothes are a woman's first duty to herself. .:" *London Daily Mail*, July 7, 1931, n.p.

146. "Wise selection of clothes will deftly conceal any defect. . .:" MGM Exhibitor Pressbook, *The Actress*, p. 3

146. "She must have a good figure, or be wise enough. . .:" MGM Exhibitor Pressbook, *After Midnight*, p. 3.

146. "in the wrong costume Shearer's figure. . .:" Lambert, p. 45.

146. "It never pays for a woman to discard her femininity. . .:" MGM Exhibitor Pressbook, *The Latest from Paris*, p. 1.

147. "The question that puzzles all feminine shoppers. . .:" MGM Exhibitor Pressbook, *A Lady of Chance*, p. 3.

147. "Norma Shearer is an Ideal Example. . .:" *Screenland*, February, 1929, p. 45.

147. "choose clothes that have grace rather than pep. . .:" *Ibid.*, p. 46.

147. "charm rather than an exotic quality. . .:" *Ibid.*, p. 46.

148. "a woman of the world, waiting for an invitation. . .:" Lambert, p. 132.

149. "on the crest of a new and powerful sexual wave. . .:" Lambert, p. 133.

149. "the typical conservative young woman. . .:" *Los Angeles Times*, August 28, 1932, n.p.

151. "Shearer's clothes are breathtaking in their daring. . .:" *Photoplay*, August, 1931, p. 42.

153. Caption: "There is no other personality on the screen today quite like Norma Shearer. . .:" MGM Exhibitor Pressbook, *Riptide*, p. 3.

153. "nobody cared any more about a beautiful. . .:" Lambert, p. 199.

153. "Style design is such a fragile thing. . .:"

153. "Adrian's designs for Norma Shearer in *Riptide*. . .:" *Ibid.*, n.p.

153. "If we can get retailers to back us on this. . .:" *Ibid.*, n.p.

154. "In Paris, they start styles by having fifty or sixty . . .:" *Ibid.*, n.p.

154. "Adrian of Metro is more mysterious than the Parisian salons. . .:" *Movie Mirror*, April, 1934, p. 48.

156. "Cukor wanted a fresh outlook on Hollywood. . .:" Charles Castle, *Oliver Messel: A Biography*, p. 101.

156. "Don't think that I'm just the MGM workhorse. . .:" Riley, p. 34.

156. "We all worked in peace and harmony. . .:" Castle, p. 102.

156. "they were both slightly embarrassed. . .:" *Louisville Kentucky Times*, July 16, 1936, n.p.

157. "Even the smallest, most insignificant item. . .:" MGM Exhibitor Pressbook, *Romeo and Juliet*, p. 8.

157. "The period is most interesting from a costume standpoint. . .:" *St. Louis Globe Democrat*, March 30, 1936, n.p.

160. Caption: "What could be more perfect than the costumes Adrian designed for *Marie Antoinette*. . . .:" Diana Vreeland, *Hollywood Costume: Glamour! Glitter! Romance!*, p. 22.

160. "Dear Toinette, you know that I have always held. . . .:" *Pictorial Review*, September, 1938, p. 21.

160. "Maria Theresa preached the same theory. . .:" *MGM Studio News*, August 8, 1938, p. 12.

164. "We have followed the gowns in Mme. Lebrun's paintings to the letter. . .:" MGM Exhibitor Pressbook, *Marie Antoinette*, p. 5.

170. "the great saint of royalism. . .:" Lambert, p. 268.

172. "Norma Shearer has a perfect passion for details. . .:" *Hedda Hopper Adrian Collection, Academy of Motion Picture Arts and Sciences*.

173. "[She] has the patience of Job in this. . .:" *Modern Screen*, July, 1934, p. 87.

173. "the right dress can triumph over any situation. . .:" *New Movie*, June, 1932, p. 35.

## Putting It All Together

175. Caption: "With 135 Women to Gown, Adrian had Field Day. . .:" MGM Exhibitor Pressbook, *The Women*, p. 5.

176. "The role is that of an outright bitch. . . .:" Alexander Walker, *Joan Crawford: The Ultimate Star*, p. 127.

176. "As a way around the censors, screenwriters Anita Loos and Jane Murfin. . .:" MGM Exhibitor Pressbook, *The Women*, p. 7.

176. "The fashion show, bursting forth in vivid colors. . . .:" *New York Herald Tribune*, October 7, 1939, p. 21.

176. "There is really no reason for the inserted fashion show. . . .:" *New York Daily News*, September 22, 1939, p. 19.

176. "Some of the new sequences are so good. . .:" *New York Times*, September 21, n.p.

178. "This vaguely belly-dancerish costume. . . .:" *New York Times Magazine*, December 1, 1974, p. 70.

178. "When Louis B. Mayer saw Crawford wearing the dress. . . .:" MGM Script Collection, *The Women*, Center for Motion Picture Study, Academy of Motion Picture Arts and Sciences.

178. "at first he refused to change the dress. . . .:" *Ibid.*

178. "Must stay home today on account of severe cold. . . .:" *MGM Production File 1091, The Women*.

182. "You will note that in some of the

stills. . . .:" Metro-Goldwyn-Mayer pressbook, *The Women*, p. 5.

184. "Mary suffers by contrast. . . .:" *New York Eagle*, September 21, 1939, n.p.

185. "The cinema's leading wearer of clothes. . . .:" *New York Daily News*, October 21, 1938, p. 24.

185. "Regarding the production as a whole. . . .:" *Hollywood Reporter*, September 15, 1939, p. 11.

185. "At the end of one sequence. . . .:" Metro-Goldwyn-Mayer pressbook, *The Women*, p. 5.

185. "when the two meet, farmers for miles around. . .:" *Look*, March 28, 1939, p. 36.

185. "and with it would come the Twilight of the Goddesses. . . .:" Mark Vieira, *Hollywood Portraits*, p. 184.

## An End of an Era

187. Caption: "The prologue . . . sums up the way the marriage. . . .:" Gavin Lambert, *On Cukor*, p. 126.

188. "echoed the popular rejection of 'Katharine Hepburn. . .'": Foster Hirsch, *Acting Hollywood Style*, p. 225.

190. "When France declared an armistice with Germany. . .:" MGM Exhibitor Pressbook, *The Philadelphia Story*, p. 16.

191. "The functions of the two dynamic fashion capitals. . .:" *The New York Times Magazine*, August 18, 1940, p. 12.

191. "Quite casually, Adrian held up the beaded party dress. . .:" Joseph Simms to author, January 6, 1989.

191. "In 1933, the Morris Nagel Company in New York. . .:" *MGM Employment File, Gilbert Adrian, Contract File 616 [42617–000]*.

192. "The obvious purpose of this firm is to lead the public. . .:" *MGM Employment File, Gilbert Adrian, Contract File 616 [42617-000]*.

192. "To furnish Weil with the dresses and a pattern of each said dress. . .:" *MGM Employment File, Gilbert Adrian, Contract File 616 [42617–000]*.

192. "While his use of the best materials is somewhat expensive. . .:" *MGM Employment File, Gilbert Adrian, Contract File 616 [42617–000]*.

192. "We have always been concerned as to the risk of impairing. . .:" *MGM Employment File, Gilbert Adrian, Contract File 616 [42617–000]*.

193. "Adrian informed studio manager M. E. Greenwood. . .:" *MGM Employment File, Gilbert Adrian, Contract File 616 [42617–000]*.

193. "The New Garbo Hat Will Be One of the Most Talked About Things. . .:" MGM Exhibitor Pressbook, *Ninotchka*, p. 9.

194. "the studio thinks nothing of cutting up those beautiful things. . .:" *Hedda Hopper Adrian Collection, Library of the Academy of Motion Picture Arts and Sciences*

194. "My father once told me. . .:" Robin Adrian to author, February 11, 2000.

194. "Fall, winter and spring are the seasons for raincoats. . .:" MGM Exhibitor Pressbook, *Keeper of the Flame*, p. 14.

194. "The contract provides we may extend term for period. . .:" *MGM Employment File, Gilbert Adrian, Contract File 616 [42617–000]*.

194. "My mother always told me. . .:" Robin Adrian to author, February 11, 2000.

195. "No one can forget Adrian's romantic period clothes. . .:" *Women's Wear Daily*, September 15, 1959, p. 5.

195. "he created a type of clothes so individual. . .:" *Ibid.*, p. 5.

195. "was the one who really started the couture here. . .:" *Ibid.*, p. 5.

195. "one of the greatest influences in design. . .:" *Ibid.*, p. 5.

# Bibliography

## BOOKS

Bailey, Margaret. *Those Glorious Glamour Years*. Secaucus, N.J.: Citadel Press, 1982.

Baral, Robert. *Revue: A Nostalgic Reprise of the Great Broadway Period*. New York: Fleet Publishing, 1962.

Barthes, Roland. *Erté*. Translated by William Weaver. Parma, Italy: Franco Maria Ricci, 1972.

Bego, Mark, ed. *The Best of Modern Screen*. New York: Arbor House, 1981.

Bordwell, David. *The Classical Hollywood Cinema: Film Style and Mode of Production to 1960*. New York: Columbia University Press, 1960.

Broman, Sven. *Conversations with Greta Garbo*. New York: Viking Press, 1991.

Calistro, Paddy, and Head, Edith. *Edith Head's Hollywood*. New York: E. P. Dutton, 1983.

Carstairs, John Paddy. *Behind the Screen: How Films Are Made*. London: Barker Publishing, 1938.

————. *Movie Merry-Go-Round*. London: Newnes Publishing, 1937.

Carter, Ernestine. *20th Century Fashion: A Scrapbook—1900 to Today*. London: Eyre Methuen, 1975.

Carter, Randolph. *The World of Flo Ziegfeld*. New York: Praeger, 1974.

Castle, Charles. *Oliver Messel: A Biography*. London: Thames and Hudson, 1986.

Chierichetti, David. *Hollywood Costume Design*. New York: Harmony Books, 1976.

Christian, Margaret, and Kidwell, Claudia. *Suiting Everyone: The Democratization of Clothing in America*. Washington, D.C.: The Smithsonian Institution Press, 1974.

Cooper, Miriam. *Dark Lady of the Silents: My Life in Early Hollywood*. New York: Bobbs-Merrill, 1973.

Costantino, Maria. *Fashions of a Decade: The 1930s*. New York: Facts On File, 1992.

Cox, Stephen. *The Munchkins of Oz*. Nashville, Tenn.: Cumberland House, 1996.

Crawford, Joan. *A Portrait of Joan: The Autobiography of Joan Crawford*. New York: Doubleday, 1962.

Crawford, M.D.C. *The Ways of Fashion*. New York: Fairchild Publications, 1948.

Crump, Irving. *Our Movie Makers*. New York: Dodd, Mead and Sons, 1940.

Daum, Raymond. *Walking with Garbo*. New York: HarperPerennial, 1991.

Daves, Jessica. *Ready-Made Miracle: The American Story of Fashion for the Millions*. New York: Putnam's, 1967.

Davies, Dentner. *Jean Harlow: Hollywood Comet*. London: Constable, 1937.

Davis, Ronald. *The Glamour Factory: Inside Hollywood's Big Studio System*. Dallas: Southern Methodist University Press, 1993.

Debrix, J. R. and Stephenson, Ralph. *The Cinema as Art*. Baltimore: Penguin Books, 1965.

DeMille, Cecil B. *The Autobiography of Cecil B. DeMille*. Englewood Cliffs, N. J.: Prentice-Hall, 1959.

Erté. *Things I Remember: An Autobiography*. New York: Quadrangle Books, 1974.

Etherington-Smith, Meredith. *Patou*. New York: St. Martin's Press, 1983.

Field, Alice Evans. *Hollywood USA: From Script to Screen*. New York: Vantage Press, 1952.

Floherty, John. *Moviemakers*. New York: Doubleday, 1935.

Forslund, Bengt. *Victor Sjöström: His Life and Work*. New York: Zoetrope, 1988.

Gaines, Jane and Herzog, Charlotte. *Fabrications: Costume and the Female Body*. New York: Routledge, 1990.

Gish, Lillian, with Ann Pinchet. *The Movies, Mr. Griffith, and Me*. Englewood Cliffs, N.J.: Prentice-Hall, 1968.

Glynn, Prudence. *In Fashion: Dress in the Twentieth Century*. New York: Oxford University Press, 1978.

Greene, Graham. *The Graham Greene Film Reader*. New York: Applause Books, 1995.

Greer, Howard. *Designing Male*. New York: Putnam's, 1949.

Harmetz, Aljean. *The Making of The Wizard of Oz*. New York: Alfred A. Knopf, 1977.

Harrington, Michael. *The Other America*. New York: MacMillan, 1962.

Hawes, Elizabeth. *Fashion is Spinach*. New York: Random House, 1938.

Hay, Peter, ed. *MGM: When the Lion Roars*. Atlanta: Turner Publishing, 1991.

Haye, Amy, and Tobin, Shelley. *Chanel: The Couturiere at Work*. Woodstock, N.Y.: The Overlook Press, 1996.

Heisner, Beverly. *Hollywood Art: Art Direction in the Days of the Great Studios*. Jefferson, N.C.: McFarland, 1990.

Herzberg, Max. *Romeo and Juliet: A Motion Picture Edition*. New York: Random House, 1936.

Higham, Charles. *Merchant of Dreams*. New York: Donald Fine Publishing, 1993.

Higham, Charles. *Ziegfeld*. Chicago: Henry Regnery Company, 1972.

Hirsch, Foster. *Acting Hollywood Style*. New York: Harry N. Abrams/AFI Press, 1991.

Hirschhorn, Clive. *Great Hollywood Musicals*. New York: Crown Publishers, 1981.

Hoadley, Ray. *How They Make a Motion Picture*. New York: Crowell, 1939.

Hopper, Hedda. *From Under My Hat*. New York: Doubleday, 1952.

Keisling, Barrett. *Talking Pictures*. Richmond, Va: Johnson Publishing, 1937.

Kinden, Gorham. *The American Movie Industry: The Business of Motion Pictures*. Carbondale: Southern Illinois University Press, 1982.

Klumph, Helen and Inez. *Screen Acting: Its Requirements and Rewards*. New York: Falk, 1922.

Lambert, Gavin. *Norma Shearer: A Life*. New York: Alfred A. Knopf, 1990.

LeRoy, Mervyn. *It Takes More than Talent*. New York: Alfred A. Knopf, 1953.

Ley, Sandra. *Fashion for Everyone: The Story of Ready-to-Wear*. New York: Scribners, 1975.

Loos, Anita. *Kiss Hollywood Goodby*. New York: Viking Press, 1974.

Loy, Myrna, with James Kotsilibas-Davis. *Myrna Loy: Being and Becoming*. New York: Alfred A. Knopf, 1987.

Lurie, Alison. *The Language of Clothes*. New York: Random House, 1981.

Martin, Richard, ed. *The St. James Fashion Encyclopedia*. Detroit: Visible Ink Press, 1997.

Marx, Samuel. *Mayer and Thalberg: The Make-Believe Saints*. New York: Random House, 1975.

McCarthy, Todd. *Howard Hawks*. New York: Grove Press, 1997.

McClelland, Doug. *Down the Yellow Brick Road: The Making of The Wizard of Oz*. New York: Pyramid Books, 1976.

McConathy, Dale and Vreeland, Diana. *Hollywood Costume: Glamour! Glitter! Romance!* New York: Harry N. Abrams, 1976.

Millbank, Caroline Rennolds. *New York Fashion: The Evolution of American Style*. New York: Harry N. Abrams, 1989.

————. *Couture*. New York: Stewart, Tabori & Chang, 1985.

Mordden, Ethan. *The Hollywood Studios*. New York: Alfred A. Knopf, 1988.

Morris, Mark. *Madam Valentino*. New York: Abbeville Press, 1991.

Newquist, Roy. *Conversations with Joan Crawford*. Secaucus, N.J.: Citadel Press, 1980.

Paris, Barry. *Garbo*. New York: Alfred A. Knopf, 1995.

Prichard, Susan Perez. *Film Costume: An Annotated Bibliography*. Metuchen, N.J.: Scarecrow Press, 1981.

Riley, Robert, ed. *American Fashion*. New York: Quadrangle Press, 1975.

Robinson, David. *Chaplin: His Life and Art*. New York: McGraw-Hill, 1985.

Ross, Clark. *Stars and Strikes: The Unionization of Hollywood*. New York: Columbia University Press, 1941.

Sarris, Andrew. *You Ain't Heard Nothin' Yet*. New York: Oxford University Press, 1998.

Schatz, Thomas. *The Genius of the System*. New York: Pantheon, 1988.

Schiaparelli, Elsa. *Shocking Life*. New York: Dutton, 1954.

Schumach, Murray. *The Face on the Cutting Room Floor: The Story of Movie and Television Censorship*. New York: Morrow, 1964.

Spencer, Charles. *Erté*. New York: Clarkson N. Potter, 1970.

Stine, Whitney. *The Hurrell Style*. New York: The John Day Company, 1976.

Swenson, Karen. *Greta Garbo: A Life Apart*. New York: Scribner's, 1997.

Thomas, Bob. *Joan Crawford*. New York: Simon and Schuster, 1978.

Thorp, Margaret Farrand. *America at the Movies*. New Haven, Conn.: Yale University Press, 1939.

Verdone, Mario. *La Moda e il Costume nel Film*. Rome: Bianco e Nero, 1952.

Vieira, Mark. *Hollywood Portraits*. Greenwich, Conn.: Portland House, 1988.

Walker, Alexander. *Joan Crawford: The Ultimate Star*. New York: Harper and Row, 1983.

Watts, Stephen. *Behind the Screen: How Films Are Made*. London: Barker, 1938.

White, Palmer. *Schiaparelli: Empress of Paris Fashion*. London: Aurum Press, 1995.

Wilcox, Ruth Turner. *The Mode in Hats and Headdress*. New York: Scribner's, 1946.

Williams, Beryl Epstein. *Fashion is Our Business*. Philadelphia: Lippincott, 1945.

Zierold, Norman. *Sex Goddesses of the Silent Screen*. Chicago: Regnery, 1973.

## NEWSPAPERS AND PERIODICALS

*American Film, American Magazine, Chicago Herald and Examiner, Christian Science Monitor Magazine, Cinema Arts, Collier's, Dallas News, Film Daily, Films in Review, Fortune, Good Housekeeping, Harper's Bazaar, Hollywood, Hollywood Reporter, Ladies' Home Journal, Los Angeles Daily News, Los Angeles Herald Examiner, Los Angeles Sunday News, Los Angeles Telegraph, Los Angeles Times, Louisville Kentucky Times, Metro-Goldwyn-Mayer exhibitor pressbooks, MGM Studio News, Modern Screen, Motion Picture, Moving Picture, Nation's Business, New Movie, New York American, New York Daily News, New York Eagle, New York Evening Journal, New York Morning Telegraph, New York Review, New York Sun, New York Times, New York Times Magazine, The New Yorker, Omaha News, Photoplay, Quarterly Review of Film and Video, St. Louis Globe Democrat, Screenland, Seattle Daily News, Silver Screen, Time, Variety, The Velvet Light Trap, Vogue, Wide Angle, Women's Culture.*

## INTERVIEWS

Robin Adrian, Kevin Brownlow, David Chierichetti, Tony Duquette, Joan Fontaine, Leonard Gershe, Katharine Hepburn, Hedy Lamarr, Myrna Loy, Roddy McDowall, Maureen O'Sullivan, Anita Page, Margaret Pellegrini, Aileen Pringle, Robert Riley, Joseph Simms, Loretta Young.

# Gilbert Adrian Filmography

**1925:** *Her Sister from Paris* (Joseph M. Schenck Prod., Sidney Franklin), Constance Talmadge, Ronald Colman; *The Eagle* (Art Finance Corp., Clarence Brown), Rudolph Valentino, Vilma Banky; *Cobra* (Ritz-Carlton Prod., Joseph Henabery), Rudolph Valentino, Nita Naldi. **1926:** *The Volga Boatman* (DeMille Studios, Cecil B. DeMille), William Boyd, Elinor Fair; *Fig Leaves* (Fox, Howard Hawks), George O'Brien, Phyllis Haver; *For Alimony Only* (DeMille Studios, William C. DeMille), Leatrice Joy, Lilyan Tashman; *Young April* (DeMille Studios, Donald Crisp), Joseph Schildkraut, Bessie Love; *Gigolo* (DeMille Studios, William K. Howard), Rod La Rocque, Louise Dresser. **1927:** *The Little Adventuress* (DeMille Studios, William C. DeMille), Vera Reynolds; *Vanity* (DeMille Studios, Donald Crisp), Leatrice Joy; *His Dog* (DeMille Studios, Karl Brown), Joseph Schildkraut, Julia Faye; *The Country Doctor* (DeMille Studios, Rupert Julian), Rudolph Schildkraut, Virginia Bradford; *The Fighting Eagle* (DeMille Studios, Donald Crisp), Rod LaRocque, Phyllis Haver; *The Angel of Broadway* (DeMille Studios, Lois Weber), Leatrice Joy; *The Wise Wife* (DeMille Studios, E. Mason Hopper), Phyllis Haver; *Dress Parade* (DeMille Studios, Donald Crisp), Bessie Love; *The Forbidden Woman* (DeMille Studios, Paul Stein), Jetta Goudal; *The Wreck of the Hesperus* (DeMille Studios, Elmer Clifton), Virginia Bradford; *The Main Event* (DeMille Studios, William K. Howard), Vera Reynolds; *My Friend from India* (DeMille Studios, E. Mason Hopper), Elinor Fair; *Chicago* (DeMille Studios, Frank Urson), Phyllis Haver; *Almost Human* (DeMille Studios, Frank Urson), Vera Reynolds. **1928:** *A Ship Comes In* (DeMille Studios, William K. Howard), Joseph Schildkraut, Louise Dresser; *Let 'Er Go, Gallegher* (DeMille Studios, Elmer Clifton), Elinor Fair; *What Price Beauty?* (UA, Tom Buckingham), Nita Naldi; *Stand and Deliver* (DeMille Studios, Donald Crisp), Rod LaRocque, Lupe Velez; *The Blue Danube* (DeMille Studios, Paul Sloane), Leatrice Joy, May Robson; *Midnight Madness* (DeMille Studios, F. Harmon Weight), Jacqueline Logan; *Skyscraper* (DeMille Studios, Howard Higgin), Sue Carol; *Walking Back* (DeMille Studios, Rupert Julian), Sue Carol; *The Masks of the Devil* (MGM, Victor Sjöström), John Gilbert, Eva Von Berne; *Dream of Love* (MGM, Fred Niblo), Joan Crawford, Aileen Pringle; *A Lady of Chance* (MGM, Robert Z. Leonard), Norma Shearer, Johnny Mack Brown; *A Woman of Affairs* (MGM, Clarence Brown), Greta Garbo, John Gilbert. **1929:** *A Single Man* (MGM, Harry Beaumont), Lew Cody, Aileen Pringle; *Wild Orchids* (MGM, Sidney Franklin), Greta Garbo, Nils Asther; *The Bridge of San Luis Rey* (MGM, Charles Brabin), Lili Damita; *The Godless Girl* (DeMille Studios, Cecil B. DeMille), Lina Basquette; *The Trial of Mary Dugan* (MGM, Bayard Veiller), Norma Shearer; *The Last of Mrs. Cheyney* (MGM, Sidney Franklin), Norma Shearer, Basil Rathbone; *The Single Standard* (MGM, John S. Robertson), Greta Garbo, Nils Asther; *Our Modern Maidens* (MGM, Jack Conway), Joan Crawford, Douglas Fairbanks, Jr.; *The Unholy Night* (MGM, Lionel Barrymore), Dorothy Sebastian; *The Thirteenth Chair* (MGM, Tod Browning), Conrad Nagel, Leila Hyams; *The Kiss* (MGM, Jacques Feyder), Greta Garbo, Lew Ayres; *Untamed* (MGM, Jack Conway), Joan Crawford, Robert Montgomery; *Dynamite* (MGM, Cecil B. DeMille), Kay Johnson; *Their Own Desire* (MGM, E. Mason Hopper), Norma Shearer, Robert Montgomery; *Devil May Care* (MGM, Sidney Franklin), Ramon Novarro, Dorothy Jordan; *Marianne* (MGM, Robert Z. Leonard), Marion Davies. **1930:** *Not So Dumb* (MGM, King Vidor), Marion Davies; *Anna Christie* (MGM, Clarence Brown), Greta Garbo, Charles Bickford; *A Lady to Love* (MGM, Victor Sjöström), Vilma Banky; *Montana Moon* (MGM, Malcolm St. Clair), Joan Crawford, Johnny Mack Brown; *This Mad World* (MGM, William C. DeMille), Kay Johnson; *The Divorcee* (MGM, Robert Z. Leonard), Norma Shearer, Chester Morris; *Redemption* (MGM, Fred Niblo), John Gilbert, Renée Adorée; *The Rogue Song* (MGM, Lionel Barrymore), Lawrence Tibbett, Catherine Dale Owen; *In Gay Madrid* (MGM, Robert Z. Leonard), Ramon Novarro, Dorothy Jordan; *The Lady of Scandal* (MGM, Sidney Franklin), Ruth Chatterton, Basil Rathbone; *The Floradora Girl* (MGM, Harry Beaumont), Marion Davies; *Our Blushing Brides* (MGM, Harry Beaumont), Joan Crawford, Robert Montgomery; *Let Us Be Gay* (MGM, Robert Z. Leonard), Norma Shearer, Marie Dressler; *Romance* (MGM, Clarence Brown), Greta Garbo, Gavin Gordon; *Madam Satan* (MGM, Cecil B.DeMille), Kay Johnson, Lillian Roth; *A Lady's Morals* (MGM, Sidney Franklin), Grace Moore; *Paid* (MGM, Sam Wood), Joan Crawford; *Passion Flower* (MGM, William C. DeMille), Kay Francis, Charles Bickford; *New Moon* (MGM, Jack Conway), Grace Moore; *Anna Christie* (MGM, Jacques Feyder), Greta Garbo, Salka Viertel. **1931:** *The Bachelor Father* (MGM, Robert Z. Leonard), Marion Davies; *Dance, Fools, Dance* (MGM, Harry Beaumont), Joan Crawford, Clark Gable; *Strangers May Kiss* (MGM, George Fitzmaurice), Norma Shearer, Robert Montgomery; *Laughing Sinners* (MGM, Harry Beaumont), Joan Crawford, Clark Gable; *A Free Soul* (MGM, Clarence Brown), Norma Shearer, Lionel Barrymore, Clark Gable; *The Guardsman* (MGM, Sidney Franklin), Lynn Fontanne, Alfred Lunt; *Son of India* (MGM, Jacques Feyder), Ramon Novarro, Madge Evans; *Daddy Longlegs* (Fox, Alfred Santell), Janet Gaynor; *Five and Ten* (MGM, Robert Z. Leonard), Marion Davies, Leslie Howard; *This Modern Age* (MGM, Nicholas Grinde), Joan Crawford; *Susan Lenox: Her Fall and Rise* (MGM, Robert Z. Leonard), Greta Garbo, Clark Gable; *Possessed* (MGM, Clarence Brown), Joan Crawford, Clark Gable; *Private Lives* (MGM, Sidney Franklin), Norma Shearer, Robert Montgomery; *Mata Hari* (MGM, George Fitzmaurice), Greta Garbo, Ramon Novarro. **1932:** *Emma* (MGM, Clarence Brown), Marie Dressler; *Polly of the Circus* (MGM, Alfred Santell), Marion Davies, Clark Gable; *Arsène Lupin* (MGM, Jack Conway), John and Lionel Barrymore, Dorothy Jordan; *The Wet Parade* (MGM, Victor Fleming), Dorothy Jordan, Myrna Loy; *But the Flesh is Weak* (MGM, Jack Conway), Robert Montgomery, Nora Gregor; *Grand Hotel* (MGM, Edmund Goulding), Greta Garbo, Joan Crawford, John and Lionel Barrymore; *Letty Lynton* (MGM, Clarence Brown), Joan Crawford, Robert Montgomery; *As You Desire Me* (MGM, George Fitzmaurice), Greta Garbo, Melvyn Douglas; *Red-Headed Woman* (MGM, Jack Conway), Jean Harlow, Chester Morris; *Unashamed* (MGM, Harry Beaumont), Helen Twelvetrees; *Blondie of the Follies* (MGM, Edmund Goulding), Marion Davies, Robert Montgomery; *Smilin' Through* (MGM, Sidney Franklin), Norma Shearer, Fredric March, Leslie Howard; *Faithless* (MGM, Harry Beaumont), Tallulah Bankhead, Robert Montgomery; *Red Dust* (MGM, Victor Fleming), Clark Gable, Jean Harlow; *The Mask of Fu Manchu* (MGM, Charles Brabin), Boris Karloff, Myrna Loy; *Washington Masquerade* (MGM, Charles Brabin), Lionel Barrymore, Karen Morley; *Strange Interlude* (MGM, Robert Z. Leonard), Norma Shearer, Clark Gable; *Rasputin and the Empress* (MGM, Richard Boleslawski), John, Lionel, and Ethel Barrymore; *Huddle* (MGM, Sam Wood), Ramon Novarro, Madge Evans. **1933:** *Men Must Fight* (MGM, Edgar Selwyn), Diana Wynyard, Lewis Stone; *Gabriel Over the White House* (MGM, Gregory LaCava), Walter Huston, Karen Morley; *Today We Live* (MGM, Howard Hawks), Joan Crawford, Gary Cooper; *Looking Forward* (MGM, Clarence Brown), Lionel Barrymore, Benita Hume; *The Barbarian* (MGM, Sam Wood), Ramon Novarro, Myrna Loy; *Peg O' My Heart* (MGM, Robert Z. Leonard), Marion Davies; *When Ladies Meet* (MGM, Harry Beaumont), Ann Harding, Robert Montgomery; *Midnight Mary* (MGM, William Wellman), Loretta Young; *Hold Your Man* (MGM, Sam Wood), Clark Gable, Jean Harlow; *Another Language* (MGM, Edward H. Griffith), Helen Hayes, Robert Montgomery; *Dinner at Eight* (MGM, George Cukor), Marie Dressler, John and Lionel Barrymore, Jean Harlow, Wallace Beery; *Beauty for Sale* (MGM, Richard Boleslawski), Madge Evans; *Penthouse* (MGM, W.S. Van Dyke), Warner Baxter, Myrna Loy; *The Solitaire Man* (MGM, Jack Conway), Herbert Marshall, Mary Boland; *Stage Mother* (MGM, Charles Brabin), Alice Brady, Maureen

O'Sullivan; *Bombshell* (MGM, Victor Fleming), Jean Harlow, Lee Tracy; *Dancing Lady* (MGM, Robert Z. Leonard), Joan Crawford, Clark Gable; *Should Ladies Behave?* (MGM, Harry Beaumont), Lionel Barrymore, Alice Brady; *Going Hollywood* (MGM, Raoul Walsh), Marion Davies, Bing Crosby; *The Stranger's Return* (MGM, King Vidor), Miriam Hopkins; *The White Sister* (MGM, Victor Fleming), Clark Gable, Helen Hayes; *Turn Back the Clock* (MGM, Edgar Selwyn), Lee Tracy, Mae Clarke; *Storm at Daybreak* (MGM, Richard Boleslawski), Kay Francis, Nils Asther; *Secrets* (UA, Frank Borzage), Mary Pickford; *The Secret of Madame Blanche* (MGM, Charles Brabin), Irene Dunne; *Reunion in Vienna* (MGM, Sidney Franklin), John Barrymore, Diana Wynyard; *Made on Broadway* (MGM, Harry Beaumont), Robert Montgomery, Sally Eilers; *Queen Christina* (MGM, Rouben Mamoulian), Greta Garbo, John Gilbert. **1934:** *The Cat and the Fiddle* (MGM, William K. Howard), Jeanette MacDonald, Ramon Novarro; *The Mystery of Mr. X* (MGM, Edgar Selwyn), Robert Montgomery, Elizabeth Allen; *Riptide* (MGM, Edmund Goulding), Norma Shearer, Robert Montgomery; *Men in White* (MGM, Richard Boleslawski), Clark Gable, Myrna Loy; *Sadie McKee* (MGM, Clarence Brown), Joan Crawford, Franchot Tone; *Hollywood Party* (MGM, Various), Laurel and Hardy, Lupe Velez; *Paris Interlude* (uncredited; conceived and executed fashion show) (MGM, Edwin L. Marin), Madge Evans; *The Girl from Missouri* (MGM, Jack Conway), Jean Harlow, Franchot Tone; *Chained* (MGM, Clarence Brown), Joan Crawford, Clark Gable; *The Painted Veil* (MGM, Richard Boleslawski), Greta Garbo, Herbert Marshall; *The Merry Widow* (MGM, Ernst Lubitsch), Jeanette MacDonald, Maurice Chevalier; *Forsaking All Others* (MGM, W. S. Van Dyke), Joan Crawford, Clark Gable, Robert Montgomery; *Women in His Life* (MGM, George B. Seitz), Muriel Evans; *What Every Woman Knows* (MGM, Gregory LaCava), Helen Hayes, Brian Aherne; *Outcast Lady* (MGM, Robert Z. Leonard), Constance Bennett; *Operator 13* (MGM, Richard Boleslawski), Marion Davies, Gary Cooper; *Nana* (Samuel Goldwyn, Dorothy Arzner), Anna Sten; *The Barretts of Wimpole Street* (MGM, Sidney Franklin), Norma Shearer, Fredric March, Charles Laughton. **1935:** *Biography of a Bachelor Girl* (MGM, Edward H. Griffith), Ann Harding, Robert Montgomery; *After Office Hours* (MGM, Robert Z. Leonard), Clark Gable, Constance Bennett; *Naughty Marietta* (MGM, Robert Z. Leonard), Jeanette MacDonald, Nelson Eddy; *Reckless* (MGM, Victor Fleming), Jean Harlow, William Powell; *No More Ladies* (MGM, Edward H. Griffith), Joan Crawford, Robert Montgomery; *China Seas* (MGM, Tay Garnett), Clark Gable, Jean Harlow, Wallace Beery; *Broadway Melody of 1936* (MGM, Roy Del Ruth), Robert Taylor, Eleanor Powell; *I Live My Life* (MGM, W. S. Van Dyke), Joan Crawford, Brian Aherne; *Mark of the Vampire* (MGM, Tod Browning), Lionel Barrymore, Bela Lugosi; *Anna Karenina* (MGM, Clarence Brown), Greta Garbo, Fredric March. **1936:** *Rose Marie* (MGM, W.S. Van Dyke), Jeanette MacDonald, Nelson Eddy; *The Great Ziegfeld* (MGM, Robert Z. Leonard), William Powell, Myrna Loy, Luise Rainer; *San Francisco* (MGM, W. S. Van Dyke), Clark Gable, Jeanette MacDonald, Spencer Tracy; *The Gorgeous Hussy* (MGM, Clarence Brown), Joan Crawford, Lionel Barrymore; *Romeo and Juliet* (MGM, George Cukor), Norma Shearer, Leslie Howard; *Born to Dance* (MGM, Roy Del Ruth), Eleanor Powell, James Stewart; *Love on the Run* (MGM, W. S. Van Dyke), Joan Crawford, Clark Gable. **1937:** *Camille* (MGM, George Cukor), Greta Garbo, Robert Taylor; *Maytime* (MGM, Robert Z. Leonard), Jeanette MacDonald, Nelson Eddy; *The Last of Mrs. Cheyney* (MGM, Richard Boleslawski), Joan Crawford, William Powell, Robert Montgomery; *Parnell* (MGM, John M. Stahl), Clark Gable, Myrna Loy; *The Emperor's Candlesticks* (MGM, George Fitzmaurice), William Powell, Luise Rainer; *Broadway Melody of 1938* (MGM, Roy Del Ruth), Robert Taylor, Eleanor Powell; *The Bride Wore Red* (MGM, Dorothy Arzner), Joan Crawford, Franchot Tone; *Double Wedding* (MGM, Richard Thorpe), William Powell, Myrna Loy; *Conquest* (MGM, Clarence Brown), Greta Garbo, Charles Boyer; *The Firefly* (MGM, Robert Z. Leonard), Jeanette MacDonald, Allen Jones; *The Last Gangster* (MGM, Edward Ludwig), Edward G. Robinson, James Stewart; *Between Two Women* (MGM, George Seitz), Franchot Tone, Maureen O'Sullivan. **1938:** *Love is a Headache* (MGM,

Richard Thorpe), Gladys George, Franchot Tone; *The Girl of the Golden West* (MGM, Robert Z. Leonard), Jeanette MacDonald, Nelson Eddy; *The Toy Wife* (MGM, Richard Thorpe), Luise Rainer, Melvyn Douglas; *The Shopworn Angel* (MGM, H. C. Potter), Margaret Sullavan, James Stewart; *Mannequin* (MGM, Frank Borzage), Joan Crawford, Spencer Tracy; *Marie Antoinette* (MGM, W. S. Van Dyke), Norma Shearer, Tyrone Power; *Three Loves Has Nancy* (MGM, Richard Thorpe), Janet Gaynor, Robert Montgomery; *The Great Waltz* (MGM, Julian Duvivier), Luise Rainer; *The Shining Hour* (MGM, Frank Borzage), Joan Crawford, Melvyn Douglas; *Dramatic School* (MGM, Robert Sinclair), Luise Rainer, Paulette Goddard, Lana Turner; *Sweethearts* (MGM, W. S. Van Dyke), Jeanette MacDonald, Nelson Eddy; *Sky Giant* (RKO, Lew Landers), Joan Fontaine. **1939:** *Idiot's Delight* (MGM, Clarence Brown), Norma Shearer, Clark Gable; *I Take This Woman* (MGM, W. S. Van Dyke), Spencer Tracy, Hedy Lamarr; *Honolulu* (MGM, Edward Buzzell), Eleanor Powell, Robert Young; *Ice Follies of 1939* (MGM, Reinhold Schünzel), Joan Crawford, James Stewart; *Broadway Serenade* (MGM, Robert Z. Leonard), Jeanette MacDonald, Lew Ayres; *It's a Wonderful World* (MGM, W. S. Van Dyke), Claudette Colbert, James Stewart; *The Wizard of Oz* (MGM, Victor Fleming), Judy Garland; *Ninotchka* (MGM, Ernst Lubitsch), Greta Garbo, Melvyn Douglas; *The Women* (MGM, George Cukor), Norma Shearer, Joan Crawford, Rosalind Russell; *Balalaika* (MGM, Reinhold Schünzel), Nelson Eddy, Ilona Massey; *Lady of the Tropics* (MGM, Jack Conway), Robert Taylor, Hedy Lamarr. **1940:** *Broadway Melody of 1940* (MGM, Norman Taurog), Fred Astaire, Eleanor Powell; *Waterloo Bridge* (MGM, Mervyn LeRoy), Robert Taylor, Vivien Leigh; *The Mortal Storm* (MGM, Frank Borzage), James Stewart, Margaret Sullavan; *Strange Cargo* (MGM, Frank Borzage), Joan Crawford, Clark Gable; *New Moon* (MGM, Robert Z. Leonard), Jeanette MacDonald, Nelson Eddy; *Boom Town* (MGM, Jack Conway), Clark Gable, Claudette Colbert, Spencer Tracy, Hedy Lamarr; *Escape* (MGM, Mervyn LeRoy), Norma Shearer, Robert Taylor; *Susan and God* (MGM, George Cukor), Joan Crawford, Fredric March; *Bitter Sweet* (MGM, W. S. Van Dyke), Jeanette MacDonald, Nelson Eddy; *The Philadelphia Story* (MGM, George Cukor), Katharine Hepburn, Cary Grant, James Stewart; *Comrade X* (MGM, King Vidor), Clark Gable, Hedy Lamarr; *Pride and Prejudice* (MGM, Robert Z. Leonard), Laurence Olivier, Greer Garson. **1941:** *Rage in Heaven* (MGM, W. S. Van Dyke), Robert Montgomery, Ingrid Bergman; *A Woman's Face* (MGM, George Cukor), Joan Crawford, Melvyn Douglas; *They Met in Bombay* (MGM, Clarence Brown), Clark Gable, Rosalind Russell; *Blossoms in the Dust* (MGM, Mervyn LeRoy), Greer Garson, Walter Pidgeon; *Dr. Jekyll and Mr. Hyde* (MGM, Victor Fleming), Spencer Tracy, Ingrid Bergman, Lana Turner; *When Ladies Meet* (MGM, Robert Z. Leonard), Joan Crawford, Robert Taylor, Greer Garson; *Ziegfeld Girl* (MGM, Robert Z. Leonard), Judy Garland, Hedy Lamarr, Lana Turner; *Smilin' Through* (MGM, Frank Borzage), Jeanette MacDonald, Gene Raymond; *Come Live With Me* (MGM, Clarence Brown), James Stewart, Hedy Lamarr; *Lady Be Good* (MGM, Norman Z. McLeod), Eleanor Powell, Ann Sothern; *Two-Faced Woman* (MGM, George Cukor), Greta Garbo, Melvyn Douglas; *The Feminine Touch* (MGM, W. S. Van Dyke), Rosalind Russell, Don Ameche; *The Chocolate Soldier* (MGM, Roy Del Ruth), Nelson Eddy, Risë Stevens. **1942:** *Woman of the Year* (MGM, George Stevens), Katharine Hepburn, Spencer Tracy; *Keeper of the Flame* (MGM, George Cukor), Katharine Hepburn, Spencer Tracy. **1943:** *They Got Me Covered* (Goldwyn-RKO, David Butler), Bob Hope, Dorothy Lamour; *Flight for Freedom* (RKO, Lothar Mendes), Rosalind Russell, Fred MacMurray; *Shadow of a Doubt* (Universal, Alfred Hitchcock), Teresa Wright, Joseph Cotten; *His Butler's Sister* (Universal, Frank Borzage), Deanna Durbin, Franchot Tone; *Hi Diddle Diddle* (UA, Andrew Stone), Adolph Menjou, Martha Scott, Pola Negri. **1946:** *Humoresque* (WB, Jean Negulesco), Joan Crawford, John Garfield. **1947:** *Possessed* (WB, Curtis Bernhardt), Joan Crawford, Van Heflin. **1948:** *Rope* (WB, Alfred Hitchcock), James Stewart, Farley Granger; *Smart Woman* (AA, Edward A. Blatt), Constance Bennett, Brian Aherne. **1952:** *Lovely to Look At* (MGM, Mervyn LeRoy), Kathryn Grayson, Red Skelton.

# Index

Page numbers in *italics* refer to illustrations

# Credits

## ILLUSTRATION CREDITS

Courtesy the Academy of Motion Picture Arts and Sciences:
Cecil B. De Mille Collection: 68 below, 69; Herrick Core
Collection Production Files: 122; John Truwe Collection: 62, 63
below; MGM Collection: 1, 2, 6, 9, 26, 27, 28, 29, 30, 31, 32, 34, 35,
36, 37, 39, 40, 41, 42, 43, 44, 45, 46, 49, 50, 52, 53, 54, 55, 56, 58,
59, 60, 61, 63 top, 64, 65 below, 66, 67, 68 top, 70, 71, 72, 75, 77,
78, 79, 81, 82, 83, 85, 86, 88, 89, 90, 91, 92, 93, 94, 96, 97, 99,
101, 102, 105, 106, 107, 109, 111, 112, 113, 115, 117, 118, 119, 120, 121,
123, 125, 126, 127, 128, 130, 131, 132, 133, 134, 135, 136, 137, 138, 139,
141, 142, 144, 147, 148, 149, 150, 151, 152, 154, 155, 157, 158, 159,
164, 165, 166, 167, 168, 169, 170, 171, 172, 173, 174, 177, 179, 180,
181, 182, 183, 184, 185, 186, 188, 189, 190. Author's Collection.
Photograph by Dennis Barna: 65 top; Courtesy Glenn Brown and
Associates: 162 top, 162 below, 163; Courtesy Fashion Institute
of Design and Merchandising, Museum Collection. From the
Department of Recreation and Parks, City of Los Angeles: 51;
Courtesy Larry McQueen. The Collection: 161; Courtesy the
Museum of the City of New York, Department of Collections: 15;
Courtesy The Museum of Modern Art/Film Stills Archive: 18,
20, 21, 23; Courtesy New York Public Library for the Performing
Arts, Billy Rose Theater Collection: 10, 12, 13 top, 13 below, 14, 16,
17; Courtesy Vogue, Conde Nast Publications, Inc: 95, 160.

## TEXT CREDITS

Grateful acknowledgement is made for permission to reproduce
material from the following texts:
Michael Arlen, *The Green Hat*. New York: George M. Doran Co.,
1925: 73; Jane Gaines and Charlotte Herzog, eds. *Fabrications:
Costume and the Female Body*. New York: Routledge Publishing Co.,
1990: 45; Hedda Hopper, *From Under My Hat*. New York, Doubleday and Co., 1952: 81, 83. Myrna Loy with James Kotsilibas-Davis,
*Being and Becoming*. New York, Alfred A. Knopf, 1987: 21; Metro-
Goldwyn-Mayer Exhibitor Pressbooks. Copyright Turner Entertainment Co. All Rights Reserved: 62, 64, 67, 73, 76, 83, 87, 91,
92, 96, 98, 108, 109, 116, 134, 146, 147, 157, 164, 175, 176, 182,
185, 190, 193, 194; Andrew Sarris, *You Ain't Heard Nothin' Yet*.
New York, Oxford University Press, 1998: 79.

# Acknowledgments

This book has been made possible by the invaluable assistance of a great many people who have generously given of their time and expertise.

First and foremost, I want to acknowledge my enormous debt to Leonard Gershe, who championed the project during the early stages of its development. His expert advice and unflagging enthusiasm helped more than anything to make this book possible.

I am also greatly indebted to Robin Adrian, who graciously answered my questions and granted me permission to review his father's personnel files from Adrian's tenure at Metro-Goldwyn-Mayer. To that end, I also want to thank Roger Mayer and Rolinda Wittman of Turner Entertainment for allowing me access to those files, as well as the production files from some of Adrian's most important films.

To the librarians at the Academy of Motion Picture Arts and Sciences, my heartfelt thanks for making the sometimes arduous process of reviewing thousands of photos and illustrations as easy and painless as possible. I am continually amazed at their level of expertise, and their swift response to all requests. In particular, I wish to extend my gratitude to Faye Thompson, Robert Cushman, Kristine Krueger, Ellen Harrington, Janet Lorenz, and Matt Severson.

Louise Coffey-Webb at the Fashion Institute of Design and Merchandising in Los Angeles gave generously of her time, helping me to track down photographs and allowing me to reproduce stills in the institute's collection. I also wish to thank Larry McQueen and Glenn Brown for providing me with access to costumes in their collections. Their meticulous restoration work keeps Adrian's designs—and the costumes of so many other designers who worked during the great studio era—alive for their many fans.

Michael Stier at the Condé Nast Archive, Marty Jacobs at the Museum of the City of New York, and Mary Corliss of the Museum of Modern Art, New York, helped me track down sketches and photographs of Adrian's early work, and graciously gave me permission to reproduce them in this book. I am indebted, too, to the librarians at the New York Public Library for the Performing Arts for their able assistance, and for allowing me to reproduce photographs in their collection that document Adrian's early stage work.

Ned Comstock at the University of Southern California speedily responded to all my inquiries, tracking down elusive articles and clippings, and granting me permission to review the Norma Shearer scrapbook collection at USC. In addition, his occasional "surprise" packages of clippings that I was not even aware existed contributed substantially to the book.

My sincere thanks to the following people who graciously submitted to interviews, sharing either their knowledge of costume design, or their personal and professional memories of Adrian with me: David Chierichetti, the late Tony Duquette, Joan Fontaine, Leonard Gershe, Katharine Hepburn, the late Hedy Lamarr, the late Myrna Loy, the late Roddy McDowall, the late Maureen O'Sullivan, Anita Page, Margaret Pellegrini, the late Aileen Pringle, Robert Riley, Joseph Simms, and the late Loretta Young.

Much appreciated assistance also came from the following friends and colleagues: Cari Beauchamp (who taught me that persistence pays off), Kevin Brownlow, Elizabeth Nielsen, Robert Dance (who made several insightful comments during a crucial stage in the development of the manuscript), and those two ace copy editors—and wonderful friends—Bobby Kelly and Charles Attardi.

My dear friend Karen Severns offered endless support both in New York and by e-mail from Tokyo. Similarly, Shane Lewis sent me the benefits of her research on film costume via e-mail from Australia. My friends Rick Brouillard and Charles Dickey offered their hospitality during my research trip to Atlanta, and have been supporting this endeavor for as long as I can remember. My sincere thanks to you both.

Michael Lonero and Joan Toland offered much needed technical support—and the loan of a powerbook—during several trips to Chicago in 2000. Alice Boynton and Ed Harris covered for me at work during the summer of 2000, when Adrian consumed most of my waking hours. I can't thank either of them enough. And my friend Dennis Barna generously offered his photographic expertise when deadlines were staring me in the face.

The following friends either read and commented on the manuscript in various stages of development, offering me the benefit of their insight, or were there when I needed encouragement. I thank all of them: Cindy Wiora, Lauren Weidenman, Judy Rosenbaum, Pat Cella, Leslie Feierstone Barna, Toby Barna, Cindy Chapman, Patricia Grossman, Ellen Geist, Marijka Kostiw, Eve Spencer, Marla Felkins Ryan, Roberta Schrader, Joyce Mallery, Dorothy McDermott, and my brother, Robert Gutner.

Finally, I want to thank my agent, Frank Weimann of the Literary Group, for finding the perfect publisher. Last, and certainly not least, I am indebted to my editor at Abrams, Ruth Peltason. She championed this book from the beginning, and never raised her voice in the face of crumbling photo deadlines.

HOWARD GUTNER
New York City, 2001